The System Made Me Do It

CORRUPTION IN POST-COMMUNIST SOCIETIES

RASMA KARKLINS

DISCARD

M.E.Sharpe
Armonk, New York
London, England

The EuroSlavic fonts used to create this work are © 1986–2002 Payne Loving Trust.
EuroSlavic is available from Linguist's Software, Inc.,
www.linguistsoftware.com, P.O. Box 580, Edmonds, WA 98020-0580 USA
tel (425) 775-1130.

Library of Congress Cataloging-in-Publication Data

Karklins, Rasma.
  The system made me do it : corruption in post-communist societies / by Rasma Karklins.
     p. cm.
  Includes bibliographical references and index.
  ISBN 0-7656-1633-5 (hardcover : alk. paper)—ISBN 0-7656-1634-3 (pbk. : alk. paper)
  1. Political corruption—Europe, Eastern. 2. Political corruption—Europe, Central.
  3. Political corruption—Former Soviet republics. 4. Political corruption—Former
  communist countries. I. Title.

JN96.A56C654 2005
364.1′323′091717—dc22   2004025860

Printed in the United States of America

The paper used in this publication meets the minimum requirements of
American National Standard for Information Sciences
Permanence of Paper for Printed Library Materials,
ANSI Z 39.48-1984.

BM (c)   10   9   8   7   6   5   4   3   2   1
BM (p)   10   9   8   7   6   5   4   3   2   1

The System Made Me Do It

"*The System Made Me Do It* breaks new ground in its comprehensive and empirical analysis of the phenomenon of corruption—a very difficult topic to research, given that corruption is so hidden. The book will be of interest to anyone seeking to come to grips with what is arguably the most important obstacle to the creation of viable democratic regimes and capitalist economies in the post-communist countries."

—Mark Beissinger
University of Wisconsin

"Rasma Karklins shows us why corruption matters and how it can be realistically mitigated. She mixes theory with specific examples . . . to provide insights that challenge conventional wisdoms. This book will change the way we think about the role of the press, non-governmental organizations, and culture in deterring individuals from acquiescing to corrupt practices."

—Roger Petersen
Massachusetts Institute of Technology

"Rasma Karklins masterfully blends general scholarship on corruption and democracy with an overview of the special case of countries making the transition from communism. She combines a neo-institutionalist approach with first-hand knowledge of the transition process to produce a book that should be of interest both to reformers in the region and to those interested in corruption's impact on democracy worldwide."

—Susan Rose-Ackerman
Yale Law School

2/06

Contents

——— List of Tables and Figures ———

Tables

Figures

Preface

Although corruption is a destructive force worldwide, the social science literature on it is surprisingly underdeveloped, rarely going beyond description and the presentation of data. A part of this theoretical and analytical gap is being filled by an upsurge of scholarly interest in recent years, and I am grateful for having had the privilege of participating in several intellectual forums crystallizing this new focus. I am especially grateful to the School of Social Sciences of the Institute for Advanced Study in Princeton, for inviting me to be a Visiting Member during academic year 2002–3 and for asking me to participate in its workshop on corruption. Being part of a group of fellows at the Institute who for an entire year discussed their work on this topic within an interdisciplinary and comparative framework was an invaluable experience. The convener of the workshop, political theorist Michael Walzer, deserves special thanks, as does the "elder statesman" of the group, Michael Johnston.

I am also deeply grateful to Susan Rose-Ackerman and Janos Kornai who led the "Honesty and Trust" research project at Hungary's Institute for Advanced Study, the Collegium Budapest. Their skill in bringing together an international group of scholars in a number of conferences in 2001–2 provided another forum that stimulated my thinking about the meaning and consequences of corruption and its opposites. A similar experience was provided by the Amsterdam School for Social Research anniversary conference on corruption in December 2002.

The research for this study was also supported by a number of grants. I gratefully acknowledge the support the International Research and Exchanges Board gave to my work by providing me with one of their short-term travel grants in May 2002. My home institution, the University of Illinois at Chicago, was generous in providing me with several internal grants: UIC's Humanities Institute in spring 2002 selected me for one of their research awards from the Office of the Vice-Chancellor for Research; the Office for Social Science Research supported one of my research trips in June 2003; and the Department of Political Science supported my travel to national and international conferences where I had an opportunity to present my ongoing research to colleagues. To all those colleagues and friends who over the years reacted constructively to my emerging arguments about the issue of corruption in the post-communist region, many thanks!

I also thank the editors and referees of *Problems of Post-Communism* for publishing my initial "Typology of Post-Communism Corruption" in their July/August 2002 issue. Chapter 2 is a signifiantly revised version of this article.

The System
Made Me Do It

1

Introduction:
All Corruption Is Not the Same

Strike up a conversation with anyone in the post-communist region and the topic of governmental corruption will invariably come up. People are convinced that corruption is widespread, and they all have stories to tell, either from their own experiences or heard from others, including the media. They are frustrated because so little is being done about the situation and because they feel helpless and see themselves as being played for fools. Many cynically believe that in order to get along they have to "play the game"— that "the system" compels them to do so. But what "system" exactly? What are the prototypical structures and processes involved in post-communist corruption, and how are others drawn into its web? Why is this corruption so pervasive and hard to fight? Most importantly, how can one contain corruption?

This study will provide some answers, but these will be convincing only if readers accept some underlying propositions. First, political corruption is in fact a serious problem in the post-communist region. Second, all corruption is not the same; the most harmful involves systemic acts that go beyond wrongdoing by individual citizens or officials. Third, corruption can be contained—and this matters—even if it cannot be eliminated altogether. Absolutely clean politics is a utopia that does not exist anywhere in the world, but stating the truism that "there always will be corruption" undermines efforts for improvement. There are huge differences in levels and types of corruption between countries and institutions, and it does matter that it be controlled as much as possible.

These three propositions provide the main themes as well as the structural framework for the study. It starts by outlining the different types of corruption, how corruption is experienced by the populations of the region, and how people talk about it. The middle part of the book focuses on its origins and depicts an alternative ideal polity. And last, but by no means least, the final chapters focus on the institutions, rules, and strategies to contain corruption. The ultimate goal of this book is to show how corruption can be limited, but this involves defining it, identifying its origins, illustrating its forms, and outlining the meaning of non-corrupt politics.

What Is Corruption?

Before one can deal with corruption, one needs to identify and define it. An often-used definition is that corruption is "the misuse of public power for private gain." Although simple, this statement contains several important assertions, a basic one being that public power as entrusted to officials is to be used for the public's good rather than that of the officials themselves. Another underlying thought is the democratic idea of explicitly public roles of politicians and administrators, who are accountable to the governed.[1] Such a political definition of corruption also includes the notion of its concrete consequences for public life.[2] Corruption has real political costs and that is why governments try to contain it.

States often have legal definitions of what constitutes corruption, which most often refer to the bribing of officials to break the rules they are mandated to uphold. But in addition to the legal approach to corruption there are the public opinion and public good approaches. Besides being defined by law, corruption is socially unacceptable as a breach of ethics and politically illegitimate as a breach of promise to serve the citizenry. Corruption scholar Robert Klitgaard states that "corruption exists when an individual illicitly puts personal interests above those of the people and ideals he or she pledged to serve."[3]

Since corruption is the self-serving misuse of official authority and a breach of public trust, corrupt actors hide it and thereby acknowledge that they know that what they are doing is wrong. They may also recognize that corruption has victims who may seek redress and that there can be negative political or legal consequences for them.

Corruption involves hidden power rather than public power. As argued by James C. Scott, corruption distorts the formal system of rules and governance.[4] The misuse of power includes more than mere money and other physical "goods." When officials trade public power for private profit, they gain both concrete benefits as well as intangible goods such as increased personal power, position, prestige, access to information or cultural goods, and the gratitude of friends or kin. The reverse of this balance sheet is that corruption has multiple costs to non-corrupt actors as well as the citizenry at large. The costs of political corruption involve much more than money; they also involve the loss of equal access to public power and position. This then leads to the loss of public trust and belief in the political system.

Corruption is a highly contested concept that triggers heated discussions and lengthy scholarly arguments. To avoid replicating the latter, this study first adopts the simple operational definition of corruption as "the misuse of public power for private gain." After this, the entire book is a definition of corruption in that each chapter examines it anew in a concrete context and what it means to the people involved.

Due to its many meanings and expressions, even mentioning the word corruption tends to trigger emotional debates. Socially the word is used as a metaphor for everything that is not right, that is impure, and that leads to decay and depravity. One of several dictionary definitions of corruption is "impairment of integrity, virtue, or moral principle."[5] Due to its pejorative overtones, the term triggers emotional reactions to implicit value judgments that people do or do not identify with. Although some people are concerned about corruption mostly because it violates their sense of what is right, others resent the moralizing thrust and argue that corruption has its good side, for example when it helps circumvent red tape and humanizes oppressive systems. This argument too is addressed throughout the book.

Some scholars warn of applying an ethnocentric Western view of corruption and say that corruption is difficult to define because it is related to cultural constructs. Indeed, cultures differ in what specific acts are viewed as corrupt, but "the misuse of public office for private gain" is culturally neutral and can be applied to all kinds of contexts and political systems. Differences in the way that corrupt acts express themselves does not change the core meaning of the concept.[6]

Differences between Types of Corruption

All corruption is not the same. This study focuses on the abuse of official power in public institutions and among politicians, especially at higher levels. This perspective is in accord with the view of the many people in the post-communist region who believe that corruption is systemic and linked to prominent and powerful political forces. A representative survey undertaken in Latvia in the fall of 1999 found that 79 percent of respondents thought that corruption will diminish only if it is fought at the highest level. Similarly, 78 percent of respondents agreed that "the current state bureaucratic system forces one to give bribes."[7] Besides this view that corruption is systemic, 72 percent of respondents affirmed a statement that "the state provides the conditions under which corruption can develop."[8] Most survey participants felt that corruption was harmful and that their country would have accomplished much more with less governmental corruption.[9]

There is a paradox in that most people in the post-communist region angrily reject corruption, yet often participate in it themselves. In the words of

William Miller and his coauthors, they are both victims and accomplices.[10] A part of this paradox can be explained by people recognizing that corruption takes many forms, some of which are accepted more easily than others. Average citizens are most angry about corruption among top government officials and politicians, less so about malfeasance by lower-level officials, and readily make excuses for petty corrupt acts committed by themselves or their peers. This study too is most concerned about grand corruption involving politicians and agrees with the following definition: "Political corruption involves a wide range of crimes and illicit acts committed by political leaders before, during, and after leaving office. It is distinct from petty or bureaucratic corruption insofar as it is perpetuated by political leaders or elected officials who have been vested with public authority and who bear the responsibility of representing the public interest."[11]

Corruption is much more than bribery; it involves many other venal acts as well. As outlined in the next chapter, subtypes of political corruption include administrative extortion and asset-stripping, illicit procurement and privatization, the forming of collusive power networks, and much more. Types of corruption also differ depending on whether they occur as everyday interactions between citizens and officials, as administrative corruption within public institutions, or as political corruption at the highest levels of government. At times the misuse of public power for private gain has become so widespread that analysts speak of "state capture" or the "stealing of the state"; both terms refer to the institutional capture and hidden privatization of public institutions.

Why Be Concerned about Corruption?

The most important reason to be concerned about corruption is that it undermines the workings of democracy, especially in regard to rule of law, political competition, and regime legitimacy.[12] Abuse of public office is a betrayal of public trust and erodes the citizenry's belief in its representatives and government. Untrustworthy officials undermine the values of public spiritedness and serving the public good, which are crucial for good governance.

The effects of corruption are especially disruptive in democracies and lead to their delegitimation. Corruption undermines basic democratic principles such as the equality of citizens before public institutions, the openness of decision making, and accountability.[13] In democracies, the press is always on the lookout for corruption, and although this serves as an important constraint it also constitutes a tragic paradox in that due to its free press, people in a democracy tend to hear much more about corruption than in nondemocratic systems that censor the news. To quote Carl J.

Friedrich, "in open societies corruption is often uncovered by the opposition and brought to public notice by a free press, whereas in autocratic regimes it remains largely hidden."[14] This can mislead people to believe that democracies are more corrupt, causing support for authoritarians or even nostalgia for a previous dictatorship, as has happened among some segments of post-communist society.

Survey data from the region indicate low degrees of public trust, democratic legitimacy, and the credibility of the rule of law. The high political costs of corruption are illustrated by the research findings of Richard Rose and his team, who have undertaken extensive comparative surveys in Eastern Europe and the former Soviet Union. They report that "the higher the level of corruption in a new democracy, the less likely individuals are to support the new regime (–.24) and . . . the less likely individuals are to reject undemocratic alternatives (–.21)."[15] This clear correlation between the experience of political corruption and support for authoritarianism is a warning to people who believe in the importance of democracy.

Nondemocratic forces are adept at seizing the anti-corruption agenda and demanding a "strong hand" to bring change by authoritarian means.[16] If prodemocracy forces fail to lead anti-corruption movements or to do so effectively, they leave the field open for authoritarians, be they from the left or right. Corruption needs to be taken seriously, because it often leads to dangerous disenchantment with existing regimes—including democratic ones—and is one of the triggers of revolutions.

Every day newspapers report on corruption worldwide, especially if a major change of government is demanded or in fact occurs. This also is the case in the post-communist region. In November 2003 Eduard A. Shevardnadze was forced to resign as president of Georgia after huge protests about intolerable levels of corruption along with economic collapse during his nearly twelve-year rule.[17] As later chapters report, charges about corruption are a leading issue in election campaigns and other political battles throughout the post-communist region. Here as well as elsewhere in the world, politicians recognize the power of using the corruption card: "In recent years a remarkable feature of many governmental changes of command has been the promise to do something about the corruption of the previous regime."[18]

The statement that corruption is a serious problem in the post-communist region may appear to be uncontroversial, but surprisingly many analysts argue that the issue is exaggerated, that corruption can be functional, or that it is unfair to single out post-communist regimes for their corruption and overlook corrupt regimes in other countries.[19] The last point is the easiest to rebut in that this study does not claim that other parts of the world are immune to corruption; on the contrary, much of the literature cited deals with corruption as a global issue. Yet this study focuses on Eastern Europe and the former Soviet Union because they are important in themselves.

Some scholars have argued that corruption should not be demonized, since it can make systems work better and often is linked to a stage in a country's political development.[20] Samuel Huntington has written that like clientelistic politics in general, corruption provides immediate, specific, and concrete benefits to groups that might otherwise be thoroughly alienated from society. "Corruption may thus be functional to the maintenance of a political system in the same way that reform is. Corruption itself may be a substitute for reform and both corruption and reform may be substitutes for revolution."[21] This may be true for some countries, for some time, and in fact was the case in the communist countries before their eventual collapse, as is argued in Chapter 5. Yet these regimes did collapse in the end, because corruption also creates many inefficiencies, and more importantly, undermines political legitimacy.

The political consequences go beyond the immediate loss to the public purse: corruption undermines the citizenry's trust in public institutions and the state, discourages honest officials and makes them leave office, and tarnishes a country's international image.

Some analysts speak of "useful corruption" when it cuts red tape and reduces bureaucratic rigidity; it can also provide people with a sense of control over their lives and in this sense humanize the interaction between the population and public officials.[22] In the past, some authors have argued that corruption can promote economic growth,[23] but this notion has been decisively repudiated by Paolo Mauro's systematic comparative study of economic growth in dozens of countries. He shows that corruption lowers private investment, thereby reducing economic growth, and that this holds true even for countries in which bureaucratic regulations are very cumbersome.[24]

Although some petty corrupt acts may help individuals overcome red tape, corruption has high costs to society at large. Corruption involves direct costs to the citizenry as funds are diverted from paying for public goods such as safety, social services, infrastructure upkeep, and decent salaries for teachers and public servants. Corruption has been found to lower tax revenues and to be strongly correlated with a declining provision of public services.[25] Poor governance pauperizes people.

It is estimated that globally the money lost to corruption adds up to approximately 5 percent of the world economy, and an even higher percentage in countries with high levels of corruption. Nevertheless, comparatively little public money is used to investigate and prevent corruption, although experience shows that higher investment in specialized anti-corruption services can boost the detection and prosecution of offenders.[26] Public procurement represents about 15 percent of the GDP in the European Union.[27] If one applies this average to the ex-communist new members of the EU and calculates that about 10 percent of procurement moneys represent kickbacks and other illicit payments,[28] one can say that between 1 and 2 percent of GDP is spent on corruption in procurement alone.

Violence and general crime frequently accompany corruption. Organized crime groups often rely on corrupt politicians and provide them with security by violence or the manipulative use of the legal process. They have proven good at hiring expert legal help to ward off investigative journalists by initiating expensive litigation abroad and at using violence to strike at their competitors or reporters who threaten their economic monopolies and their power base.[29]

Corruption is more complex than is often thought and has major political costs and consequences. It involves administrative, legislative, and judicial malpractice and squanders political capital through such things as the loss of judicial security, public accountability, and international prestige.

Theories and Findings about Corruption: Integrating Levels of Knowledge

There is no universal formula that tells us about corruption and how to control it, but much can be learned by integrating existing knowledge from the global, regional, and local levels. Corruption occurs in all political systems, and is the subject of a developed universal literature.[30] Social scientists have devised helpful theories and findings about corruption as a generic and global phenomenon. Much good research also exists on the regional level, and on specific countries and institutions. Thus, in analyzing corruption, it is crucial—just as in other comparative politics research—to merge three levels of analysis and comparative knowledge: first, one needs to examine generic theories and findings based on worldwide experience; second, one needs to look at the specificity provided by regional contexts and regime types— "post-communism" in our case; and third, one needs to be alert to the particular conditions of individual countries, institutions, and political contexts.

The chapters of this book typically start with the broader findings of corruption research worldwide, then go to the regional level of the distinct experience of post-communist states—the legacies of the old regimes as well as the formative context in transition from them—and finally hone in on country and context specifics. Thus, the study contributes to knowledge on all three levels of analysis: the universal, the regional, and the local.

Although a comparative framework illuminates corruption in the post-communist region, this study hopes to make its own contribution to comparative knowledge by using the post-communist cases to rethink the concept of political corruption. Any analytical study focusing on a particular region needs to use general social science theory and concepts to escape pure description, but as noted by Valerie Bunce, area studies contribute new knowledge to comparative political science in that they question common assumptions. Speaking about insights from the study of the post-communist region, she aptly argues that "political institutions may be a facade with real politics taking place elsewhere; these institutions often have perverse consequences because they lack many of those associated characteristics that in the West create predictable incentives that in turn produce predictable patterns of political behavior."[31] As she notes, a minimalist definition of democracy is insufficient to assess how democratic the new states are,[32] and one must go beyond the institutional facade to see how the system really works.

The need to look behind facades is especially important in the study of political corruption. Most post-communist regimes have succeeded in putting in place the structures of democracy, including many laws and regulations designed to limit corruption, yet they rarely work in practice due to the lack of enforcement capacity and political will. As outlined in the middle part of this study, the absence of decisiveness and will is linked to the role of corrupt networks and old-time habits of mutual covering up and evasion of responsibility.

Thus, although generic comparative knowledge illuminates politics in the post-communist region, in-depth learning about its hidden side can provide unexpected insights about similar phenomena in other parts of the world, including the established democracies. While the application of what is known generally about corruption helps to understand post-communist corruption, a closer look at the latter promotes understanding corruption worldwide.

How Can We Know about Corruption?

Much skepticism about claims that a regime or institution is corrupt is based in questions about evidence. By its very nature corruption is hidden and difficult to prove. People talk about it, newspapers write about it, investigations are launched, and there clearly exists an impression of corruption, but what do we really know about it? And is not knowing about it even more of a challenge in the post-communist region, with its tradition of secretiveness, obfuscation, and Orwellian distortions of reality? Yes, it is, but there are also things one can learn, data one can collect, and analyses one can perform. This study uses a multitude of approaches because each has specific strengths that complement each other in depicting the larger phenomenon. Corruption is complex and can best be approached by integrating multiple perspectives and methodological tools.

Representative sociological surveys are a major source of data that establishes the perception and experience of corruption among the population of specific countries. By early 2004, local scholars as well as international teams had undertaken many surveys that will be cited extensively here. The advantage of surveys is that they tell us about illicit acts engaged in by respondents or their households, they provide data on popular attitudes about corruption, and they indicate how average citizens rate various public institutions. Yet one should beware of using representative surveys too frequently because most respondents have direct experience only with low-level corruption in everyday contexts, such as the bribing of a traffic cop. Average citizens can report on high-level corruption only as they know it from the media and other sources.

Targeted surveys of firms, experts, and officials measure the experience of corruption among intermediate and high-level public officials and politicians. Scholars at the World Bank Institute in 1999 conducted an exemplary study of this sort that resulted in indexes for "administrative corruption" and "state capture" for most of the states in Eastern Europe and the former Soviet territory. Aside from providing measures for individual countries, these indexes have the great advantage of allowing comparisons across the entire post-communist region.[33] One of the crucial findings is that there are major differences in levels of corruption in specific post-communist countries and subregions. The differences are confirmed by the "Corruption Perception Index" compiled by Transparency International. As shown in Figure 1.1, the index for the year 2004 indicates that the Central European and Baltic states have notably lower levels of corruption than other subregions, especially the Caucasus and Central Asia. Rankings in preceding years are similar, in part because this index only provides rough scores and has some methodological problems, as do all measures of corruption.[34]

The compilation of case study data integrates various materials, most importantly those that emerge from investigations undertaken by law enforcement agencies, the courts, and the media. The advantage of these materials is that they provide details about actual cases and how existing laws and institutions have dealt with them. In-depth commentary in the media and interviews with anticorruption experts and activists provide additional insights about how corrupt deals occur and what new laws and policies are needed. The European Union monitoring reports as well as those written by experts at GRECO (Group of States against Corruption, Council of Europe) are excellent examples of this genre of analysis.[35] The accession of the new Central and East European members to the European Union has led to a score of corruption assessments by joint teams of local and international experts.

Figure 1.1 **Sub-Regional Pattern of Corruption Intensity** (Transparency International Corruption Perceptions Index, 2004)

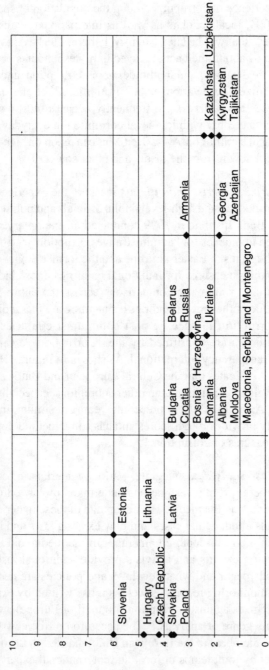

Source: Scores are from www.transparency.org; in the worldwide index Finland had the best corruption score with 9.7 points, and Bangladesh as well as Haiti scored worst with 1.5 points. The TI Corruption Perceptions Index (CPI) ranks countries in terms of the degree to which corruption is perceived to exist among public officials and politicians. It is a composite index, drawing on 14 different polls and surveys from seven independent institutions carried out among business people and country analysts, including surveys of residents, both local and expatriate.

Although this study refers to all post-communist states, its main empirical focus is on the Central European and Baltic states. For one, significantly better data are available. In addition, as illustrated by Figure 1.1, this group of states has lower levels of corruption than others in the post-communist region. These states also are ahead on the corruption containment path and can serve as guides to what steps to take toward cleaner government.

The collection of ethnographic and discourse data vividly relates experiences of corruption by individual people and the ways they talk about it. Besides anthropological studies,[36] much illustrative material can be gathered by spending time in the societies studied and by exposure to local media. Such material is used throughout this study.

Reviews of the press yield a variety of material, often focused on specific instances of corruption or changes in anticorruption laws and policies. The media relate statements by politicians and narratives about major scandals and thus illuminate grand corruption and how it is dealt with over time. Much can be learned from systematic studies of the press, of which there unfortunately are only a few to date.

As implied throughout this overview of how we can learn about corruption, the research methods one uses influence the findings. This study casts its net widely to capture as many aspects of corruption as possible, without claiming to provide definitive knowledge or proof. There are few phenomena in the social sciences that can be proven beyond a shadow of doubt, but this does not mean that they do not exist.

Although this study relies on a multitude of approaches and data sources, the nature of the topic limits the availability of the precise empirical material that social scientists like. The data, cases, and examples cited are used mostly illustratively, not exhaustively or conclusively.[37] Whenever country-specific examples are given, they were chosen to be as representative of the region as possible.

The Meaning of "System"

"System" is one of the terms around which this study revolves. The dictionary defines the word *systemic* as "relating to, or common to a system," and *systematic* as "relating to or consisting of a system," "marked by thoroughness and regularity."[38] Analytically, these concepts are used in several ways. For one, political regimes and institutions matter and need to be referred to in the analysis of corruption. Systemic structures and processes influence public behaviors and this must be kept in mind both when discussing corruption and when deliberating about how it can be controlled. Institutional theories help understand the workings of post-communist corruption, suggesting, for example, that the upheavals during regime change favored the emergence of certain types of corrupt behaviors, with the opportunities provided by the massive privatization of state assets being a case in point.

Another basic tenet is that political institutions form an autonomous source of the way politics works,[39] that political institutions can be agents of change, and that appropriate institutional settings can help prevent corruption. The neoinstitutional perspective relied on throughout this book draws attention to informal structures, including patterns of behaviors. Dominant political habits are linked to unofficial "rules of the game," which again tend to take on a systemic nature. This is especially true in regard to inherited and newly enhanced habits of people in the post-communist region relying on networks of friends and peers to get things done. Furthermore, controlling corruption implies providing the right incentives for the various actors. Any successful anti-corruption strategy must assess incentives systematically and change the calculus of the people involved. Finally, people in the post-communist region themselves often use the term "system" when they refer to corruption, both in the sense of what it constitutes and also when they make excuses for themselves because "the system made me do it."

The Meaning of "Post-Communist"

In its simplest sense, the term "post-communist" refers to a geographic region: the territory of the USSR and the East European communist state system until 1989/91. More importantly, the term implies that these states still have something in common. Political regimes and political history matter, and these countries continue to be influenced by their past. A crucial legacy is that they were ruled by a handful of communist party elites that had exceptional powers and were above the law. An example involves the so-called telephone law whereby communist party leaders would pick up the telephone and call prosecutors and judges and tell them what outcome the party expected in specific cases. Although we have only scattered evidence that this practice continues, the exceptional political influence of the ruling elites on law enforcement persists.

Throughout the region, prosecutors and judges rarely dare to challenge leading officials even though much of post-communist corruption occurs at the highest levels of the state. And, even though laws and other means of institutional control over corruption proliferate, they rarely lead to concrete accountability due to lack of political will and the communist-era legacy of informal rules dominating political behavior. This informal system includes elite cartels and the division of spoils among them. It is backed up by a tradition of collecting compromising material on rivals to be used for political blackmail whenever someone tries to break the informal rules of collusion. More broadly, one can say that the post-communist regimes tend to have a special relationship between formal and informal institutions, with the latter often being decisive.

Established habits of the mind among many people living in the region also can be called "post-communist." One defining aspect is that because the Soviet-type regimes and their institutions were repressive and illegitimate, most people felt it was legitimate to not observe laws and to engage in informal illicit activities. This attitude persists, but is inappropriate in legitimate democratic systems that the new states have struggled to become. Another attitude revolves around the notion of "good" corruption, which is thought to be functional in the sense of overcoming oppressive red tape for which the communist regimes were notorious.[40] In addition, there is little recognition that in a democracy public institutions can be designed to serve the public good and that the citizenry has a stake in their not being undermined by corruption.[41] There also is a widely held view, established during the communist era and confirmed during the last decade, that established elites are able to act with impunity no matter what.

The term "post-communist" also refers to the experience of these states undergoing the transition from communism, which created many opportunities for new forms of corruption. Although countries elsewhere also have experienced regime transitions, the post-communist region is unique in simultaneously going through a radical restructuring of the political, economic, and social systems. New states emerged or were reconstituted, a process that also involved huge changes. These extraordinary upheavals—including in some cases civil war and anarchy—provide the context for exceptional opportunities to forge corrupt deals. The radical change away from the former systems created unique contexts, such as temptations provided by an unprecedented privatization of state property—the communist states having owned nearly everything—and the challenges of having to construct new legal and judicial systems. The exceptionally extensive privatization of state-owned property led to the appearance of transition profiteers, political oligarchies, and elite cartels.

Although corruption in the post-communist region has similarities to corruption found in other parts of the world, it also has specific institutional and political cultural roots and expressions that need to be identified if any counterstrategy is to work. A comparative study speaks of "the observed international diversity in forms of corruption."[42] Since this study focuses on political corruption, its explanations of the distinctiveness of the post-communist variety focus on political factors. The full implications of political corruption have to be analyzed with reference to systemic regime features.[43]

An underlying thesis is that regime types matter and that there are specific traits that formerly communist states have in common. Post-communist systems, especially those in the Baltic and East European region, are regimes in flux in which traits of the old systems coexist with those that already are truly democratic and others that are transitional.

Plan of the Book

After this introductory chapter, the study outlines a typology of post-communist corruption and provides examples of the many forms of corrupt acts beyond simple bribery. The typology differentiates between forms of low-level administrative corruption, profiteering by officials, and institutional capture. It also discusses collusive networks and corrupt practices such as the use of compromising material in mutual blackmail. By assessing which acts are the most costly politically, Chapter 2 identifies priority targets for anti-corruption strategies. According to the analysis presented and popular perceptions in the region, priority should be given to containing corrupt deals at the highest levels, especially in privatization and procurement.

Chapter 3 provides a summary of how people in the post-communist region experience corruption in everyday encounters with public officials, as well as through accounts by close associates and the media. The findings of surveys of individuals, households, enterprise managers, and public officials relate concrete experiences. Sociological surveys also indicate different degrees of corruption among public institutions and allow the comparison of profiles and the intensity of corruption across the region.

Chapter 4 depicts how the people in the region view corruption and probes their core attitudes. Many believe that it does not "pay" to be honest and that their own dishonesty is justified by official corruption. The chapter traces the patterns of thinking and talking about this. Talk reflects values, perceptions, and expectations. It is important to know the themes of discourse, underlying assumptions and claims, and popular suggestions for reform, because effective corruption control needs the normative support of the citizenry.

Under the heading "Political Legacies: Old Habits Die Hard," Chapter 5 examines how the structures and processes of the new states are influenced by the preceding regimes. Neoinstitutional thinkers urge focusing on unofficial rules and patterns of behavior. This chapter outlines what they are. The tendency to form informal networks has its roots in the communist era, where patronage, clientelism, and the exchange of favors were common. These habits, as well as a tradition of mutual covering up, contribute to the persistence of illicit behavior and hinder efforts to contain corruption.

Corruption can be better understood by examining its opposites. Chapter 6 uses political theory to outline the values of good citizenship and public spiritedness and argues that there are concrete benefits to civic virtue. It proposes that corruption is linked to the extent of a regime's political legitimacy. It highlights the distinction between public and private ethics, which is often blurred in post-communist political practice. Other concepts that create contrasts and thus are important to understanding corruption are integrity, accountability, transparency, and good governance. Although laws address corruption in the narrower criminal law sense, these general principles influence public perceptions of its meaning.

Corruption is a problem worldwide, and this has led to a huge literature on how to deal with it. Chapter 7 uses this store of anti-corruption handbooks to outline the role of institutions and systems that work. The common thread in all advice is an emphasis on countervailing powers, checks and balances, and monitoring by media and civic society. Especially relevant to the post-communist region is a clarification of the boundaries between public and private behaviors by laws, rules, and ethics codes. Following a general inventory of instruments that help contain corruption, Chapter 7 discusses a "typical" post-communist public health-care system in order to illustrate the main points.

Although institutions matter greatly, they can be a Potemkin village. Chapter 8 establishes a balance sheet of real accountability, which is measured by electoral upsets, resignations of officials, the quality of media reporting and parliamentary hearings, reversals of corrupt deals, and investigations and convictions. While outlining the issues for the entire post-communist region, the empirical analysis focuses on the new East and Central European members of the European Union due to their progress in putting corruption prevention laws and institutions in place. Instances of success that others could learn from are emphasized.

Chapter 9 focuses on promising strategies for containing corruption. Effective corruption control needs to address how actors calculate their risks and benefits, and the chapter examines this calculus in both theoretical and practical terms. Tangible deterrence revolves around how other people act. To capture this interactive dynamic it is useful to apply notions of strategic action theory to outline various scenarios. The chapter also assesses alternative anti-corruption strategies, in particular the choice of whether to target everyday corruption, high-level corruption, or corruption within a single institution. The latter two options appear to be most promising as they more easily can trigger a downward spiral of corruption levels. Any real democracy needs to have working mechanisms of institutional checks and balances as well as an engaged citizenry that participates in enhancing the public good.

The concluding chapter summarizes the main arguments of the book on how to contain corruption.

2

The Typology of
Post-Communist Corruption

The boundaries of corruption are hard to define and depend on
local laws and customs. The first task of policy analysis is to
disaggregate the types of corrupt and illicit behavior in the
situation at hand and look at concrete examples.

Robert Klitgaard, Controlling Corruption[1]

Post-communist corruption has many subtypes, some of which are institutionalized. Aside from petty acts like bribing traffic cops or building inspectors,
there is the grand corruption of exercising illicit influence at the highest levels
of government. Post-communist corruption also includes the stripping of public assets by self-serving officials who, at times, transform entire public institutions into private fiefdoms. Although the extent and specific mix of corrupt
practices differs from one post-communist country to another, they are similar
across the region. This suggests that corruption is rooted in systemic features
of the preceding regimes and the transition from them. A typology clarifies
what these systemic features are and provides a list of corrupt acts.

When talking about corruption, people often think only of bribery, but it
exists in many other forms, such as extortion, profiteering from procurement, and institutional capture. These often involve the accessory acts of
fraud, dereliction of duty, and the violation of multiple laws. Corrupt
privatization or procurement deals tend to include collusion or blackmail
and the corruption of others, including legislators or journalists. One needs
to look beyond the simple act of illicit self-enrichment or bribery and ask
what else this act is linked to.

The categorization of corrupt acts in the post-communist region at times
calls for new concepts, such as when scholars from the World Bank Institute
coined the term "state capture." Other concepts useful for the understanding
of political corruption in post-communist states include corruptive over-
regulation and predatory licensing requirements, power grabbing by collu-

sive networks, deliberate dereliction of oversight and legislative duty, and the use of *kompromat* (compromising material) to undermine investigations.

Differentiation is at the root of all comparative analysis. In addition to differentiating among similar-looking corrupt acts, such as bribery, by their scope and effects, one needs to ask whether these acts are incidental or systemic, that is, whether they emerge from the moral failing of an individual or from an institutional failing. The latter are more difficult to deal with, especially if they involve a network of people.[2] Corrupt acts can be ranked by their political costs. The types of corrupt practices are listed in Table 2.1 and the political damage each inflicts on the public is assessed throughout the text. Surveys show that the citizens of post-communist countries are much more critical of the misconduct of politicians than of street-level officials.[3]

Many analyses of post-communist corruption focus too much on how private citizens or businesses corrupt public officials and pay insufficient attention to the reverse. The corruption of the public sector by private interests presupposes a Western-type business world that in fact has been slow in emerging. During the transition from state-controlled command economies, post-communist officials themselves often initiate corrupt deals. There is a difference between public money being misused for private gain and private money being misused to influence public policy. There is a difference between corruption of the state by outside forces and corruption by the state itself. If officials initiate corruption, the political costs are much higher, especially if entire state institutions become extortionist. Then they not only prey on the public, but also fail to serve their official purpose. Thus a study of traffic police in Hungary found that "a considerable proportion of police time and effort is devoted to corrupt money collection instead of maintenance of order."[4] In cases like these the public pays a dual cost, one consisting of money and the other of the public good of orderly and safe traffic.

Level I. Everyday Interaction between Officials and Citizens

Bribery of public officials to bend rules. Corruption in everyday encounters between officials and citizens typically involves bribes to officials to break rules and regulations. Surveys of households in post-communist countries show that payments to police, particularly the traffic police, and the health services, account for about half of all bribe expenses. Bribes associated with the educational system, especially its higher levels, are also common.[5] Such bribery is a more or less an open social secret, yet some cases have been proven in court. One example involves the selling of admissions examination materials for the prestigious Legal Faculty of Prague's Charles University in 1999.[6] Cases like this suggest that new cohorts of lawyers and other professionals are socialized into corrupt behaviors. The resulting bribery carries the social cost of universities focusing on the sale of grades and diplomas rather than the production of knowledge. Also, educators extorting students by selling grades or forcing them into private tutoring constitutes misuse of authority over dependent individuals.[7]

The latter example illustrates that "a bribe is not a bribe, is not a bribe," meaning that it has costs beyond the exchange of money and these social costs vary depending on the case in question. Instances where individual citizens initiate the giving of a bribe—for example, to a traffic officer—are politically less consequential than instances where public officials—for example, a group of police officers—extort bribes from citizens in an organized manner. When an individual driver bribes a traffic cop, this indirectly undermines public safety, but when police officers demand bribes for drivers licenses, both public safety and the rule of law are systematically undermined.[8] There is even more political damage if the bribe taking is institutionalized, as for example when employees of a public agency collaborate to extort bribes and then divide the spoils, often according to a set formula. A study of Russia in the late 1990s reports that police officers who received bribes were part of an organized scheme and passed part of their bribes up the law enforcement hierarchy.[9] A highly publicized case in Poland involved a team of police officers in a provincial town who forced money from farmers coming to market.[10]

Once this happens, official rules and laws will have been replaced de facto and a new political regime will exist in this specific administrative office. If unofficial rules and payments start to dominate public institutions, the political regime of an entire state will be changed. If corruption affects just a few branches of public administration, the extent of political damage will depend on what branches are involved. The damage is less serious if corruption involves the de facto purchase of public services such as health care or access to higher education. The legitimacy and functioning of the state are much more seriously damaged if judicial decisions are for sale, because the rule of law is at the heart of democracy and whenever it is undermined, accountability is undercut. When a judge takes a bribe, the most significant aspect is the undermining of justice, which is more serious than a surgeon in a state hospital taking an unofficial "fee" to expedite a surgery. The corruption of the tax collection service probably is somewhere in the middle range of political damage, although the bribing of building, fire, and sanitary inspectors can also be highly damaging to the public if they lead to unsafe conditions.

Deliberate over-regulation, obfuscation of rules, and disorganization are related to bribery, but are separate corrupt acts of officials who want to induce the public to offer more bribes. Extortionist bureaucrats deliberately obfuscate and expand the number of rules, procedures, regulations, and fee-paying requirements.[11] Excessive regulation, often paradoxically combined with excessive discretion on some issues, costs money, time, and energy and thus elicits bribes.[12] Self-serving bureaucrats also have an incentive to hold short office hours, withhold information, and aggravate the bureaucratic process as much as possible, because this makes it more likely that citizens will look for illicit ways to overcome the obstacles put before them. As noted by Susan Rose-Ackerman, bureaucrats tend to behave like monopolists, who profit from increasing prices created by scarcity.[13] Or, in the words of Robert Klitgaard, "corruption thrives on disorganization."[14] Chaos and obfuscation also provide a shield behind which to hide in the case of investigations, as those bureaucrats who are interested in using their office for enrichment are well aware. In contrast, it is in the interests of the citizenry to work toward efficient public organization and the de-monopolization of governance.

Corruption by over-regulation can also be due to self-important bureaucrats getting satisfaction from wielding power. Whatever their motives, officials engaging in deliberate disorganization have a stake in preventing reformers from effectively cutting red tape. In those instances when they have prevailed, the defense of turf and self-serving use of office have become systemic features of post-communist public administration. Hungarian scholar Andras Sajo goes so far to say that in post-communist states the regulatory system is enacted to create opportunities to extort bribes.[15]

Misuse of licensing and inspection powers. Every state issues licenses to professionals and for specific activities that involve the public good, such as public safety or the protection of the environment. Yet licensing is susceptible to corruption, especially during the transition from communism as established systems are changed and new needs arise. In the case of Russia, a number of scholars have concluded that many licensing officials and inspectors make it a habit to extort businesspeople. Besides the withholding of crucial certificates and permits, a common tactic is to deliberately have contradictory rules so that businesses have no choice but to break one or the other law: an example is that police authorities require that all jewelry stores install bars on their windows, but fire inspectors decree that windows must not be barred.[16]

At times inspectors become predatory. Eighty-seven percent of Russian businesspeople surveyed in 1997–98 noted extortionist bureaucratic pressures and cited the demand for bribes for licenses and permits as the main example.[17] A comparative study of shopkeepers in Russia and Poland found that on average, shopkeepers in Moscow were inspected by 3.9 different agencies, resulting in nineteen visits per year. Shopkeepers in Warsaw were inspected by an average of 2.6 agencies, whose officials came to the shop only nine times per year.[18]

A study of Ukraine in 1999 found that the average business owner spends fifty-five days registering a business, though it may take up to ninety days. There are twenty-six agencies authorized to inspect businesses and impose fines for infractions of rules, yet these rules are not published. In addition, the inspectors refuse to tell the business owner what the fine is for; the way to get a license faster and to avoid official fines is to bribe.[19]

Level II. Interaction within Public Institutions

Many of the corrupt deals found in the post-communist region are initiated by self-serving bureaucrats who use their power over the resources under their purview to enrich themselves and their cronies rather than work for the public good. A systemic context for the self-enrichment of officials has been that during the communist era the state owned practically everything: real estate and enterprises, service companies and infrastructure, land and natural resources. The transition to private ownership and a market system has involved huge and manifold assets and provided much opportunity for private enrichment for those in charge. This has included the assets of the many quasi-public organizations, such as sports and cultural clubs, universities, labor unions, and the Red Cross, all of which have had to make a transition to becoming genuine civic associations.

The self-enrichment from public resources comes in many forms including extravagant civil servant spoils, influence peddling, and profiteering from illicit privatization and procurement deals (see Table 2.1). These practices typically occur in collusion with other officials and can turn public institutions into private fiefdoms serving the whims of entrenched lords. The extraction of spoils, rents, and tributes tends to be systematic, since formal rules have to be broken repeatedly and on a long-term basis. To sustain the accumulation of corrupt profits and power, the perpetrators have to become skilled in cover-ups, deception, and the corruption of others involved in the transactions. Therefore the consequences involve more than misdirection of public monies and assets—a hidden political regime is substituted for the formal one. Below are some examples of the many practices of self-enrichment and asset stripping.

Diverting public funds for civil servant spoils. One practice is to divert money into hidden "second" budgets that can equal the official budgets of ministries or state offices. Quite often the salaries of state officials and civil servants are supplemented with hidden second salaries and bonuses. Bonuses typically involve five extra monthly salaries, and second salaries can also be significant. After a scandal about unauthorized expenditures in the State Chancellery of Latvia, a state audit found that additional pay, "although not exactly illegal, in some cases meant a 300% addition to salary."[20] Bonuses and special salaries are paid at the discretion of supervisors. This discretionary power often forms a tool to force compliance and even collusion in corrupt practices. Second salaries are agreed upon between the supervisor and an individual employee, who often has to sign a statement that he or she will not divulge this to anyone. This secrecy about how public money is used indicates that the people involved realize what they are doing is illicit and possibly illegal.

Officials use many other spoils to enrich themselves and their cohorts. Public outrage tends to focus on visible and grating instances of overspending, such as the purchase of luxury cars, pompous receptions, or spurious foreign travel such as the fall 2000 revelation that the Hungarian Ministry of Agriculture "had spent large amounts on irregular activities, including several trips to the Far East."[21] This is just the tip of the iceberg. There are other hidden benefits carried over from the communist era during which personal well-being was tied to the workplace. Places of employment were in charge of providing access to apartments, cars, special shops and cafeterias, vacations, sports facilities and saunas, better medical and day care, burial plots, and many other benefits. In this employment culture, formal salaries mattered much less than nonmonetary payments and privileges dispersed by the bosses. These practices continue depending on specific country and workplace, with the misuse of official cars, travel, and dachas typically being seen as "normal." These illicit "fringe benefits" explain why many officials of the former communist regimes were eager to retain their positions, despite very low formal salaries. The opening to the West and foreign aid provided new opportunities for illicit profit making in the form of consultants fees, travel to foreign conferences and meetings, scholarships for study abroad for oneself or for one's children, and access to foreign businesspeople and politicians.

Mismanagement and profiteering from public resources take many forms. One practice with long-term consequences involves the exploitative use of natural resources and the environment by state-appointed managers and their political friends. Examples include the deforestation of a large part of East Central Europe for the sake of timber exports, the breaking of rules about hunting rights for well-paying clients, and the dumping of nuclear waste.

Those in charge at times embezzle public assets outright. In 1993 and 1994 alone, Russian generals are believed to have embezzled the equivalent of almost $65 million from officially authorized military property sales intended to help pay for military housing.[22] Other favorite targets of misuse

Table 2.1   **Typology of Corrupt Acts**

Level I. Everyday Interaction between Officials and Citizens

1. Bribery of public officials to bend rules
   —citizen-initiated
   —initiated by individual official
   —organized extortion by group of officials
2. Obfuscation and over-regulation by officials
   —in order to extort more bribes
   —in order to enhance power and control
3. Misuse of licensing and inspection powers by officials
   (partial overlap with subcategories of 1 and 2)

Level II. Interaction within Public Institutions

1. Self-serving use of public funds
   —bonuses and hidden salaries
   —overspending on luxury cars, travel, receptions, equipment, etc.
   —appropriating cars, apartments, dachas, etc.
2. Profiteering from public resources
   —selling off environmental assets
   —leasing offices, equipment, etc. for personal gain
   —using public employees for private work
   —quasi-privatization of state-owned enterprises and property
   —paying exorbitant board of directors' fees to self/cronies
3. Malpractice and profiteering from privatization and public procurement
   —steering business and assets to self and cronies
   —disregarding conflicts of interest
   —breaking rules of competitive bidding
   —taking kickbacks and bribes
   —corrupt government subsidies and tax write-offs
4. Influence-peddling, manipulation of personnel decisions
   —engaging in nepotism, clientelism, favoritism
   —extorting favors from subordinates or job candidates
   —sabotaging personnel reform to preserve turf

Level III. Influence over Political Institutions

1. "State capture," e.g., de facto takeover of state institutions
   —building of personal fiefdoms
   —exploiting public institutions for enrichment of self and network
2. Forming secret power networks to collude in corrupt acts
3. Undermining elections and political competition
   —illicit campaign and party financing
   —buying hidden political advertising
   —secretly creating spheres of influence for exploitation
4. Misuse of legislative power
   —"selling" laws to private interests
   —blocking anti-corruption legislation
   —deliberately passing poor laws
   —dereliction of duty to oversee executive branch
   —ineffective parliamentary investigations
5. Corruption of the judicial process
   —"selling" court decisions
   —false prosecution, scapegoating
   —lack of prosecution
6. Misuse of audits and investigatory powers
7. Using kompromat for political blackmail
8. Corruption in and of the media

involve official cars, computers, various types of supplies, and equipment. Some practices endanger lives, such as when crucial police or military equipment is sold or rented out on the black market. The Russian Northern Fleet is reported to have rented out its most advanced rescue equipment to private oil companies and was therefore handicapped in rescuing the *Kursk* submarine.[23] There is no mention of who received the payment for this deal.

Another practice involves the renting out of public space, such as state-owned enterprises, transportation systems and harbors, parks and land, office and apartment buildings, sanatoriums and vacation homes, stores and restaurants, universities and schools. The last are an example of publicly owned real estate that one usually does not think of as such, yet many school officials have rented out space to private firms. One can argue that this does not constitute corruption if the rent is used for the upkeep of the school, but lack of transparency in such dealings suggests that this has rarely been the case.

A common practice is to misuse public labor, such as military officers using conscripts to build private dachas.[24] Individuals on the public payroll often "rent out" themselves for secondary jobs, shortchanging the clients in need of their services on their official full-time jobs. This includes police officers working as private security guards, surgeons taking on private patients from abroad, and professors at state universities giving privately paid lessons instead of scheduled university lectures. In 2001 the Polish Audit Chamber noted that the widespread practice of public agencies outsourcing their functions, often to their own employees, is inherently vulnerable to corruption.[25] In Romania similar practices are widespread and often lead to conflicts of interest such as when employees of the Ministry of Finance hold supplementary jobs as auditors or accountants in private firms, "thereby ensuring the protection of the firms that hired them."[26]

A subtype of the mismanagement of public assets involves the quasi-privatization of state-owned enterprises where state-appointed managers act as if they owned them. Usually there is very little public accountability. If there is any oversight at all, it is engaged in by politically appointed boards of directors receiving huge payments that are, again, hidden from the public eye. In Romania the media have covered "the apparently universal practice of state secretaries and other senior officials sitting on the administrative councils of companies where the State is shareholder."[27] Many of these cases also involve blatant conflicts of interest.

Malpractice and profiteering from privatization and public procurement often overlap with other corrupt acts, such as the bribing of politicians, lawmakers, and even judges. They involve huge sums of public monies. Although the prices that the state receives from privatization deals typically are far too low compared to their real value, the prices that the state pays in procurement typically are much too high. According to a study conducted by the World Bank, misprocurement on large state contracts in Poland can mean that market prices are exceeded by a factor of two or three.[28] Illicit profiteering from privatization and procurement often involves highly sophisticated schemes that are hard to detect and even harder to prove. The media throughout the region report new scandals on a daily basis, yet few cases are ever brought to a satisfactory conclusion by investigators, the courts, or the media themselves. The inability of the authorities to check what appear to be clear cases of corruption is a source of public frustration and forms an argument many use to justify their own illicit acts such as not paying taxes or engaging in low-level corruption (see Chapter 4).

Suspect privatization and procurement deals mean that officials steer profitable assets or contracts to themselves, their cronies, or whoever provides the highest bribe. This involves the sidestepping of rules about competitive bidding and conflicts of interest. At times public institutions purchase faulty products or products they do not need. In 2001 the Czech Ministry of Defense signed a contract for $16.7 million without a tender to purchase parachutes from a firm that did not legally exist. The inventor of the parachute was also an employee of the ministry department responsible for the purchase. The parachutes turned out to be unsafe, resulting in the death of a soldier.[29]

Throughout the region, procurement involves many scandals involving blatant conflicts of interest, for example high-ranking officials of the Moscow city government sitting on boards of numerous companies doing business with the city.[30] The taking of bribes and kickbacks is typically worth 5 to 10 percent of the value of the contract, but the cost to the public can be even higher if firms collude among themselves. In Sofia, rampant collusion is said to raise the price of contracts by around 20 percent on average.[31] A European Union monitoring report notes that in Romania "corruption appears to be systemic in public procurement, ranging from collusion and strong patron-client networks to standard bribery."[32]

Privatization has been another locus of corruption where huge gains can be made. After the communist regimes nationalized nearly everything in the early years of their rule, the state owned most land, real estate, enterprises, shops, and other property. One of the biggest issues in the transition to a market economy and democracy has been how to privatize many of these assets. All too often state property funds and privatization agencies have acted with little transparency and there have been numerous suspect deals, most of which will never be untangled. Privatization throughout the region has been marked by conflicts of interest, collusion, fraudulent assessments, and other corrupt behaviors. As noted by Czech scholar Ivan Miklos, in the initial privatization phase in the early 1990s, privatization also involved such criminal activities as blackmail, extortion, intimidation, fraud, forgery, pilfering of assets, and loan and bank fraud.[33] Many deals amounted to little more than looting.

Corrupt privatizations abound across the region, including in Estonia, which is ranked as one of the least corrupt states formerly under communist rule. The city of Tallinn sold its Central Market to individuals connected to the market's governing body for half its market value, losing close to one million euros.[34]

Other aspects of corruption during privatization are examined in more detail in Chapter 5, but here it is important to note that "corruption has played a key part" in the process of privatization, as summarized by the comprehensive study of corruption in the post-communist region conducted by the World Bank.[35] The specific techniques differ from case to case, yet the common denominator is that public officials responsible for privatizing public assets for the sake of the public good have chosen instead to concentrate on their personal enrichment. This has tainted the image of all politicians, since few among them made a visible effort not only to avoid personal involvement, but to look for effective countermeasures to constrain their colleagues. The lack of preventive work by more honest politicians is a significant part of the corruption experience. Besides the economic costs of such practices, there are political costs to the public, such as loss of trust in public representatives and state institutions.

Although corruption in privatization and procurement has been covered relatively well in various reports, corrupt state subsidies and tax relief have rarely been investigated. Huge sums of money are involved, for example in Poland, where widespread abuse of tax relief provisions in the mid-1990s included 40 percent of corporate tax revenue.[36] Another example involves the tolerance of rampant tax evasion by alcohol producers in Romania, who make huge contributions to parliamentary candidates. "It is estimated that only ten percent of total alcohol production is officially taxed. In addition to tolerance of tax evasion, after the elections the same companies received huge tax exemptions and debt rescheduling."[37] An illustration of governmental ministries being involved in the corrupt allocation of subsidies comes from the Czech Republic, where state officials referred applicants for subsidies to consultancy firms to which they had relationships.[38]

Nepotism, clientelism, and the political "selling" of positions occur as separate corrupt acts as well as the means to facilitate other corrupt dealings.

High-level appointments to offices in charge of significant public assets are a prime target. Examples include financial, economic, and transportation ministries; privatization agencies; the management of state-owned enterprises; harbors and other infrastructure facilities; and customs and tax inspectorates. A 1998 World Bank study of Albania, Georgia, and Latvia found that the prices of "high rent" public positions were "well-known among public officials and the general public, suggesting that corruption is deeply institutionalized."[39]

The misuse of power to make job appointments can occur at all levels of public administration and in all sorts of institutions, including state universities, the diplomatic corps, state-owned media, the judicial system, and the armed forces. Corruption again takes the form of commission as well as omission. Often the candidacies of people who present a reform alternative— be they local reformers or Western-trained professionals—are undermined. Networks of old comrades or schoolmates guarantee that friends retain their positions. Rhetorical arguments that "nobody else is available," or that special experience is a job requirement, mask a self-serving and cynical agenda whereby the empowerment of new and well-trained personnel is prevented to preserve turf.[40] An example is the refusal of many post-communist agencies to recognize foreign academic degrees, even if they are conferred by world-famous universities. Other examples include the deliberate prevention of new training programs designed to produce competitive alternative cadres by scholars who made their careers under the old regimes.[41]

The misuse of power over personnel decisions takes other forms as well, including the use of appointments as bribes or the threat of firings as blackmail, to make someone collude in corruption.

Level III. Influence over Political Institutions

Institutional capture. Many forms of corruption occur at the highest levels of politics. A core phenomenon is that of institutional capture, or "state capture," which refers to the de facto takeover of entire state or public institutions, typically by an elite cartel of political and business oligarchs. The concept was coined by scholars at the World Bank Institute, who noted that it involved "so-called oligarchs manipulating policy formation and even shaping the emerging rules of the game to their own, very substantial advantage." They block any policy reforms that might eliminate these advantages, and as a result, "the capture economy is trapped in a vicious circle in which the policy and institutional reforms necessary to improve governance are undermined by collusion between powerful firms and state officials who reap substantial private gains from the continuation of weak governance."[42]

"State capture" is the systematic high-level corruption that establishes a hidden political regime at odds with the constitutional purpose of state institutions. Analysts note that the capturing may be done not only by private firms or narrow interest groups, but also by political leaders. Furthermore, "distinctions can be drawn between the types of institutions that are captured—the legislature, the executive, the judiciary, or regulatory agencies."[43] The capturing goes hand in hand with other corrupt acts, for example decisions by law enforcement agencies and the judiciary whether to pursue investigations of suspicious acts. Political oligarchs also engage in illicit party financing, buying of media, and various schemes to neutralize political competitors. Allegations about institutional capture tend to focus on ministries dealing with financial and economic matters. Since powerful people are involved and much is at stake, this form of corruption is especially difficult to prove and fight.

Extreme cases of state capture involve the de facto takeover of public institutions not just for business interests, but for outright criminal activity. This consists of the strategic penetration of executive institutions by criminal networks. For instance, a case of alleged institutional takeover implicated drug-fighting offices in some Central Asian states. Another example involves Georgia in 2000, where an international investigation found that "the police, the customs and the courts, those very agencies responsible for fighting corruption, are most widely affected by it."[44] In Romania, an investigative journalist was told by an unsuccessful candidate for the post of head of the Customs Authority that the "price" to secure the post was $1.3 million.[45] Many observers believe that in Russia some security services run substantial criminal enterprises and represent a separate form of organized crime. As one analyst has argued, "the problem is not simply corruption, such as bribe taking, that infects the public sphere, but actual criminal activity by governmental and law-enforcement agencies."[46] An example is a scandal in early 2002 when several Russian newspapers alleged that high officials had organized a scheme to illegally import furniture for sale in a chain of warehouses in Moscow.[47]

The forming of hidden power networks to collude in corrupt acts is a form of post-communist corruption that is quasi-institutional and systemic. As noted by Andras Sajo, "clientelist corruption is a form of structural corruption, which should be distinguished from discrete individual acts of corruption."[48] This needs to be emphasized, because many commonly used definitions of corruption are so narrow that they do not capture phenomena such as patron-client and other illicit network relationships.[49] The forming of secretive political cartels is a corrupt practice in and of itself. These corrupt networks are predatory groupings that search for ways to use public institutions for their private gain, often through illegal party financing and state capture. Even in Slovenia, one of the best-ranked post-communist countries, reports speak of "networks of clientelistic or nepotistic social relationships that are corrupt but not characterized by direct exchanges of money or benefits."[50] One example mentioned is the influence of personal connections on criminal proceedings, particularly during investigations. Another involves political influence on the media through personal connections and multiple board memberships across banks as well as media and other companies, many of which remain under state control.[51]

Networking has been used in an exploitative and corrupt way both by old comrades' cliques and the newly privileged managerial class. Interestingly, some authors also see a constructive side to post-communist networking in that it mobilizes social capital.[52] Thus, the main questions to be asked in any specific case are whether a political network serves the public good or is self-serving, and whether it honors the law and other rules governing the political system.

Post-communist countries differ in the extent to which the old power holders survived the change of regimes and continue to hold on to accumulated power, but in many instances there has been a marked continuity in elite composition.[53] The Russian banking network is a prime example of extensive elite survival, since "on a scale from one (party secretary at the local level) to ten (party secretary in the Central Committee) the banking elite gets an average of eight."[54] Although one would assume that at least some leading cadres survive regime change, the core issue is the extent to which old elites continue to work in an organized and collusive manner and deliberately exclude counter-elites, thus limiting the citizenry's choice of representation. Peter Eigen has said that "corruption gives rise to oligarchy," but one could also reverse the statement and say that oligarchy gives rise to corruption.[55]

As in all patronage networks, those active in the post-communist region function on the basis of benefit and obligation; that is, rules of reciprocity. Corrupt networks tend to self-perpetuate, since members have a strong motive to keep non-corrupt individuals out of politics or to try to co-opt anyone slipping through their net. Fear of disclosure is another motive for perpetuating the network and its dealings, and thus many decisions are made with the consideration of protecting implicated officials, be they in someone's own network or involved in a collusive quid pro quo. In addition, any renegade member has to fear severe retribution.[56]

It would be important to learn more about the internal workings of these networks, but such research is by its nature highly problematic. It appears that special rules of silence, similar to those previously imposed on KGB personnel as well as on Gulag victims, exist and are enforced. Nevertheless, there are occasional revelations such as when the president of Romania stated in 2001 that "in the past four years, we have witnessed a growing complicity between the structures of organized crime and high officers in the Police, Gendarmerie, and secret services, judges, and politicians. This complicity represents a great threat for the national security."[57]

The undermining of free elections through illicit party financing and electoral slush funds appears to be widespread. In Slovakia, more than one-third of public officials interviewed in 2000 reported that "political payoffs to benefit political parties or a political campaign" are frequent.[58] Payoffs often are linked to power oligarchies that own media or pay for hidden political advertising in supposedly objective media. Such practices are especially problematic if candidates pay journalists for image-building interviews that are presented as neutral reportage. Another corrupt practice that undermines democratic elections involves candidates who seek election for the sake of parliamentary immunity from prosecution, as has been reported in several cases. A European Commission report states that according to estimates as many as half of Romanian members of parliament bribed political parties to be placed in a favorable position on their candidate lists, many doing so to gain immunity from legal prosecution.[59] Similar practices have been reported for Russia.[60] Grigory Yavlinsky, himself a prominent politician and former member of the Duma, has commented that "the large number of criminals running for Duma seats to gain immunity is repulsive. How can a legislature fight corruption when its members have their own deals on the side?"[61]

The post-communist states tend to have proportional electoral systems, and elections typically result in several parties having to form a coalition government. This process can involve constructive negotiation and policy compromise, but also the division of spoils and spheres of interest that specific parties can exploit without interference by their coalition partners. This has been alleged to be a common practice in city government.[62] Political coalitions can be based on the division of spoils and fiefdom building, but elite cartels are held together by the possibility of mutual blackmail over past misdeeds as well as by a joint interest in holding off economic and political competition.

To the degree that secretive power networks limit political competition they seriously undermine democratic development. Just as market economies cannot function properly if monopolies or cartels rule, democracies cannot function if collusive power blocs capture the political market. Competition in elections and decision making is a hallmark of democracy, and it is also a crucial means of empowering those candidates and programs that best represent the public good—as defined by the citizenry.

Misuse of legislative power. Bribery may occur when legislators at various levels of government have the power to select candidates for desirable positions. Researchers also speak of laws being "purchased" by business or criminal interests, meaning that legislators are bribed to pass specific laws. Romania has been reported to be seriously affected by state capture, particularly through the purchase of parliamentary votes and political party funding.[63] In addition to this active corruption of legislators, there also is passive corruption in the sense of omission and dereliction of duty. Many post-communist parliaments and regulatory bodies have been derelict in their public duty to pass not only effective laws and regulations on party financing, conflicts of interest, money laundering, off-shore assets, the review of income declarations of public officials, but even a corruption law itself. As argued by Louise Shelley, the corruption of the privatization process in Russia resulted, in part, from the deliberate absence of laws that could have prevented individuals from promoting their interests at the expense of others and the larger financial good of society.[64] Conflict-of-interest laws have been especially slow in being written. At the same time many state officials have profited from their positions as regulators of the economy by starting private businesses in the area that they themselves regulate.[65]

Most post-communist legislatures have been passive when asked to pass laws on witness protection, sting operations, and similar programs that are crucial for anti-corruption struggles. At times, drafts of promising laws have been deliberately blocked. Yet this does not mean that there is no anti-corruption legislation—often there is plenty of it, just not the right kind. More than twenty laws to fight corruption were passed in Ukraine between 1992 and 1999, and seven government ministries and departments were assigned to implement these laws, yet "no one is actually doing the fighting."[66] Whenever real anti-favoritism measures are proposed, the beneficiaries of the existing system mobilize, thus, "the more promising the measure, the less likely it will be implemented."[67] Nevertheless, legislators and governments are eager to create the appearance of anti-corruption to further mask illicit dealings. According to Hungarian legal scholar Andras Sajo, post-communist regimes deliberately use dubious laws and legal standards to provide supposed democratic legitimacy to governmental sleaze, which arguably is worse than doing nothing.[68]

Confusing and contradictory legislation also promotes corruption, especially in Russia where a plethora of often conflicting laws and decrees emanates from a variety of jurisdictions.[69] Although this is partially the result of disorganization emanating from the transition process, it provides room for corrupt maneuvers. A variant of this misuse of lawmaking involves lawyers who become short-term legislators in order to create complicated laws and then return to private practice where they command high fees as the sole experts who can negotiate the same confusing laws.

The corruption of the judicial process too takes many forms, some overlapping with previous categories, such as the de facto sale of favorable decisions by courts. For Russia, Louise Shelley speaks of "massive pay-offs to the police, procuracy, and judiciary."[70] Selective or false investigations and prosecutions constitute other corrupt misuses of the judicial system. Revelations about corruption are often used in power struggles, rather than in promoting transparency in society.[71] The Russian Interior Ministry under Putin serves as a textbook case: Thirty criminal cases against officials in the Moscow city government were opened in August 2000 after Mayor Luzhkov opposed a new tax plan.[72] During corporate battles, executives "often bribe prosecutors and judges, who earn an average of about $200 a month, to open baseless criminal investigations of their competitors or to let them snatch companies from their legitimate owners through forced bankruptcies."[73] Practices like these mean that instead of rule of law, a country rules through law, that is, abuses laws and the legal system for political purposes.[74]

Worse even than absence of law is the abuse of law to promote corrupt deals. It has been reported that by 1996 in Bulgaria privatizations were routinely corrupted under the rule of law. If insiders lost out on their bid for a company, they merely went to court and had a friendly judge annul the auction. Slanches Dan, once a luxury spa for high-ranking communist apparatchiks, was clawed back by its managers through such dubious court proceedings.[75]

Another politically devastating form of corruption is judicial complicity in it. All too often, prosecutors decline to open investigations into cases where corruption is highly indicated, as evidenced by the many large banking and financial scandals that have plagued the post-communist region. When powerful players seem to be involved, prosecutors typically start to investigate only after a repeated public outcry and then fail to resolve the case. Lack of evidence is often cited as the main reason for discontinuation of cases, but at times ludicrous arguments are brought in as well, possibly to deliberately enhance public cynicism about the judicial system.[76] A court in Hungary in 2001 acquitted a powerful politician of bribery charges related to campaign financing, stating that although formally bribery was performed, "danger to society" could not be established and hence a crime could not be proven to have occurred.[77]

There is a curious paradox in the judicial prosecution of corruption. The naive observer may think that if just a few cases are prosecuted, this indicates a low level of corruption. In fact, just the opposite is likely to be true: the scarcity of prosecutions can indicate a very high level of corruption, including corruption that has overtaken the judicial branch as well. This seems to be the case in Russia. As one author notes, the relatively small number of corruption cases that have gone to court suggests that corruption plagues law enforcement agencies as well.[78] Similarly, if many corruption cases are brought to trial, this can indicate an active fight against corruption and a low level of it, or a decreasing trend line. Commenting on cross-country data that show that Singapore and Hong Kong have exceptionally high conviction rates for corruption, an analyst notes that these "exceptionally high conviction rates confirm the suspicion that such data, when aggregated, may tell more about the police and the judiciary than about corruption."[79] This illustrates that numerical measures need to be treated very carefully as one tries to measure corruption levels.

Misuse of auditing, investigatory, and oversight powers to hide and promote corruption rather than fight it is related to judicial corruption, but can take special forms, including the corruption of anti-corruption agencies. This is an especially difficult issue to study, but accusations in this area have been frequent. A former head of the KGB's analytical department has claimed that Russia's Federal Security Bureau has become too riddled with corruption to fight it.[80] In addition to individual cases of delinquency, an entire anti-corruption agenda may become misdirected. This apparently happened in the case of the "Clean Hands" campaign launched in the Czech Republic in 1998, which drew enormously bad reviews and was terminated in May 2000 under suspicions of politically motivated decisions.[81]

Dereliction of oversight duty by offices of the procuracy, parliamentary investigation committees, the supervisory arms of ministries and central banks, tax authorities, general accounting offices, and similar bodies usually represents a passive form of corruption and collusion. As noted, the careful hiding of corruption is part of its definition and indicates that the perpetrators are well aware they are misusing the public power entrusted to them. Fearing exposure, they have an incentive to corrupt other officials, especially those charged with oversight duties. In order to check corruption it is therefore crucial that the separation of powers be taken seriously and that public and state institutions use various mechanisms to check on each other. Public oversight and the demand for accountability are core features of democracy and the rule of law. Unfortunately, this has emerged as one of the weakest links in the new post-communist democracies, be it due to inexperience or to deliberate neglect and collusion.

Using "kompromat" for political blackmail and coercion. A politically
damaging practice is to misuse investigative and judicial power to intimi-
date citizens and political rivals. This is a concrete legacy of the Soviet-
type systems where lawbreaking became a means of coercion in the sense
that everybody was bound to break the law somehow to survive and then
could be picked out for prosecution if needed.[82] Recently, Keith Darden
has outlined the systematic use of the threat of prosecution for political
control on the basis of secret recordings in the presidential office of Ukraine.
These materials suggest that state leaders deliberately encouraged corruption in order to secure compromising materials (kompromat) to use for
political blackmail whenever needed. After first encouraging an atmosphere
of impunity, state surveillance organs were used to document corruption
among officials, and then compliance was secured by the threat of exposure and prosecution.[83] Darden describes how this method was used in the
1999 presidential election to get the vote out for Leonid Kuchma. He also
argues that using kompromat as a tool of political pressure is common in
Ukraine and other post-communist countries and has become an "institutional base of the blackmailing state."[84]

Kompromat is most often used by corrupt individuals and networks to
protect themselves against rivals. Yet this knowledge of guilt is mutual and
therefore acts mostly as a deterrent to preserve the status quo. "There is only
one adequate response to kompromat, i.e. counter-kompromat. To this, you
can respond with a newer, even more powerful counter-kompromat."[85] This
is reminiscent of the arms struggle and peace being preserved by the implicit
doctrine of "mutual assured destruction," that is, when both sides in a struggle
have powerfully destructive weapons, each side is careful not to start a battle.
In the case of grand corruption, this is one more reason why few cases ever
get to trial.

Thus corruption is perpetuated not only due to the common interests of
many of the individuals involved, but also due to mutual blackmail, that is,
many powerful politicians have compromising material on other politicians,
which keeps collusion going.[86] Such a systemic explanation also fits the fact
that many clearly illegal and corrupt activities have been conducted for years
with impunity. In the real estate market in Russian cities, officially registered
prices of real estate (subject to taxation) are often only a small fraction of
amounts actually paid. The real prices are common knowledge, so that local
authorities, if they really wanted to, could crack down.[87] They rarely do,
suggesting both complicity and an institutionalized pattern of collusion.

Besides deliberate perpetuation, corruption tends to be self-perpetuating.
Fear of exposure of previous corrupt dealings leads to additional corrupt
acts, whether through blackmail or bribery to prevent investigations. Unless

there is a decisive and institutionally based break in the spiral of corruption, it is likely to pursue an upward trend.

Corruption of and in the media. Next to the judiciary, the media are the crucial player in promoting or hindering successful anti-corruption activities. There are many examples of individual journalists or media outlets having effectively exposed corruption, but there are also indications of occasional media collusion in cover-ups and other corrupt practices. This relates to both newly private and remaining state-owned media. The latter are now directed by public media oversight boards, but there often is little transparency of personnel and program decisions. As for private media, they tend to be controlled by business interests that have been capturing state institutions.[88]

Hidden advertisements for politicians and businesspeople frequently are cloaked in the mantle of public information. One also finds innuendo and false accusations being spread against political or economic rivals. The pay-off to journalists and editors may be in the form of tax favors or direct payments. As reported by the *Financial Times*, "stories are for sale in most of the Russian media, with a very few honorable exceptions. There are price lists available from public relations firms in Moscow, spelling out what different publications charge: one sum for a positive story, another for a bit of black propaganda and the highest price of all for a guaranteed news blackout."[89]

Conclusion

More than a decade after the beginning of the transition from communism, it has become clear that corruption is the key obstacle to democratic and economic progress in the post-communist region. The emerging research has begun to identify the roots of corrupt practices as well as promising strategies for combating them, but in order to do so successfully, a basic task is to identify and categorize what it is we are dealing with. A typology can do that. It helps us understand the nature, context, and political implications of post-communist corruption.

The typology presented here focuses less on the currency of corruption and more on the political nature of the corrupt act. "The misuse of public power for private gain" has political consequences that need to be spelled out and assessed. Analysts tend to focus on the "private gain" part of the definition of corruption, and to discuss the details of bribery and other forms of illicit profiteering. Although this is important, one needs to focus on the meaning of the "misuse of public power." When officials in charge of securing the public good prefer to focus on their private good, the basic purpose of public institutions is undermined. This means that besides lost funds there is a cost to the citizenry in terms of public safety, services, judicial enforcement of contracts and laws, and democratic representation. Not surprisingly, the public reacts with anger, distrust, and cynicism.

Corruption has three dimensions that affect the quality of politics: the currency of the corrupt act, its institutional aspects, and the consequences it has for the polity. "Currency" refers to the means of the illicit exchange. This can include bribery, profiteering, favoritism and nepotism, building collusive networks, extortion and blackmail, and other illegitimate or illegal dealings. The extent to which such practices pervade a country influences the quality of its politics. The political damage is less serious if bribery, for example, consists mostly of individual acts of citizens wishing to secure public services or circumvent red tape. Bribery is more damaging if it involves systemic extortion by officials and if it encourages institutional pathologies such as deliberate over-regulation or its opposite, the deliberate dereliction of oversight or legislative duty. Similarly, various forms of profiteering from public assets are less damaging if they originate from the avarice of individuals and much more damaging if they are due to systematic action by collusive networks. If so, then one can speak of an institutionalization of corruption and a change in the foundations of the political system.

3

The Experience of Corruption

A reality show that is only too real has transformed daytime
Polish TV in recent weeks and kept millions glued to their
screens. Starring an Oscar-nominated film producer,
the country's prime minister, and one of Poland's most
respected anti-Communist dissidents, live coverage of
parliamentary hearings into influence peddling is tearing
the veil from an allegedly tight group of rich and powerful
Poles accused of corruptly controlling the country.

Peter Ford, "Poland Lifts Veil on Corruption"[1]

People living in the post-communist region experience corruption in many
ways. Most often they learn about it from the media, through attention-
grabbing situations as in the above quote. This refers to the so-called
Rywingate, a huge corruption scandal that ended in April 2004 with Polish
filmmaker Lew Rywin being sentenced to prison.[2] Media reports about scandals at the highest levels of power greatly heighten popular views that corruption is widespread. It has been argued that the media, focusing too much
on real and suspected scandals, can create a "culture of mistrust" that is
overdrawn and hampers effective governance.[3]

A similar argument has been made by the Bulgarian scholar Ivan Krastev,
who emphasizes that analysts know less about the real experience of corruption than its perception in public opinion. Krastev's "perceptionalist" argument about corruption holds that the public's image of corruption in particular
countries changes depending less on its actual level than on the level of revelations about it. Perceptionalists distrust the consensus that corruption is on
the rise and see it as something created by scandal-loving media. Another
origin of this "black myth" of transition is that in the post-communist world,
anti-corruption rhetoric is the favorite weapon for anybody seeking power.[4]

Such arguments are true in part, but just because the corrupt nature of
politics often is exaggerated does not mean that it does not exist. Besides

reporting scandals, the media cover other aspects of corruption, with the newspapers being especially vigilant. They publicize parliamentary investigations and court cases such as the one involving Rywin and publish their own investigative reports, the findings of police investigations and audits, and much commentary. The media relate what local or international experts say about corruption, for example, how a particular country ranks in the annual Transparency International Corruption Perceptions Index. As they provide a host of information on corruption, the media evaluate its meaning and discuss what one can do to combat it.

Besides experiencing corruption as presented by the media, many people personally encounter it in contacts with public officials or when hearing about such encounters from family members, friends, or colleagues. After outlining such personal experiences, this chapter presents some regional comparisons about the types and pervasiveness of corruption, and concludes with an analysis of the role of the media in relating the corruption experience. The underlying issue throughout is how reality relates to perception.

The Scale of the Problem: Daily Life

A crucial part of the corruption experience is when individuals or members of their household encounter it personally (Level I). Studies undertaken in the region indicate that the scale of the problem differs from one post-communist country to another, however the overall thrust of the findings is similar. Romanian surveys show that the public not only sees corruption to be widespread, but that among households surveyed in 2000, 42 percent themselves had paid a bribe during the last twelve months. Of a representative sample of Romanians, about two-thirds stated that "all" or "most" officials are corrupt, and 44 percent of public officials said the same.[5] The latter is striking as it underlines that in addition to average citizens believing that corruption is widespread, officials believe so as well, although understandably at somewhat lower levels.

The corrupt tinge of bureaucratic encounters between citizens and public servants was evident during the communist era,[6] and is evident in all post-communist countries, although with different intensities. In Latvia, the local branch of Transparency International sponsored a large survey in fall 1999 that asked a cluster of questions about interactions with officials. The results show that 31 percent of respondents have personally had one or more interactions where they had to give an unofficial payment, and more than half (54 percent) would be willing to give a bribe to get a better result. The latter ratio might have been even higher if people were wealthier, since 39 percent of respondents say that they cannot afford any unofficial payments.[7]

Table 3.1

Experiences with Corruption, Slovakia, 1999

Households	Percent making unofficial payments in previous two months	14.4
	Percent making unofficial payments in previous three years	41.3
Enterprises	Percent making unofficial payments in previous two months	17.6
	Percent making unofficial payments in previous three years	41.4
Public officials	Percent offered a small gift in previous two years	42.3
	Percent offered money or an expensive gift in previous two years	9.7

Source: James H. Anderson, *Corruption in Slovakia: Results of Diagnostic Surveys* (Washington, D.C.: World Bank, 2000), p. 5.

A similar picture emerges from a Slovak population survey in the fall of 1999, as well as separate surveys of 350 public officials and 400 enterprise managers. Respondents were asked about their direct experience of making unofficial payments or receiving gifts. As Table 3.1 illustrates, about half of all three respondent groups reported involvement with unofficial payments or gifts during the past two or three years. Households were also asked whether the payments made were voluntary or not. It emerges that in about two-thirds of all cases the payments were non-voluntary, either because officials had requested them or respondents knew that "this is the way it goes."[8] The latter comment reflects a climate of public interactions where unofficial payments are unexceptional and people offer them fearing that otherwise they will not receive the service due to them.

These findings are complemented by the results of surveys undertaken by William Miller and colleagues between 1997 and 1998. Their comparative study of several post-communist countries reveals that officials at times specifically asked for bribes, but mostly gave indirect signals that they expected something. As Table 3.2 illustrates, this practice differed only slightly among the four countries studied. Ukraine has the highest score for officials directly asking for money or a present, while Slovakia has the highest score for respondents saying that officials "seemed to expect" money or a present. However, in the Czech Republic and Bulgaria about half of the respondents stated that officials neither asked for, nor seemed to expect, something. Since one-third of the respondents in Slovakia and Ukraine also said so, one can conclude that although many officials expect some unofficial payment, this is by no means the general rule.

In instances where illicit payments are expected, officials often convey their demands by hints, by complaints about their workload, or by comments

Table 3.2

Experience of Extortion, 1997–98

"In these last few years, did an official ever ask you or your family for money or a present, or not ask directly but seem to expect something?"

	Czech Republic (%)	Slovakia (%)	Bulgaria (%)	Ukraine (%)
Asked directly	2	4	7	11
Seemed to expect	44	64	39	56
Neither	54	32	54	33

Source: William L. Miller, Ase B. Grodeland, and Tatyana Y. Koskechkina, *A Culture of Corruption? Coping with Government in Post-Communist Europe* (Budapest: Central European University Press, 2001), p. 85.

about the special efforts they are making for the client. A general tactic is "to make unnecessary problems in order to get money or a present for solving them."[9] At times officials argue that they need payment for the expenses they are incurring, such as when Bulgarian policemen asked the mother of a rape and kidnap victim for money to buy gas for their car so that they could search for the girl.[10] The staff of public hospitals and surgeries are especially direct in asking for unofficial payments, with one respondent saying that "they tell you right away that you will need that much for that, and that much for that, and that much for surgery." Another respondent received an even more explicit message: "Our mother was going to have surgery and the surgeon said that she had to give so much to him, so much to the neuropathologist, so much to the anesthesiologist, and so much to the assistant. He directly said how much."[11] In gaining access to health services, unofficial payments are most frequently made for stays in a hospital or consultations with specialists.[12]

These accounts are buttressed by the perspective of a surgeon in Latvia who told an anthropologist about his experiences. He originally was shocked when patients gave him money under the table in Soviet times, but then became accustomed to it and later felt that he needed to continue. He explained: "For the 100 lats which the state officially pays me, I [cannot] survive. It is not the fault of the doctors that they take bribes or honorariums, however people may call it. . . . Mostly people thank by money in an envelope. It is a standard now. It happens in my office when we are alone with the patient."[13] The same anthropologist recounts how a patient with an inflammation of the lymph nodes could not get good treatment from a specialist who supposedly had no time for her. "Of course, she understood that giving a bribe or a gift to that specialist would make her one of his patients. She said she felt like a loser because she did not know how to bribe . . . [and] besides, she was not well off and was afraid that the little amount she could afford to give would make the situation even worse."[14]

Surveys conducted in Slovakia in 1999 by James Anderson and other scholars at the World Bank Institute cover the actual experience of corruption, its assessment, and perceptions. The last are included here because the authors convincingly argue that perceptions should be part of an analysis of experiences, even though some analysts disagree and say that perceptions can be distorted. This can be true, especially if the media provide skewed news, but perceptions also are shaped by the concrete experiences of respondents. The survey authors argue that the data for Slovakia demonstrate clearly that several of the governmental bodies that are perceived as the most corrupt are the very same ones with which respondents have had the most experience with corruption. Also, an approach focusing entirely on actual experiences would not be balanced, since ordinary people and enterprise managers are generally not party to certain forms of high-level corruption, which would therefore be underreported in the surveys.[15]

Anderson and his colleagues add a third point, namely, that perceptions themselves are important, even if not completely reflective of reality, because they influence behavior. People calculate the usefulness of corruption when they decide whether to take a case to court or seek potentially expensive medical treatment.[16] As elaborated upon in Chapter 9, the perceived level of a society's corruption influences people's calculus of whether they themselves should participate in it. The same calculus affects whether people will get involved in fighting corruption: If "everybody" does one or the other, it is much more likely that others will participate. In commenting on the region, some analysts speak of a self-sustaining system of corruption in which officials seek bribes, yet citizens are willing to pay and even offer them on their own to get what they need.[17] This system is built on a pattern of anticipation of what others in society expect or how they will act.[18] Perceptions and expectations are linked to behavior.

Public institutions differ by the degree to which illicit payments and practices play a role. The three parallel Slovak surveys depicted in Figure 3.1 demonstrate broad agreement among Slovak households, public officials, and enterprise managers that corruption is widespread in the health and justice systems, the National Property Fund, and customs and the police. As a rule, household respondents perceive the levels of corruption to be somewhat higher than do enterprise managers and public officials. This gap is especially noticeable when households presumably have had more direct interaction with an institution, such as health care, the tax authorities, and edu-

Figure 3.1   **Perceptions of Corruption in Public Institutions, Slovakia, 1999**

Percent believing corruption is "very widespread" in:

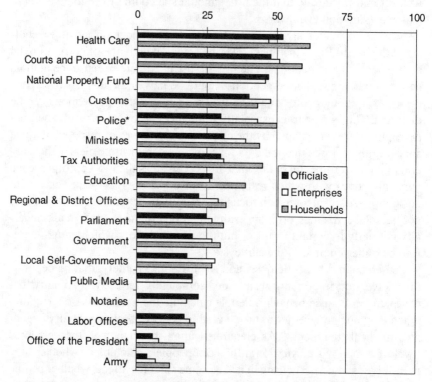

Source: James H. Anderson, *Corruption in Slovakia: Results of Diagnostic Surveys* (Washington, D.C.: World Bank, 2000), p. 8, revised presentation.

Note: The absence of a bar indicates that household perceptions of corruption in that organization are not available.

*On the enterprise and household surveys, separate responses were provided for traffic police and other police. These were averaged to arrive at the aggregate for police.

cation. Customs is the one instance where enterprise managers clearly see a state institution to be more corrupt than do the others. This again is an institution with which the particular respondents presumably have had more interactions than the others. Compared to enterprise managers, officials have a higher score in saying that corruption is widespread in the National Property Fund and among notaries (households were not asked this question).

Parallel studies undertaken in late 1998 in Latvia and in 2000 in Romania by the same team of World Bank Institute researchers show very similar results.[19] Politically, the most troubling aspect of these findings is that the courts and prosecutors' offices register so high in the corruption rankings. This illustrates the crucial weakness of the post-communist judicial systems, which should be at the forefront of fighting corruption rather than participating in it. One reason for courts being a risk zone is that there are huge delays between the filing of cases and their resolution, and thus many people are tempted to pay "speed money" to resolve a case.[20]

Corruption in the educational system is centered mostly around universities and focuses on admissions and grading. Even though such practices tend to be hidden, at times "price lists" have been published. A newspaper in the Ukrainian city of Donetsk reported that one had to pay $30–$50 for a good exam grade in local colleges and universities, with a group price as low as $10 per student, and a premium rate of $80 for students who only paid after failing an exam.[21] Many believe that one cannot get into a law or medical school without paying bribes, with more than half of all survey respondents in Slovakia in 2000 saying so in regard to law schools.[22] This is hardly a hopeful sign for the future of lawfulness in that country.

All these data indicate that corrupt practices play a significant role in everyday interactions between citizens and public institutions. William L. Miller and his colleagues talk of a climate of petty corruption in which most people (between 76 and 90 percent) believe that whenever someone needs something from a public official, a personal contact or a payment is required to get what is needed. They note that while many think so, fewer people report their own individual experiences of needing to give a present or bribe.[23] However, one must consider that not everyone has personal contact with all public institutions: healthy people do not go to hospitals, and housewives rarely have reason to go to court. People base their assessments not only on direct personal experience but also on the experience of family members, friends, and colleagues, as well as on what they read in the press.

Nevertheless, as Table 3.2 shows, many respondents also relate that in their experience officials did not demand or expect gifts or unofficial payments. Some say that bribes are unnecessary; others say that they are being refused when offered. Especially in small villages, Bulgarians reported that "people know each other there. Bribes are not expected."[24] Yet when there is a widespread practice of bribe giving and bribe taking, people who do not participate can get into trouble. In a focus group in Sofia, a university lecturer had this to say about how bribes affect the grading of student exams: "I know the price is 300 dollars, but I have not given any mark without examining the student. So I have become the black sheep among my fellow-lecturers and they have become nasty toward me."[25]

Some observers argue that bribes often are small and that one should not make a fuss about them. A counter-argument is that the practice leads to unequal treatment of people, as expressed by a respondent from Slovakia in saying that there are "special [maternity] deliveries—paid for, fast, painless. And naturally the attitude of the nurses to those patients was different."[26] From the perspective of the recipient of the unofficial payments, the sums add up. To again cite a respondent from Slovakia, "My cousin cannot praise it enough, being a customs officer. He says: 'Yesterday I brought home slippers for the entire family. I get so many chickens that I do not know where to put them. I need a second fridge.'"[27] Many officials in the region probably feel the same about abundant bribes in the form of flowers, chocolates, and bottles of cognac, but hardly about money.

In addition to representative surveys of the general population, the research team led by William Miller conducted focus group discussions and surveys with public officials. They found that as a rule the experiences related by officials were similar to those of the general public, except that when it came to their own profession the acknowledgment of corruption went down perceptively. "When hospital doctors were asked about hospital doctors, schoolteachers about schoolteachers, or customs officials about customs officials, and so on, the numbers of those who said presents or bribes were likely to be necessary went down from 70 percent to 51 percent on average. But at the same time, even slightly different professions were highly critical of each other," for example schoolteachers when commenting on university staff.[28]

In the entire region, corruption among politicians is a prominent political issue, and at times increasingly so. In Poland the proportion of respondents in national surveys who consider corruption to be a "very great problem" has increased steadily, from 33 percent in 1991 to 46 percent in 2000 and 68 percent in August 2001. In this last survey, 70 percent of respondents expressed the view that many top officials make improper profits. Politicians themselves are only slightly more generous in their opinion of their peers: when a random sample of 101 deputies of Poland's House of Deputies answered a questionnaire in 1998, 18 percent stated that corruption is frequent or very frequent among politicians, 40 percent believed it to be "medium," and 32 percent thought it rare or very rare.[29]

Corruption perceptions also are triggered by the sudden unexplained wealth of public officials and politicians. A typical observation made by a Latvian politician is "if someone drives an upscale Mercedes or other fancy car and his official annual income is one hundred lats [less than $200], I cannot take him to be an honest man."[30] Similar comments are often made in regard to other observations of unexplained riches and conspicuous consumption, such as the building of grandiose villas or taking the family on a trip down the Nile. Although people have occasions to personally witness the luxurious lifestyle of many politicians, the media also like to publish stories about it.

For an entire year a popular newspaper in Armenia featured on its front page photographs of hotels, villas, restaurants, and other expensive properties belonging to ministers, deputies, judges, and their families. While there was no reaction by law enforcement agencies, the consumers of such information must have wondered how all this came about.[31]

Regional Comparisons of Administrative and Grand Corruption

In 2000, scholars at the World Bank published an important study of corruption that covered most countries in the post-communist region. It differentiates between administrative corruption (Level II) and state capture (Level III) and provides sophisticated measures for each, specifically an Administrative Corruption Index and a State Capture Index. The indexes are based on a 1999 survey of more than 3,000 enterprise owners and senior managers in twenty-two countries in Eastern Europe and the area of the former Soviet Union. In addition to being exceptional in providing comparative data across the region, this study stands out by focusing on the experience of firms with a presence there.[32]

The Administrative Corruption Index is an aggregate measure of administrative corruption in the transition countries surveyed. Enterprise managers were asked what share of their annual revenues they typically pay unofficially to public officials in order to "get things done." This refers to bribes to gain licenses, to smooth customs procedures, or to be given advantages in procurement and other government contracts.[33] As Figure 3.2 illustrates, the size of the bribes for the twenty-two countries listed differ considerably, with Croatia scoring best and Azerbaijan scoring worst. The magnitude of differences is considerable, with Russia scoring twice as high as Latvia, and Kyrgyzstan scoring twice as high as Russia. Although these measurements cannot be taken to be exact, they suggest a broad range in the pervasiveness of corruption in interactions between businesses and public administrators. In addition, they indicate that corruption is not just in the minds of people; there is a reality to it, and it is, in this case, measurable in terms of firm revenues.

A different ranking emerges in the State Capture Index, which measures political corruption at the highest levels of government (see Figure 3.3). As outlined in Chapter 2, state capture subverts legitimate and transparent channels of political influence, "reducing the access of competing groups and interests to state officials."[34] Empirically, "the survey identified a number of specific activities that fall within the definition of state capture, including: the 'sale' of Parliamentary votes and presidential decrees to private interests; the sale of civil and criminal court decisions to private interests; corrupt mis-

Figure 3.2   **Administrative Corruption Index, 1999**

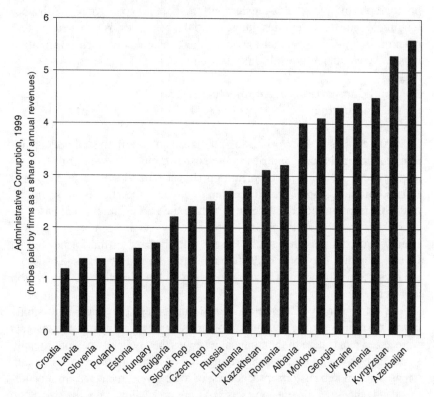

Source: Revised presentation of data from World Bank, *Anticorruption in Transition: A Contribution to the Policy Debate* (Washington, D.C., September 2000), p. 8.

handling of central bank funds; and illegal contributions by private actors to political parties. Firms were asked to measure the *direct impact* on their business from each of these activities, regardless of whether they engaged in such activities themselves."[35]

Compared to the measure used in the Administrative Corruption Index, which asks about the bribe-giving activities of the firms themselves, this index asks for an estimate by firm managers as to whether the various forms of high-level political corruption have had an impact on their enterprises. In this instance Armenia, Hungary, and Slovenia are tied for the cleanest record, whereas Azerbaijan again has the worst rating, followed by Moldova, Russia, and Ukraine. The scale of differences is big, with Ukraine rating four times as badly as Slovenia or Hungary. It is important to note that, like the Administrative Corruption Index and aggregate indexes generally, the State

49

Figure 3.3 **State Capture Index, 1999**

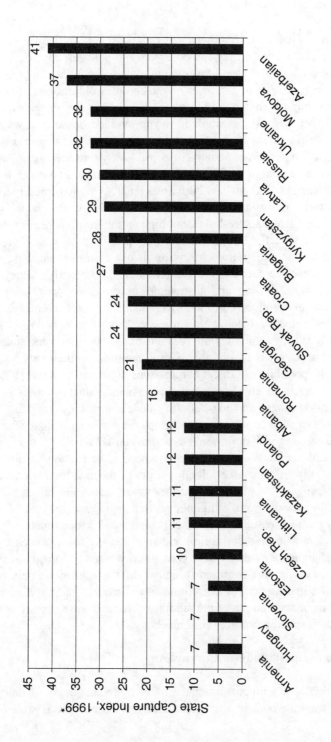

Source: World Bank, *Anticorruption in Transition: A Contribution to the Policy Debate* (Washington, D.C., September 2000), p. 13, revised presentation.

*Share of firms affected by state capture.

Capture Index is just a rough indicator that masks more subtle differences in the patterns of corruption between countries and between specific institutions. As the authors of these indexes caution, they should not be taken as a definitive categorization of countries on the complex dimensions of corruption.[36] Yet the huge advantage of these measures is that they provide empirical data on two major dimensions of corruption, and do so in a way that allows comparisons with most countries in the region. The two indexes also allow a rough comparison of patterns of corruption within specific countries. Some countries rank high on both indexes (Azerbaijan and Ukraine, for example), and some others rank low both times (such as Slovenia and Estonia), while still others show a divergent pattern, especially Armenia, which ranks very low on the State Capture Index, but high on the Administrative Corruption Index. The data for Latvia indicate the opposite pattern of high state capture, but low administrative corruption. If one assumes that these measures are broadly accurate despite methodological complexities, they suggest on what issues anti-corruption strategies may want to focus.

The pattern of forms of corruption in individual countries changes over time, as is indicated by a follow-up survey by another team of World Bank experts in 2002. They again measured administrative corruption and state capture, but unfortunately used slightly different questions in their surveys, thus precluding the possibility of direct comparisons over time between 1999 and 2002. There appears to have been some change in individual countries, but the authors caution against drawing definitive conclusions by saying that "one cannot simply say that corruption is going up or down in individual countries, as we find a complex web of movements and mutations across different forms, features, and dimensions of corruption. We need to be cautious and modest and to constantly recognize the full complexity of the measurement effort."[37] Some of the suggestive findings nevertheless are that while bribes paid by firms in dealings with courts and public service providers appear to have declined, they have increased in tax collection and public procurement.[38]

In sum, administrative corruption and state capture as measured by the World Bank studies provide a way to compare two types of corruption and to do so over the entire post-communist region. But the indexes are only rough measures of some aspects of corruption. As noted in Chapter 2, a whole range of corrupt acts fall under the administrative and state capture categories, each with specific political consequences.

The Media as the Window to Corruption

Personal experience with corruption is limited by the nature of the daily life of average persons, both in terms of quantity of encounters as well as the actual form of corruption. The average citizen rarely learns about institutional or high-level political corruption on his own or from close associates, this experience typically being mediated through newspapers, radio, and television. That the media are a major source of the corruption experience is evident from various surveys. In Romania in 1999, 83 percent of household survey respondents stated that the media are a source of information about corruption in their country, 40 percent named personal experience, 46 percent listed relatives and friends, and 11 percent cited public officials with whom they interact (multiple replies were possible).[39] Anthropologist Klāvs Sedlenieks notes that respondents who participated in his study in Latvia were convinced about widespread corruption because newspapers often write about it and "everyone talks about it."[40] The next chapter elaborates on the content of this talk and the attitudes reflected in it; here it is important to outline the way issues of corruption and its containment come to the attention of people.

The media, especially the newspapers, play several roles in the popular experience of corruption. Their basic role is to inform about political events, yet one needs to ask how the media relate "the facts" about political corruption. Looking first at intensity of coverage, the trend has been one of rising attention. A Slovak study, replicated in Figure 3.4, shows that the coverage of corruption issues in newspapers nearly tripled between 1997 and 2001. While more exposure in newspaper reports increases awareness that corrupt acts occur, it may also raise awareness that something should be done about it. A study of press reports in Latvia for the years 1996–98 finds that the intensity of reporting is closely tied not only to exposés of corruption, but also to public discussions about draft legislation on how to contain it. Reporting intensified in the summer of 1997 when a scandal broke about many ministers and legislators having ignored conflict of interest regulations. Besides straight reporting on the scandal, the leading daily newspaper *Diena* also published thirty commentaries by public figures within three months.[41] Clearly, information and evaluation go hand in hand.

The analysis of Latvian newspapers indicates that items about high-level corruption predominate. There are many allegations of politicians and officials either misusing their offices or failing to observe laws designed to prevent corruption, such as declaring their financial interests. There has been extensive coverage of suspicious dealings in the privatization of attractive objects, disappearing foreign credits, and banking scandals in the course of which many small depositors lost their savings. Many stories appeared on the front page, including reports that law enforcement was largely ineffectual in its investigations and sanctions were rarely imposed. Editorials commented on this and tried to exert pressure on policy makers to be more active

Figure 3.4   **Number of Articles on Corruption in Slovak Print Media, 1997–2001**

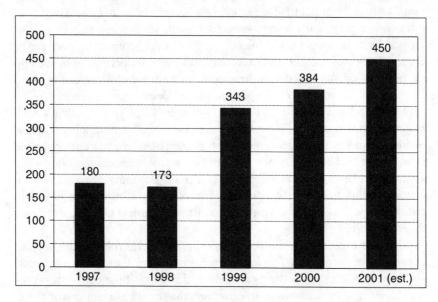

Source: Central Coordination Group, Office of the Slovak Government, *Report on the Fight against Corruption*, October 2001.

in corruption-control efforts.[42] Although this exemplifies how the media can become an advocate for cleaner government, such commentary reinforces the public's understanding that this goal has not been reached.

Newspapers, radio, and television mediate the popular experience of political corruption through their reporting on actual occurrences, such as the unexplained disappearance of millions of dollars in foreign aid, or following investigations and relaying their results. Reporting on investigations by law enforcement agencies is sometimes limited by procedural safeguards, but when access to the proceedings is granted, much information comes to light. Details about investigations by audit chambers (and similar institutions) also get much publicity that focuses on facts. The perception of Romanians that corruption in their country is very high no doubt is influenced by official reports such as the 1999 annual report to the parliament by the Court of Audit that contained scathing accounts of financial irregularities in many ministries, including the Ministry of Finance's allocation of tax relief and illegal reimbursement of taxes.[43]

Investigations by parliamentary committees of inquiry garner even more attention, since they usually involve prominent politicians and proceedings are often broadcast over national radio or television. In Romania, the chief of a Parliamentary Commission of Inquiry into the privatization of the national telecommunications company accused four ministers of having received several million dollars from the winner of the contract, Greek OTE. The state lost huge amounts of money because of the manner in which the privatization contracts were drafted.[44] Another investigation, by the prime minister's Control Department in 2001 into conflicts of interest in Bucharest, concluded that thirty-eight out of sixty-five city councillors were involved in firms that gained contracts from the city. As a result, the City Council resigned.[45] More cases that are thoroughly documented are cited in Chapters 2 and 8.

Since the media are the primary public source of information about corruption, it is of utmost importance that reporting be as accurate as possible. Either too much or too little, or false allegations, can result in serious consequences not only for the people involved, but also for the public and its knowledge about corruption. Much depends on the quality of journalists, especially investigative journalists, yet their job is very hard. In Hungary, journalists participating in focus groups during 1999–2000 noted their difficulties in obtaining good investigative material and how they rarely are able to follow a case to its conclusion due to a chronic lack of follow-up by courts and district attorneys.[46] It also takes courage to investigate cases where money and careers are at stake. Many journalists have risen to the challenge, and quite a few have paid with their lives. During the six years between 1995 and 2001 alone, eleven journalists were killed in Ukraine, one of the most prominent being Igor Aleksandrov, who had led a television program featuring investigative reporting of government corruption and organized crime. Other journalists have been victimized by acts of violence as well as groundless lawsuits and threats to themselves and their families.[47] Such occurrences again are reported in the media, as is the fact that those guilty of the attacks on journalists are usually not apprehended. These reports form another crucial piece of the corruption experience and add to the public's belief that corruption is a real and dangerous dimension of politics.

When the media cover the highly sensitive issue of corruption among politicians, they often become the subject of political pressure by those accused. Besides attempts to influence reporting from the outside, influence is also exerted from inside the media organization whenever an outlet is owned by political forces. Powerful oligarchs wish to control media to cover up their own misdeeds or to plant stories to discredit political rivals. As noted in Chapter 2, the media are often part of the corruption enterprise by selling favorable coverage or deliberately neglecting their public duty to provide accurate information. Also, the media tend to play to the public's interest in soap opera–style drama and to highlight issues that are more scandalous in popular opinion, but that are less significant in terms of political consequences or the amount of money involved. An example is the penchant of the post-communist press to comment on frivolous and often illegal official spending on luxury cars and foreign travel, while paying less attention to intricate financial schemes involving sums a thousand times larger.

There are other ways the media may distort the reality of corruption. Allegations of corruption among elites are at times false, their revelation motivated by struggles among the politically powerful, or the story is deliberately muddled to protect specific interests. The scandals surrounding the privatization of the state-owned firm Bulgartabak in Bulgaria in 2002 presents a vivid example. The enterprise was known for illegal party financing, and the government initially appointed a new director with the declared intention of limiting the possibility of inside deals. A young Bulgarian was chosen whose entire career had been with multinational companies outside of the country, none of them related to the tobacco business. After some initial controversy over his high Western-level salary, one of the contenders for privatizing the enterprise accused the new director of soliciting a bribe of half a million dollars. The accusers claimed to have tapes proving the solicitation and that they were ready to turn these over to law enforcement. For several weeks, the media extensively covered the case, openly favoring the accusers, and as a result the director was replaced. Yet the notorious tapes were never produced, and it soon emerged that the accusing party was linked to a well-known Russian businessman who had been expelled from Bulgaria as a threat to national security. Soon there were further revelations that the new director had tried to stop illegal operations between Bulgartabak and the group making the allegations, but in the end all investigations were closed for lack of evidence.[48]

The Bulgartabak scandal is illustrative of many cases in the post-communist region where a party accused of malfeasance reacts with allegations about the corruption of the accusers. In a whirlwind of accusations and counter-accusations, observers have difficulty discerning the truth. Since accusations against the politically powerful rarely lead to conclusive investigations by law enforcement, the public remains at a loss about what has really occurred. The inconclusive ending of many scandals raises the specter of possible corruption—or at least frustrating incompetence—among law enforcement and judicial authorities. The lack of accountability strengthens beliefs that public institutions and their leaders cannot be trusted.

There is an interesting analytical point here. Whenever there is a public battle of allegations among politicians and other members of the elite, the battle itself reinforces the public's belief that political corruption is rampant, even if nothing is ever proven in court. Logically, observers are unlikely to conclude that both sides are innocent; it is much more likely that they will think that both or at least one side is corrupt. Therefore the allegations as such and the content of what is alleged lead the public to think that some-one—or "everyone"—is corrupt. Effective investigations and prosecutions are needed not only to bring guilty parties to justice, but also to provide the public with reliable information.

Scandals involving allegations about grand corruption both in terms of the outcome at stake and in terms of the prominence of perpetrators have been front page news in all post-communist countries. Most have never been solved, a prominent exception being the Rywin affair mentioned at the beginning of this chapter. The scandal originated in 2002 when the Polish government drafted a bill that would have prevented any one consortium from owning a national newspaper and a national television channel at the same time. The bill threatened the interests of the media consortium Agora, which had plans to purchase a private TV station. Subsequently, Polish filmmaker Lew Rywin, co-producer of *Schindler's List* and *The Pianist*, was accused of having solicited Poland's best-known newspaper, *Gazeta Wyborcza*, into paying him $17.5 million by claiming he could use his influence with leading politicians to change the proposed law so that the newspaper's parent company, Agora SA, could purchase the TV station. The editor of the newspaper, famous dissident Adam Michnik, revealed the attempted bribery and as a result both a parliamentary investigation and court case were launched.

The affair was a huge news item in Poland from 2002 to April 2004 as detailed allegations were published in the media and the sessions of the parliamentary commission of inquiry were broadcast for several hours once or twice weekly. The public hearings implied the involvement of many prominent political figures with close ties to each other, including the president, prime minister, and minister of justice. They denied the charges, yet were contradicted by other officials. A crucial piece of evidence was the transcript of a secret tape recording of Rywin's solicitation. On the recording, Rywin claims that he is acting on behalf of "a group holding power" and that if Agora fails to pay the bribe, the prime minister will kill any legislation working to Agora's advantage. At the trial Rywin insisted that he was drunk when the crucial conversation was recorded, and that he had been set up, but he was sentenced to two and a half years in jail. Rywin's connection to Prime Minister Miller and other prominent politicians could not be proven.[49]

Even though the involvement of politicians in the affair was not proven, the scandal rocked Poland's minority social democratic government. It contributed to a dramatic fall in popularity ratings of Miller's Social Democratic Party, forcing the prime minister to promise that he would resign, which he did after Poland entered the European Union on May 1, 2004.

A complication in the effect of media monitoring of this and other scandals is that there usually is a time lag between a corrupt act and when it is brought to public attention. Corruption investigations typically refer to events that occurred in earlier periods, and this creates the paradoxical situation of people thinking that there is less corruption when there actually is more, and vice versa. When no investigations are conducted, or at least are not revealed in the media or open courts, people are likely to believe that government is cleaner than it actually is. In contrast, revelations about past corruption often occur under the stewardship of less corrupt governments, yet these revelations easily can color contemporary perceptions about rampant political corruption. A Bulgarian scholar has concluded that this phenomenon undermines the incentives for corruption cleanups.[50] The counterargument is that this is true only if the officials heading the cleanup are inept at demonstrating that things are actually changing. The discussion about considerations for an effective anti-corruption strategy in Chapter 9 will elaborate on these points.

Another occasion when the media pay more attention to corruption is during election campaigns. Since the late 1990s, many electoral candidates have been eager to align themselves which the image of less corrupt government. Concerned groups of citizens too have used elections to put the spotlight on malfeasance by politicians. In Slovakia a broad coalition of reform groups in the elections of 1998 used the issue to rally voters and oust the Meciar government. In Bulgaria civil society organizations joined together in 1997 to form the anti-corruption initiative Coalition 2000. It subsequently played a key role in assisting the new government, which came to power on a platform that included the fight against corruption as one of its main priorities. Yet despite much fanfare, the National Anti-Corruption Strategy made little progress besides raising public awareness that something was wrong. Promises of corruption cleanups and a politics of morality again were central elements in Bulgaria's elections in June 2001 and allowed the National Movement Simeon II, a party founded by Bulgaria's former king just three months prior to elections, to win an overwhelming majority in parliament.[51] Elections in many other post-communist countries have similarly focused on corruption issues, each time adding new information and perspectives.

A more routine occasion when the media raise the topic of corruption is when the findings of new research are released or when the issue comes up in discussions with international institutions, as has frequently happened in the context of accession to the European Union and NATO. In the case of Latvia, there has been extensive news coverage of all such instances, for example when the first large survey about corruption was published in late 1998.[52] The discussion was even more intense because the study—showing that corruption was a serious issue—was conducted by scholars from the World Bank Institute and was thus given more credence than tends to be the case with local studies.

Conclusion

People in the post-communist region encounter the issues of corruption and anti-corruption on a daily basis. It is not unusual for them to personally experience corruption in encounters with public officials, and they often hear about it from close associates. Additional information emerges from surveys of representative population samples, households, enterprise managers, and public officials. Most importantly, however, the media provide a daily indirect experience of the reality of corruption through their investigations and reporting. These reports mostly focus on corrupt acts by politicians and other publicly visible persons, and often involve scandals. In contrast, individual citizens personally are most familiar with routine petty corruption during bureaucratic encounters.

The media have a pivotal role in what a society knows and does about corruption since they reproduce a discourse about it, define themes, and provide accurate as well as inaccurate information. They not only report readily available news, but also engage in active investigative reporting. Besides informing, the media have a socializing role in the sense that they provide the images and language of corruption. The power of the media cannot be understated, as their actions have helped to bring down governments in post-communist societies. The public looks to the media to be its voice in the struggle with what it perceives to be a bureaucratic governmental system riddled with corruption. But there are dangers, here, too, as the media are not immune to exaggeration and lack of follow-up. One can conclude that a good anti-corruption policy should fight both corruption itself and the lack of good information about it.

4

Attitudes and Discourses about Corruption

> More than most other reform efforts, Hong Kong's was based
> upon the realization that corruption involves complex
> interactions of state and society; that cultural standards play a
> major role in defining the working meaning and the social
> significance of corruption; and that legal reforms,
> if they were to be effective, must be closely linked
> to those standards and values.
>
> *Michael Johnston, "Corruption as a Process"*[1]

As the quotation above indicates, the containment of corruption is only successful if it is based on a culturally framed approach. Although the principles evident in global strategies are useful, they fail unless they are adjusted for regional and local conditions. This chapter provides an overview of the attitudes toward corruption in the post-communist region. It relates how people view corruption, demonstrates their level of tolerance, discusses the actions they think the state—or they themselves—should take, and describes how they talk about corruption. Public talk and its underlying perceptions and attitudes are tied to behavior. Attitudes determine whether people will participate in corrupt acts or will be active in trying to contain them. There is an important interactive loop between what people think and do. If one wants to change behavior, one must consider attitudes, values, and expectations.

The post-communist region includes nearly thirty independent states and many cultures and religions. There is room for future investigations of how each distinct identity affects corruption in particular countries. This study focuses on the cultural context of the common legacy of the communist era on basic habits of political thinking and acting. As one examines attitudes toward corruption in the various countries of the region, it is striking how many similarities emerge, which points to the continuing impact of common experiences. There is something akin to a post-communist political culture:

certain ways of looking at politics are similar from one country to the next. The communist regimes put great effort into political socialization and the control of alternative perspectives, and this has had a lasting impact on many people. A fundamental socializing experience was the necessity to evade pressure from the state and obtain social and economic goods through personal contacts. The reality of everyday life under communism shaped political habits and attitudes that focused on personal concerns and unofficial methods of accomplishing things.

The upheavals of regime transition formed other commonly held attitudes. The slow and indecisive transition to the rule of law and reliable law enforcement has had a lasting impact on views about what is corrupt. Trustworthy political and economic elites were slow to emerge. However, as this chapter outlines some of the characteristic attitudes held by many people in the region, it does not claim homogeneity among individuals, contexts, and countries. The discussion of similarities is not meant to erase the role of unique traits of events and places.

Among the general population, many believe that it does not "pay" to be honest and that their own dishonesty is justified by the corrupt behavior of elites. A large segment of the public in the post-communist region sees corruption as being pervasive and very difficult to deal with. A typical statement is that of a young Latvian customs officer: "Everybody thinks [about] how to survive today and cannot afford to think [about] how good or bad corrupt practices are for the state and for the future. And, let's say I will stop doing such [things]. I'll just be a loser, because everybody else does it and [benefits] from it."[2]

Many who engage in petty corruption use similar self-serving arguments to justify their personal dishonesty by citing the corruption of others. They like to point to corruption at the top, the power elites, and "the system." Some argue that circumventing cumbersome rules humanizes the administrative and legal system of the state, which is seen as unresponsive and oppressive. Most people believe that high-level political corruption can be contained only by decisive action from the top and that there is little they themselves can do. In contrast, corruption experts argue that anti-corruption campaigns cannot succeed without public support. If ordinary people and businesses are accustomed to dealing with the state through payoffs, even if this is considered a "necessary evil," then a change in attitude is essential to achieve fundamental, systemic change.[3]

This chapter relies on surveys, anthropological studies, and discourse data.[4] It opens with studies that compare permissiveness toward corruption in various regions of the world and then moves to characterize broadly held attitudes and public talk. A differentiation between elite and mass political culture is made throughout this analysis.

The Distinctiveness of Post-Communist Attitudes

Certain views about corruption are characteristic of the people in the post-communist region, as can be illustrated by a study that measures differences in permissiveness toward corruption worldwide. Alejandro Moreno has constructed a permissiveness index based on surveys from sixty-four societies covered by the World Values Survey and European Values Survey conducted between 1981 and 2001. The index measures the extent to which certain corrupt practices are seen as culturally justifiable; specifically it measures the extent to which respondents justify "claiming government benefits to which you are not entitled," "avoiding a fare on public transport," "cheating on taxes if you have a chance," and people "accepting a bribe in the course of their duties."[5] Results show that although most societies are to some degree permissive toward corruption, these attitudes vary cross-culturally. East Asian societies are least likely to justify corruption, followed by Western democracies, and African societies. Latin America and South Asia have higher levels of permissiveness toward corruption, with formerly communist societies scoring the highest.[6] As with all empirical measures, this index has weaknesses, but it highlights regional differences in how the public views certain corrupt acts. Furthermore, it underscores the argument of this chapter when it says that "corruption not only is a problem of governing, but also a daily expectation among the mass publics."[7]

That the post-communist region shows certain attitudinal patterns is confirmed by an analysis looking jointly at data from the World Values Survey of 1995–98 and rankings in the Transparency International Corruption Index. It finds that the formerly communist-ruled societies stand out with an overemphasis on survival values, at the expense of self-expression values, including those linked to community.[8] As shown below, arguments about the necessities of daily life and survival are also prominent in public discourse, thus confirming the results of the more rigorous surveys.

But political attitudes are not static; they shift over time, especially when major changes occur in regimes, policies, or social conditions. The study of permissiveness toward corruption worldwide shows that the score of post-communist societies worsened between 1990 and 1995, which could be explained by the radical changes occurring during that period. After 1995, some countries in the region seemed to have gone in the opposite direction, although there are not enough recent data to verify this.[9] Nevertheless, the analytical conclusion is that political culture is dynamic and can change, for better or worse. That is so if one accepts a definition of political culture that links a people's political cognition, emotions, evaluations, and values to concrete political structures, experiences, and opportunities.[10] This is also in accord with the theoretical assumptions of neo-institutionalism underlying this study, as these assumptions argue that institutions can shape new attitudes and behaviors. People's attitudes toward corruption can change, and with this the overall level of corruption in specific societies can change. Yet, besides constituting a scholarly argument, this proposition refers to a crucial public attitude, and one has to ask how many people in specific post-communist states believe that such change is possible.

Discourses about Corruption

Societies experience parallel discourses about corruption. One discourse is that of people genuinely concerned about the advantages of a corruption-free society, who use arguments and language about civic virtue and the high costs of corruption. The extent of such civic views in the post-communist region will be elaborated on in later chapters, which discuss anti-corruption policies. Here the focus is on the many people at both the elite and mass level who are ambivalent about corruption. Many politicians and citizens have contradictory views about corruption: there are times when they justify it and times when they decry it. Attitudes fluctuate depending on the type of corruption people refer to, or depending on the audience. This contradictory discourse is first analyzed among members of the elite and then among the general population.

Elite Attitudes and Discourse

Paradoxically, few studies of post-communist corruption have focused on the political elites, yet in the perception of the populace they are at the core of the corruption game. Furthermore, there is a link between grand corruption and the petty corruption engaged in by citizens, since the latter excuse their behavior with that of public officials and power holders. Elites set the tone of how society discusses corruption, especially if the media relate their talk uncritically or indulge the public interest in the details of scandalous allegations. True—and false—allegations about the corruption of political rivals often are raised in the course of power struggles and especially during election campaigns. As Andras Sajo puts it, "political . . . competition is about the successful imposition of corruption labels."[11]

Although elite members at times use the corruption issue to make themselves look better during elections, or to accuse rivals during power struggles, their dominant attitudes are defensiveness and denial that corruption is a serious issue. The notably poor acceptance of criticism among the powerful often leads to counterattacks on whoever raises the issue of dirty politics. An implicit message, at times stated explicitly, is that "nobody is clean" and it thus is unwise to "point the finger" at others. A 1998 study of scholars from the World Bank stated that in Latvia, and by extension in other post-communist countries, there are "several empirical observations—denial of the damage caused to society, blaming corruption mostly on low salaries, admission that many civil servants take jobs for the unofficial benefits, and sharing bribes with colleagues—which suggest that a worrying culture of corruption within the civil service may be hindering *accountability*."[12]

When accusations of political corruption arise, officials tend to use strictly formalistic arguments, saying that the incident does not involve corruption because there is no law prohibiting the particular act in question. Ironically, although this argument takes a very narrow view of the law to excuse corruption, those wishing to make such excuses use the reverse argument as well, that is, that someone has violated a law only "formally," not in substance.[13] Another phrase favored by many politicians and others trying to refute allegations of corrupt acts is that something is "not technically illegal."[14] Other interpretative maneuvers are linked to the fact that anti-corruption laws are often badly written or have loopholes. Many laws state that they apply only to public officials, yet the definition of public official remains unclear, for example in Bulgaria.[15] This sticking to the letter and even grammar of the law ignores the spirit of the law, as well as the broader question of the public duty and responsibility of politicians, civil servants, and others employed in public service. By in essence arguing that there is no crime if there is no law, post-communist officials typically relate corruption solely to the breaking of laws, ignoring the significance of ethics and their responsibility to work for the good of the people they represent.

Elite apologists for illicit deals also ignore the special circumstances of regime change and transition to democracy where not only specific laws, but entire systems of law, had to be created anew, and thus the more basic democratic "law" of political representatives serving the common good of the public was paramount. A radical change of political system, such as the transition from communism to democracy, unavoidably leaves a legal vacuum in which references to a lack of laws are gratuitous. Moreover, politicians who justify acts widely seen as illicit by saying that they are not forbidden by law, themselves often prevented such laws from passing. In other instances, lawmakers have passed absurd provisions: until recently Poland had a law that allowed "sting" bribes by undercover officers only in the amount of 202,670 euros.[16] Evasion and circular arguments are recognized as such by the citizenry and leave it frustrated, as does the use of Orwellian language and insultingly ridiculous arguments as to why cases could not be pursued. An example is that of a defendant in Poland who was prosecuted in an organized crime case, but secured a doctor's certificate that he was claustrophobic and therefore could not be incarcerated.[17]

Prosecutors and other law enforcement officials often reject statements or specific allegations about high levels of corruption by saying that they have received "no information" of any wrongdoing. This implies that it is up to the public or media to ferret out specific proof and bring it to them, while the real issue is whether the law enforcement agencies themselves seek such proof by initiating investigations. Another rationalization for inactivity or poor results is that the funding of the law enforcement and judicial branches is inadequate, which has been the case throughout the region (see Chapter 8). Yet again, the same decision makers often are responsible. At a convention of Latvian judges and legal experts in May 2002, there was consensus that the judicial system had not been a priority for political leaders. Several former justice ministers emphasized that the finance and prime ministers usually gave them about half of the funds they asked for even though the sums involved were small in proportion to the overall budget. Several commentators thought that there was a deliberate policy to keep the judicial system weak.

Politicians and other highly placed people often challenge reports and allegations about extensive corruption. A frequent argument is that the studies mostly rely on the subjective perceptions of survey respondents rather than actual experiences.[18] At other times purely opportunistic arguments are used, such as that political corruption is unavoidable due to a lack of funding for party activities.[19] An appreciation of the negative impact of conflicts of interest has been slow to emerge, and there have been arguments that businesspeople should be active in the legislature and government, but without giving up their businesses. Thus Latvian "oligarch" and former head of the local branch of the Soviet KGB Guntis Indriksons stated in an 1993 interview that "the worldwide practice that ministers cease working for their business for the time they are in office is useless in our case, because the state lacks the funds to pay decent salaries. Therefore a minister could be a businessman who simultaneously solves his own problems and those of the state."[20] This remark also illustrates low political sensitivity to the need of politicians to at least rhetorically claim that they sacrifice their personal good to serve the public.

Widespread elite skepticism about the extent to which public officials work for the public good was found by a Norwegian study of elite attitudes in the three Baltic states and Russia. When legislators as well as top leaders from ministries, the judiciary, state and private enterprises, local government, and cultural enterprises were asked whether they agreed with the statement that public officials in their country should pursue their self-interest more than the good of the people, 39 percent agreed fully or somewhat in Estonia, 51 percent in Lithuania, 55 percent in Latvia, and 61 percent in Russia.[21]

Several articles in a magazine for Latvian businesspeople relate their thoughts about bribery. One article pinpoints a perennial theme in its heading: "Corruption in business—it pays off and is unavoidable."[22] Again arguments tend to be contradictory. On the one hand, businesspeople acknowledge that bribery exists and is used to circumvent red tape or lack of cooperation by officials; on the other hand, they claim that talk about high levels of corruption is misleading and "real proof" is lacking.[23] A similar article about a group of businesspeople in 2001 cites a banker as saying, "there is a general view, that the less a businessman gives to the state, the better, because the state gives him nothing in return."[24] People are said to dislike to inform on bribe givers, or to go to court if they are pressured, because they want to avoid trouble and "most people themselves have given something to someone."[25] The president of an investment company is quoted as saying, "it isn't my job to fight corruption in the state. Unfortunately the situation is what it is. It is difficult to compete if someone uses bribes, and someone else doesn't. The more private a business is, the less these things happen. State property that is involved in various tenders is unprotected."[26]

Many legal professionals too feel that corruption cannot be contained. The president of the Latvian Law Society, Aivars Borovkovs, has spoken quite cynically about initiatives to fight corruption, including their origination with outside institutions that impose their will on Latvia.

The following are excerpts from an interview in 2000:

> *Interviewer*: In your opinion will the formation of the Corruption Prevention Bureau help to solve the problem?
>
> *Borovkovs*: Absolutely not. If we continue in such a manner then [we must remember] there are 356 clauses in the criminal law and we could form a bureau for each one of them. This, in my opinion, is another example of the squandering of state funds. . . .
>
> *Interviewer*: Where do you see a solution to this problem?
>
> *Borovkovs*: With the rise in living standards and the resolution of various social problems in society, the disease will slowly disappear. Unfortunately, it will not happen during the lifetime of the present political generation.
>
> *Interviewer*: How do you rate the recently publicized campaign for corruption prevention?
>
> *Borovkovs*: As any other campaign. As far as I know the pinnacle in political campaigns was achieved during the Stalin period and in China during the Cultural Revolution. Khrushchev also was great at organizing campaigns for corn growing, and Gorbachev launched an absolute and totally blundering struggle against alcoholism.[27]

While the last part of this statement illustrates that communist-era experiences often serve as points of reference for evaluations of policies, it also shows the belief that anti-corruption policies are bound to fail and that the only hope lies in gradual social change.

Power holders often excuse corruption and their difficulties in dealing with it by blaming the people and referring to "culture" in the sense of a traditional culture that undermines cleanup attempts. This argument has been used by prominent Russian politicians, among them Anatolii Chubais, who has argued that "corruption depends very little on the authorities. It depends on the people."[28] President Iliescu of Romania expressed a similar view when he stated in 2002 that corruption "must be eradicated from the bottom up."[29] Yet, as illustrated below, the people on their part think that much depends on the elites, and that corruption must be tackled from the top. This leads to a standoff. As noted in the case of Hungary, "the ruling elite sets a bad example for the rest of the population by ignoring laws and court rulings and failing to resign after being found guilty of corruption."[30]

The Public Image of Elites

Popular discourse in the region reveals that many people see corruption mainly as an elite problem and that the image of politicians is very poor. The popular explanation why the powerful do little to fight corruption is that the elites themselves are part and parcel of it. After the initial euphoria about the newly won freedom following the collapse of communism, the image of politicians changed quickly. The picture of noble and honest people was replaced by the conviction that "politicians always steal." In Poland, the perception that high-ranking officials abuse their posts for personal gain rose from 42 percent in 1995 to 61 percent in 1999. Many believed that nepotism was key in filling prominent posts.[31] A 2002 Bulgarian study similarly observed a high level of disillusionment with those who enter politics, with politics being seen primarily as a means for personal acquisition rather than public service. As the author of the study noted, "Cynicism and resignation seem to be prevailing attitudes."[32]

A common view is that power elites subdivide spheres of interest, agree not to challenge each other, and then engage in a "system of covering up by silence."[33] Thus, importantly, silence about the essence of corruption is part of the discourse about it. Another popularly held view is that this silence is due to the standoff created by unspoken, or surreptitiously alluded to, mutual blackmail. When scandals do break, people suspect that ulterior motives are at play. Thus a legislator in Latvia commented during an uproar over mostly procedural malfeasance in mid-1997 that the scandal was artificially inflated to divert attention from the more serious corruption involving millions of dollars of foreign credit. "It is tragic that everyone has kompromat on everybody else, therefore everyone pretends that nothing has happened."[34]

Strikingly often law enforcement officials fail to follow up on serious allegations, thus strengthening the impression of possible cover-ups or collusion. This phenomenon is commented upon by a schoolgirl participating in a Latvian essay-writing contest about corruption. She notes that newspapers write about suspected corruption on a daily basis, "yet, if this problem is indeed this pressing in Latvia and the press writes about it this much, why is it that until now no high official has been convicted of bribery or misuse of public office?"[35] Similar points are made about other states in the region, such as Romania, where strong perceptions of high-level corruption are in stark contrast to the lack of convictions at that level.[36] A Romanian scholar sees the problem as being comprehensive: "Corruption, as a concept, does not capture the failure of politicians in these societies to construct a public-interest space, a failure that leaves blatant partisan interests to reign over every aspect of life, from privatization to the regulation of public broadcasting."[37]

Popular views about corrupt habits among power elites revolve around notions of disproportionate power, collusion, and mutual protection. A survey conducted in Armenia in 2002 found that few citizens are prepared to report bribery to the law enforcement agencies, because they do not believe that any action will be taken. In the words of a housewife: "They have it all—the power, the connections and the force. I'm not going to fight them. I'd rather give them the couple of dollars they ask for and spare myself an endless bureaucratic ordeal."[38] A Russian scholar speaks of the "massive co-optation of officials, administrations, and law-enforcement agencies," for corrupt deals and also notes the "almost total impunity of the principal actors in these processes." She hazards a quantitative estimate by saying that "only 1 percent of 'corruption crimes' are solved in Russia; only one of every thousand economic crimes ends up in court. The greater the size of the deal and the extortion, the higher the level of the 'receiving' (extorting) official, the greater the guarantee of impunity."[39]

In commenting about the Rywin scandal in Poland, a Polish anti-corruption activist noted that the case suggested much deeper connections among the media, business, the courts, and the government than she and others had expected. She added that the most dangerous aspect of Polish politics is "the Teflon effect. Politicians can go through scandal after scandal and not be affected. That does not help to create public trust or standards" in public life.[40]

People often use allusions when talking about political corruption and how it works. In Latvia common allusions involve phrases like "you need to know the rules of the game," "circles of friends help each other out," "birds of a feather do not attack each other,"[41] "a telephone call decides everything."[42] In an in-depth interview with an anthropologist, a former member of the cabinet repeated the often-used expression that "politics is a dirty business," and then explained: "I have seen it from inside and do not think I will ever go back there. There is only one set of rules for playing that game. If you cannot play by these rules, you are out. It is not possible to describe all [the] absurdities and sharing that takes place in the government. And what is the sense to get them to the Prosecutor's Office? There are no institutions to control the Prosecutor's Office. They go hand in hand, after the principle scratch my back and I'll scratch yours—I see that [the] system works that way. And if I rise up against it I'll lose everything, both job and bread. I am forced to obey the system, otherwise I cannot pull through."[43] His wife added that everyone thought him a fool for not taking bribes and that because of his refusal he was eased out of government.[44]

People also speak of "corporate ties" and at times use the Soviet-era term *blat* to denote illicit favors to acquaintances or relatives. For example, in a small town close ties and the mutual exchange of favors among local lawyers, prosecutors, and judges means that the outcomes of legal cases are most likely to favor other locals. Corporate ties are also seen to explain nepotism and cronyism in getting good jobs.[45]

Yet some think that corruption can have a positive role in getting public projects on their way: "Well, take the example of the National Library—it would be great if someone were to bribe all those who have to make decisions on this and then it would get done. . . . Otherwise nothing happens."[46] This underlines the ambivalence of public attitudes toward corruption. While generally decried, corruption is also seen as a system with specific informal rules that make for a degree of functionality in business and social affairs.

Mass Attitudes: The "Normalization" of Corruption

For many people in the post-communist region corruption is a normal phenomenon that is internalized or easily excused, if an excuse is called for. When discussing Slovakia, the 2002 European Union Monitoring report speaks of "a very high degree of internalization of bribery—or at least informal payments and gifts—as normal."[47] It finds a troubling level of popular tolerance of corruption and that its cultural acceptance hinders efforts to fight it.[48] An analysis of popular attitudes in Russia concludes that a bribe that resolves a problem is considered normal, and helping a friend receive a valuable license, state contract, or a position in a state enterprise is viewed as something akin to a moral responsibility.[49] Findings from Poland are more ambivalent, in that a 1999 survey reports 83 percent of respondents agreeing with a statement that bribes are always and everywhere immoral, although half also say that bribes are justified in certain situations. Thirty-six percent of those polled say that "even if circumstances forced me to give a bribe, I would not do so."[50] Similar findings in Latvia have led an anthropologist to conclude that as one considers anti-corruption strategies, one needs to realize that the public holds two divergent views of corruption: an idealistic view of corruption being negative, and a practical individual view that corruption is useful and worthwhile to participate in. In resolving this clash of views, the individual practical approach tends to win out, even more so as many people have a negative image of the state.[51]

In-depth interviews with twenty mid-level young entrepreneurs and state employees in Latvia in the fall of 2000 focused on what activities people associate with corruption and how they view its legitimacy. Although respondents struggled to distinguish "gifts" from "bribes" and "corruption," the issue of gifts to public officials nevertheless was often raised and thus belongs to the corruption discourse.[52] Some respondents make a point of distinguishing between "bribes," and "corruption," and see as corrupt only that which is detrimental to public interests. If a respondent feels that a bribe has no negative consequence for society, this action is seen as justifiable. The main example cited is bribes given to the traffic police, but other cases involve unofficial payments to doctors or educators. Respondents also tend to justify any illicit deal they themselves participate in, but see it as immoral when others engage in them.[53] Illicit acts are seen as justifiable if they help overcome red tape and other bureaucratic hurdles, or "if they help defend one's interests in a situation that is already corrupted."[54] The latter logic is similar to the points raised in Chapter 6 about the links between regime legitimacy and corruption.

Yet respondents also point to the negative side of corruption, saying that they feel uncomfortable when engaging in illegal acts, and that it is difficult to know exactly how to behave according to the "unofficial rules." Other costs of corruption are related to the way respondents view society and the state. Some recognize that corruption undermines faith in the state and its institutions; others mention that it is unfair to other members of society. Many respondents emphasize that corruption is bad if it occurs at the highest level of government, because that endangers the interest of the entire state, whereas individual corruption is seen to involve the interests of only a few people.[55] An illicit act often is seen as the only way to avoid hassles, as explained by an Armenian woman: "I would have had to endure several months of red tape to secure my pension. It would have been too strenuous for me physically, so I paid a small bribe and the issue was settled in a matter of days. Many people I know would rather pay a bribe than spend months running from one government office to another."[56]

The Image of the State and Public Institutions

The legitimacy of states, regimes, and their policies influence views about what is and is not corrupt. Several comparative studies of post-communist societies reveal considerable skepticism toward public institutions, although trust and levels of confidence in the state differ over time, from one institution to another, and between countries.[57] Often the police and other law enforcement agencies are viewed as a repressive part of the state administration and not as fulfilling their official functions of fighting crime, protecting the population, and providing security.[58] One comparison between various countries in Eastern and Western Europe shows that in the latter, public trust in the police and courts is more than twice as high as in the former.[59] Also, as noted in Chapter 3, in many post-communist countries the police and the judicial system are ranked among the most corrupt public institutions and this again deters people from turning to them for help.

There is a link between people engaging in illicit actions and not trusting the judicial system to help get justice. Several of the young Latvian entrepreneur interviewees noted that when they feel sure that they are in the right, they do not turn to the courts. One respondent elaborated how he only bribes if he cannot solve his problems otherwise: "I would be happy if one could resolve all problems legally. For example, you may know that you are right and could prove your case in court. If that would work, I would never bribe. . . . But the courts are seen as part of the state and therefore one cannot trust them. They support each other."[60] In short, there is little faith in the ability of law enforcement to defend people against corrupt officials, and this is taken as a justification for using illicit means to get justice. Going outside the legal domain because it is difficult to resolve disputes through formal procedures has also been cited as a major problem in Russia. Informal means are used because state institutions, including the judiciary, are widely seen as self-serving and incapable of fulfilling their obligations to the citizenry.[61]

In some countries distrust of public institutions has risen over time. Distrust rose constantly during the 1990s in Russia, indicating declining state legitimacy and with it the reciprocal behavior of citizens.[62] Asked to identify the most characteristic features of post-communist rule in Russia, 63 percent of Russians identified it as "criminal, corrupt," followed by 41 percent finding it to be "remote, alien."[63] Anthropologists working in Latvia similarly found that most people think the state machinery works against the interests of society.[64] Importantly, respondents often link their own behavior to that of the state. This is how one woman explained why she cheats on taxes: "The state does not care for our health, for our old parents—we have to do it ourselves. I would rather use my tax money for such purposes. If I would pay taxes honestly I could not survive. We are smart and know how to survive here. You [cannot] live otherwise in such a system. Those who do not live here will never understand that. People have [become] used to and are forced to live that way. It is not unethical. We need food to eat. We just take care of ourselves."[65]

Focus group participants in Latvia have similarly emphasized daily survival and the need to surmount barriers put up by the state. This view of the detrimental role of the state is crucial in legitimizing personal corrupt acts. Respondents do recognize their part in corruption, yet do not feel responsible for it: they "are made" to participate. A representative survey conducted in Latvia in 1999 found that 78 percent of the respondents feel that "the bureaucratic system forces you to give bribes."[66] A vicious circle is at play here: societal relations are based on reciprocity, and if citizens perceive that public institutions do not serve them, they themselves will become delinquent in doing their part in paying taxes, observing laws, and engaging in public service. Many analysts from the region link this to the legacy of the communist era. For example, the president of the Hungarian Audit Office has said: "In those decades when the values of public ownership were loudly praised and hypocrisy was the norm, it was almost fashionable to cheat on taxes and rob the state. . . . My opinion . . . is that formal laws have been and continue to be undermined by an attitude of open cynicism."[67]

Who Should Fight Corruption and How?

Besides viewing corruption as an unavoidable evil that originates from elites and is systemic, many post-communist citizens feel that there is little that they personally can do about it. In a typical study, the Czech Institute for Public Opinion Research repeatedly found that corruption and economic criminality are regarded as very urgent problems by a high percentage of respondents (80 percent in October 2000), yet according to another survey, in 1999 only one-fifth would report an act of corruption to the police.[68] Similarly in 1999, many Slovak officials stated that they definitely or probably would not inform on their colleagues if they learned that they had accepted bribes. Of those who said they probably would not report, many cited the fear of harming themselves (for instance, "I am afraid for my job") and a distaste for hurting colleagues (for example, "I don't want to cause problems for them").[69] Three years later, in March 2002, only 17 percent of respondents said that they would report cases of police corruption, and only 4 percent would definitely do so. Eighteen percent of respondents would not do so for fear of retaliation, while 15 percent believe that doing so "would not lead to any result."[70]

Another reason why people are reluctant to report crimes to the police is that most individuals themselves have something to hide and fear that this may come out during an investigation or in retribution. Reporting is especially difficult when officials share bribes with colleagues or superiors. Sixty-four percent of public officials in Georgia in mid-1998 reported that when mid-level bureaucrats extract bribes, they share the bribes with colleagues or supervisors.[71] The rates are much lower in Slovakia, but higher again elsewhere.[72] In a situation like the one in Georgia, one must doubt the effectiveness of any anti-corruption campaign. Superiors cannot be counted on to discipline their staff when they themselves are benefiting from illicit practices, and colleagues who get a share of a bribe cannot be expected to blow the whistle unless a special program to protect them is put in place.

At times police are unresponsive because too many crime reports reflect badly on their work. A kiosk owner in Russia who had frequently been extorted put it in these words: "The more I send reports to the militia, the more likely it is that the militia will close my kiosk, even if I am the victim. This is so because the official crime-rates in the district will increase and the local militia won't have a good image on paper."[73]

The public sees itself as helpless. When respondents to a three-time survey in Latvia in 2000 and 2001 were asked whether they personally could do anything to diminish corruption, 52 percent chose the reply that they "could do nothing because the struggle is at the state level."[74] Other answers included: not to give bribes (29%), report to responsible institutions (15%), report to the mass media (15%), and become engaged in relevant NGOs (4%). These results were largely consistent over time, with the exception that there is a correlation with older people being more likely to say that they themselves can do nothing to curtail corruption, and younger people being more likely to say that corruption should be reported to responsible institutions (19 percent among 18–24 year olds compared to 10 percent among people over 55).[75] The latter suggests that the public's willingness to cooperate with law enforcement agencies may increase over time. Some optimism also emerges from Miller's large-scale study of Ukraine, the Czech Republic, Slovakia, and Bulgaria, which concludes that both the public and street-level officials believe that reform is possible. An overwhelming majority of the public think that corruption would be controlled in their country if their government made "a strong and sincere effort" to do so. However, as Miller and his coauthors note, few people think that their government is sincerely committed to reducing corruption, and therefore such people welcome international pressure on their governments.[76]

In sum, many people in the region feel that the government should be the main force in combating corruption, yet doubt its political will to initiate the necessary steps. Prosecution and strong enforcement of anti-corruption statutes are cited as the best approach to preventing corruption. For many reformist leaders "anti-corruption" is synonymous with strong enforcement. Romanian respondents to a representative survey sympathized with this view. When answering an open-ended question about the top priorities for fighting corruption, many favored strong enforcement, at times resorting to colorful descriptions of how they would like the guilty to be dealt with. To cite a few responses: "harder penalties; seize their assets; arrest them; throw them in jail; punch them; death penalty; shoot them; strangle them; torture them. Several invoked the name of Vlad Tepes (Dracula) in explaining their proposed solutions to the problem of corruption."[77] Responses like these reveal the depth of frustration that many Romanians feel about corruption.[78] If the new democracies do not develop effective law enforcement and judicial systems, such frustration can lead to accepting more authoritarian policies.

A decade after the transition to democratic regimes, dissatisfaction with the rate of progress of reform had bred suspicion and distrust of many public institutions, including the police and the judiciary. This raises two challenges for the institutions trying to combat corruption: to gain the trust of the public and demonstrate the effectiveness of their policies by producing results.

Conclusion

People in the post-communist region have certain patterns of thinking and acting that affect the level of corruption in society. As compared to other regions of the world, there is greater permissiveness toward petty corrupt acts in daily life. People have many excuses for this: the acts they engage in are rather innocent, "everybody else does it," they need to engage in them to survive, and they would lose out by not participating. The summary view is that "the system" makes them do it, they are forced to act in certain ways due to red tape, poor laws and law enforcement, and the unresponsiveness of the state to their needs. Often a bribe that expedites the resolution of a problem is considered normal. Illicit acts are seen as justifiable if they help overcome red tape and other bureaucratic hurdles. In this light, corruption is seen as a system that operates according to informal rules and can be functional; it helps defend one's interests in a situation that is already corrupted. Many think like survey respondent Anna, who said: "I do not trust in state power which is corrupt. . . . I trust my friends."[79]

Informal means are used because formal institutions, including the judiciary, are widely seen as self-serving and incapable of fulfilling their obligations to the citizenry. Many individuals see themselves as victims of bureaucratic indifference and irrationality, and this can be an excuse for their own questionable behavior. Few people take individual responsibility or see themselves as actors in events and fewer still are prepared to report corrupt acts to the law enforcement agencies, because they do not believe that any action will be taken. Since clean government requires active citizens, the lack of feelings of agency is problematic from the perspective of anti-corruption programs. As outlined in other chapters, and especially in Chapter 9, there are exceptions—public-spirited individuals and civil society groups—yet they too need to address the issue of how to influence mass attitudes toward a decisive rejection of corrupt practices. Strategies need to be designed in such a way that they aim at changing deeply entrenched popular views. There must be a shift from familial and narrow group loyalties to loyalties to the state and rule of law. Although such a cultural change is difficult, comparative research shows that it is possible.[80]

A cultural shift may be easier for the many individuals with contradictory views about corruption. The ambivalent nature of public attitudes toward corruption is evident from much of the material cited above; while there is a tendency to depict corruption as something unavoidable, many people also understand its problematic side. Many of the same people who try to justify corruption are also angry about it and suggest that they would be much happier with public institutions that work with integrity and accountability. Emphases differ: some note the ethical dilemmas involved; some recognize the costs of corruption and how it undermines faith in the state and its institutions; a few mention that it is unfair to other members of society. There is significant consensus that corruption is bad if it occurs at the highest levels of government, because that endangers the interests of the entire state.

Citizens are most concerned about political corruption at high levels of government, especially in the form of institutional and state capture. The public image of power elites is quite poor: people like to comment about corrupt habits among politicians, who are seen as self-serving and liable to be part of collusive networks protecting each other. It is commonly believed that cleaning up corruption should start at the top and be initiated from the top. Seeing that these two imperatives are in tension with each other, many think there is little likelihood of real reform.

While these are some dominant themes in public discourse about corruption, there are other, parallel discourses among various subgroups. Aside from the discourse of civic activists eager for reform, several themes are raised by political leaders. Over time, their tendency to minimize the impact of corruption and to use the issue mostly to discredit rivals has given way to a greater acknowledgment of its high costs. Since words at times carry over into deeds, this rhetorical trend also may suggest a trend in policy.

5

Political Legacies:
Old Habits Die Hard

> Bribes are given for selling off state resources, for granting
> permits for apartments, for allotting plots of land, for granting
> pensions, for admission to higher educational establishments,
> and even for the awarding of diplomas. . . . This disease, this
> bribery, has infected some of the central departments and
> institutions, including many leading officials with
> a party card in their pocket.
>
> *Nikita Khrushchev, 1963[1]*

Whether one reads the words of Nikita Khrushchev or scholarly works about
corruption in the former communist systems, much sounds familiar to the
observer of the post-communist world. Some political habits have carried
over from the old regimes to the new democracies that emerged in the 1990s.
Analyzing past political patterns helps us to better understand the contemporary political world. Even a cursory review of the extensive literature on the
Soviet-type regimes provides important insights. As noted by Valerie Bunce,
this store of research has not become irrelevant just because the communist
regimes collapsed.[2]

Social science searches for universal laws and frameworks that explain
political, economic, and social behavior, but it also analyzes observed differences. Often, the explanation points to the role of distinct traits of political
and economic systems and institutions. Political corruption must be analyzed with reference to the systemic features of political regimes.[3] Corruption in one-party systems and under a state-administered command economy
had a distinct profile, and the profile of corruption in the post-communist
region is rooted in its political history.

This chapter outlines core facets of illicit political behavior under communism as well as the formative role of paths of transition to democracy and
market economies. Besides highlighting legacies of the formal political regime

and the command economy, it emphasizes informal institutions and their operational rules. The informal networks of power elites and regular citizens that characterized Soviet-type regimes have left an imprint on post-communist societies. Networks of political patronage and personal influence emerged in response to tight party and state control of all political, economic, and social life. Their contemporary influence differs depending on a country's quality of democratization and marketization, but certain patterns are noticeable all over the region.

Regime Type

Corrupt as well as non-corrupt behaviors are shaped by institutional incentives, including the basic structures of entire political systems. The field of comparative politics, which focuses on differences in regime types, would suggest that some traits of communist regimes have influenced their successors and have shaped the process of regime change. These crucial characteristics are: (a) the monopoly of the communist party over important decisions; (b) state control over the means of production, with extremely limited private ownership of property; (c) the unofficial use of informal networks at both the elite and mass levels. It is beyond the scope of this study to discuss the consequences of these traits in detail, but their main thrust is that post-communist politicians try to re-create monopolies of decision making, that the privatization of the huge state assets has been the defining issue for economic change, and that informal patterns of getting things done have continued to play a significant role.

Soviet-type political systems were based on the claim that the communist party must be the leading political power because it alone knew what was in the public interest. One consequence was that state administrators engaged in the micromanagement not only of the planned economy, but also the life of its citizens. The result was that vast bureaucracies emerged and created what has been called the "administered society."[4] While claiming a monopoly of political decision making, the communist parties delegated policy implementation to bureaucracies that in effect decided on many details of how things were to be done. In order to safeguard compliance with their directives, communist parties put their own parallel structures within these state bureaucracies to cross-check everyday policy implementation. Although this was expected to preclude administrative corruption, party professionals and administrators often found it to their advantage to protect each other. This tendency increased over time as the parties lost whatever youthful ideological ethos they once had.[5]

The unprecedented scope of administrative control of communist institutions created many temptations to misuse official positions for private gain, even more so as public moral norms were contradictory. The fulfillment of the economic plan was the highest state priority, but illegalities committed for its sake were justified.[6] The command economies were kept going by manifold unofficial practices, such as barter between enterprises and the managerial services of *tolkachi*, middlemen facilitating such arrangements. William A. Clark talks of the Soviet leaders developing an informal regime as they increasingly recognized the serious problems of its formal rules and institutions.[7] A considerable part of this unofficial regime entailed the "second economy," but another part consisted of the growing tolerance of officials' corrupt actions such as neglect of office and bribe taking for cutting red tape. The irrationalities of the socialist economic and administrative system became increasingly evident during the Brezhnev era, and the party elite recognized that unofficial arrangements allowed it to function better.[8]

Yet corruption has multiple public consequences: although some informal practices may promote economic growth, they can undermine other parts of the established regime. Dysfunctional practices in the Soviet system included the self-enrichment of officials by inaccurate reporting and flaws in the accounting system. Nevertheless, the priority of economic performance meant that unsavory practices were ignored if they produced success. Formal rules and law were further undermined by the informal rule that party interests superseded law for the sake of the smooth functioning of the system. Except when the communist party wanted to set an example, it protected its members from legal prosecution in order to uphold the party's image of infallibility. In sum, the meaning of corruption was uncertain due to the "overriding importance of power and institutional interests."[9]

Nevertheless, there were periodic campaigns to limit the misuse of office. As documented by Leslie Holmes, corruption not only was prevalent in communist systems, it was publicly denounced, and communist parties staged anti-corruption campaigns that revealed details about bribery, falsification of reports, misuse of public office and state funds, patronage and nepotism, and party-state complicity in concealing corruption.[10] In retrospect one can see that these campaigns—just as corruption itself—created a dualistic legacy for the post-communist systems. Rooted in the internal contradictions of the communist party states and command economies, the tension between the formal rejection of corruption and its informal toleration meant that the regimes increasingly became opportunistic and hypocritical. This was even more the case as there was also the "corruption" of Soviet reporting of corruption, in that it was often used to discredit political opponents or minority groups.[11]

At times some higher official was targeted for sanctions, yet many dismissed officials escaped real punishment and with the help of their friends were reappointed to important positions where they continued as before.[12] This de facto impunity of elite cadre is one of the striking aspects of corruption in the latter phase of the communist systems that post-communist systems have inherited. The gap between a rhetoric of anti-corruption and the actual impunity of power holders promotes popular cynicism and a rationale for "everyone" to participate in illicit practices.

In addition to communist parties protecting their members, informal networks did so also. Their considerable success indicates the power of these personal connections: one might have expected Soviet-type systems to prove adept at exposing illegalities because of their coercive apparatus and elaborate systems of monitoring the behavior of people. However, Soviet officials charged with exposing corruption frequently collaborated in perpetrating or concealing it. The Soviets recognized this pattern and gave it such labels as *krugovaia poruka* (mutual involvement) or *semeistvennost* (family-ness).[13] Officials also protected each other due to the perennial danger of being implicated in the malfeasance if it were to be uncovered.

The Communist-Era Legacy of Networking

Communist regimes outlawed independent social, communal, and civic groups, but unofficial networks flourished. These were based on personal connections, the most influential being the clientelist power networks of the nomenklatura and the everyday "blat" networks of the citizenry. The latter provided mutual assistance in overcoming red tape and shortages of goods. Both the elite and mass networks were quasi-institutional groupings that were crucial in making the Soviet-type systems work, especially in their final stage. They have had a foundational role in shaping practices and perceptions of corruption among the people who grew up and lived under communist regimes, and have retained additional influence in the form of surviving elites.

Everyday Corruption and Blat Networks

The informal networks of the communist era were a response to a scarcity: the scarcity of good jobs led to patronage and clientelism and the scarcity of consumer goods and services led to practices known as blat, the informal exchange of goods, services, and favors. Shortages arose from inefficiencies of the state planned economy as well as its prioritization of certain products. The creation of scarcity may even have been a deliberate tool of political control: "Management of scarcity ensured power over those administered."[14] Institutional power holders, be they enterprise directors, head doctors, collective-farm chairmen, or university rectors were the gatekeepers to better jobs as well as a host of services and consumer goods. Places of employment were in charge of housing complexes, day care facilities, the purchase of cars, and much more. This provided numerous illicit opportunities for the exercise of influence over people desiring or needing such goods. "Gifts" were often required to accomplish something. For example, a university dean gave a professor permission to travel abroad to a conference only after having stipulated what presents he expected to be brought back for his wife and children.[15]

In socialist shortage economies the consumers are preoccupied with how to obtain scarce goods and use personal influence and ties to get them. The blat networks in the former Soviet Union and in Eastern Europe were fluid groupings of friends and family members, neighbors, co-workers, and other social contacts. Goods were exchanged informally, at times on an immediate quid pro quo basis, at times with an implied promise of future reciprocity. In the words of Alena Ledeneva, "Blat is the use of personal networks and informal contacts to obtain goods and services in short supply and to find a way around formal procedures."[16] The latter point is significant: for many people the breaking of official rules was a daily necessity.

Communist citizens who wanted to live a halfway decent life used blat because official access to the same goods was near impossible. Since nearly all goods and services were controlled by state bureaucracies, individuals working in them used their positions to channel resources to members of their networks. Although this informal system helped people—and the regimes —to survive, it was a form of in-group favoritism that came dangerously close to corruption. Ledeneva grants that blat had negative overtones, but highlights its positive feature of being embedded in human relationships.[17] Yet, as noted by James R. Millar, "in its most attractive form, reciprocity reflects the concern of family and friends for one another. In its less attractive form it is nepotism, favoritism, and cronyism." Furthermore, "many reciprocity transactions violate either the letter or the spirit of the law."[18]

This again raises the issue of the meaning of corruption. Several scholars have linked corruption to developmental stages of political systems, at times arguing that corruption can be functional and humanizing.[19] William A. Clark speaks of "useful corruption" when it cuts red tape and reduces bureaucratic rigidity. He also notes that the citizenry attains some psychological comfort from being able to control its fate to some extent and that "the government's de facto acceptance of official corruption in this sense humanizes the interaction between the population and the public organs which go so far in controlling most aspects of social life in the country."[20] Yet Clark also notes negative aspects of Soviet corruption, such as the misuse of capital to support elite extravagances and the diversion of administrative activity from its main purpose to the pursuit of illicit profit.

Blat not only made daily life easier for many people, it also had some economic advantages for the regimes. This has been summarized most cogently by Millar, who suggests that the Brezhnev leadership struck a "Little Deal"—"a new but tacit bargain with the urban population: to tolerate the expansion of a wide range of petty economic activities, some legal, some in the penumbra of the legal, and some clearly and obviously illegal, the primary aim of which was the reallocation by private means of a significant fraction of Soviet national income according to private preferences."[21] It also included tolerance of the use of public property for personal gain, nepotism, and other forms of favoritism or even outright corruption.[22] Millar argues that in economic terms this increased the national product, and that these private transactions operated in a symbiotic relationship with state enterprise and marketing, serving to make the total system more responsive to household demand.[23]

For understanding post-communist corruption it is significant that this accommodation was tacit and pervasive, and that illicit activities were for the most part winked at by the regime. This represents a "deal" in the sense that illicit acts frequently took place in plain view of police, citizens, bureaucrats, and high officials.[24] The power holders accepted the use of blat as an informal practice to smooth socioeconomic transactions, and some payments were called "bonuses" instead of bribes. Blat and gift giving were essential lubricants in otherwise rigid and regimented political systems. But, these practices often came close to bribery, which usually is wasteful, discriminatory, and may involve extortion. There are also long-term consequences: "The Soviet press complains that official tolerance of petty violations leads to a general sense of impunity, and that this encourages more serious types of corruption, as well as other forms of economic crime."[25]

Blat was a response to the inadequacies of the formal political and economic system. Some scholars speak of "real socialism" when outlining the role of informal structures and argue they were significant way beyond the solving of everyday problems. Ilja Srubar believes that the informal practices were tolerated not only because they compensated for inefficiencies of the formal system, but also because they directed citizens' attention away from politics toward the nurturing of connections that involved numerous moral compromises and illicit dealings. With time, trust in the public good and social solidarity were undermined since the "real socialist" society was split up in an "archipelago of networks" whose members were focused on exchanges with fellow network members at the expense of outsiders. A culture of "functional friendship" served to camouflage the exchange of favors as something pleasant and kind. Dependence on personal contacts also meant that the credibility of formal institutions was undermined and a huge gap emerged between the useful private and dysfunctional public structures.[26]

A premium was put on getting jobs that controlled desirable resources, and certain jobs were sought after precisely because they offered more opportunities for illicit practices. This point is significant because it suggests a type of corruption where a public office is captured for the distinct purpose of exploitation. This is qualitatively different from a situation where an official holding a specific position occasionally succumbs to the temptation of self-enrichment at the expense of the public interest.

Antoni Kaminski has argued that the permeation of the formal facade of the state by a network of privatized relations led to a gradual privatization of the state: "At the individual level, this is manifested in the incumbents' attitudes toward their official positions which they regard as private endowments rather than as official functions. These strategies . . . also weaken the political support for reforms."[27] This pinpoints the political cost of blat and other illicit practices. To the extent that these practices were illegal, they distorted popular attitudes toward law, equal opportunity, merit, and fairness. The de facto complicity of the regime undermined the readiness for decisive political reform or even revolution. Corruption served the system by being an informal alternative to institutional reform.[28] At the same time the communist system itself was undermined since its ideological and rhetorical legitimacy depended on the appearance of being non-corrupt, efficient, and concerned about equality and social justice. When Gorbachev in the late 1980s allowed glasnost to publicly reveal numerous corrupt schemes, this only confirmed what most people already knew from personal experience, and consequently the regime was doomed.[29]

Elite Networks, Patronage, and Political Cartels

Many contemporary power cartels in the post-communist region originated in the nomenklatura elites of the communist era, consisting of the professionals of the communist party as well as its appointees to the leading positions in the country. The legacy of the party's monopolistic power over elite selection created habits of self-selection, patronage, and the elimination of counter-elites. Analysts differ as to whether clientelism constituted a central or a supplementary aspect of the institutional pattern of Soviet-type societies.[30] Wherever one puts the emphasis, there is considerable consensus that the nomenklatura cliques, their power and privileges, and their functional and dysfunctional sides as informal systems of influence became increasingly prominent during communism's declining years.[31]

John Willerton's study of patronage and elite behavior in the final phases of the Soviet Union provides many insights into how this worked. Due to the insecurity of the political domain, Soviet officials had to rely on informal mechanisms and political reciprocity. Willerton sees patronage as involving "a mutual exchange of political goods . . . in a commerce of support, ideas, and favors."[32] Patronage has a positive side, for example as a means of unifying politicians and providing slack in a rigid decision-making process. Even though it was an extralegal arrangement, clientelism was informally accepted because it overcame barriers and permitted effective ties to different institutions and locales. By establishing political hierarchies, clientelism helped compensate for the lack of procedure for the succession of leaders. Coalition building was made easier, and given the paucity of legal constraints, patronage became a functional equivalent to law.[33] Yet, although the unofficial practices lubricated the wheels of the cumbersome state machine, they limited pressures for the formation of an effective legal and judicial system.

The Soviet press lamented the dysfunctional side of patronage in that self-dealing and the creation of local fiefdoms undercut central programs. Officials tried to develop countervailing practices such as the rotation of cadres, but this rarely was effective unless more than the head of the network was removed. Clientelism meant jobs were given to those aspirants who were most likely to advance the patron's interests without question, regardless of merit and individual initiative.[34] In addition, Willerton depicts the meaning of loyalty in the Soviet context as involving "some mutual covering up, so that the taut plan can be fulfilled and various assignments met. Indeed, the nature of the Soviet hierarchical political structure all but requires such covering up by a politician to be successful. Mutual covering up benefits the system in that it reinforces the very set of informal political relationships that must function if the overriding economic mission is to be realized."[35]

This tradition of mutual covering up does not speak well for the consolidation of legality in the post-communist context. It also suggests that the informal arrangements were integral to the political and economic regime and its priorities. Although the arrangements were functional in the narrow sense of making the system work, they were dysfunctional in terms of long-term goals as they fostered misinformation, opportunism, and other pathologies that led to the system's eventual collapse. Individuals and their circles were focused not just on individual positions of power, but on the control of entire state institutions. "Control over those bureaucracies—obtained by penetrating one's network into those bureaucracies—became a top political and career priority for the leader."[36] This practice is strikingly similar to what recent studies of post-communist corruption have called state capture.

The qualities and nature of the elites inherited by post-communist systems matter. In the case of the last stages of the Soviet state, Ken Jowitt speaks of the progressive corruption of the communist cadres and their transformation into traditional-type patrons who received tribute from subservient units and subordinated the interests of their posts to personal and particular interests. This transformation was not limited to a small number of cadres, but rather overcame the entire party by 1980. In short, the late Soviet regime was a system dominated by an exclusive, self-serving, and "organizationally corrupt status elite,"[37] earlier forms of which were diagnosed by Milovan Djilas and Michael Voslensky, among others.[38] Djilas was among the first to identify the emergence of a privileged "new class" in supposedly classless communist societies. In Poland, this contradiction to ideological claims as well as the visible luxury in which many corrupt officials lived while many poor people suffered was a core reason for the Solidarity-led protests and eventual regime change.[39]

Willerton wrote his study of patronage during the late Gorbachev era. He concludes that the normalization of public service would only come with a fundamental restructuring of the Soviet system and a resetting of elite rules of behavior. Notions of public accountability would have to become preeminent, otherwise informal mechanisms of influence would continue to structure elite interactions.[40] This admonition continued to be relevant throughout the 1990s.

Regime Change and Privatization

Once the communist systems began to change, new contexts for corruption emerged. In early 1988 Antoni Kaminski summarized the fateful dilemma faced by the communist elites: They had to rely more and more upon corrupting the society and its own apparatus by accepting the growing unofficial privatization of the state, or to enter the risky path of reform, which included policies that had been brutally rejected as bourgeois inventions by communists when they took power.[41] In this stark choice between corruption and reform, reform won out in that new regimes, new states, and new institutions were created. Corruption won as well, however, since a segment of the established elite saw the breakdown of the old regimes as an opportunity to legalize past illicit gains and expand them.

Privatization in the transition countries was unprecedented both in its scale and in its character because it involved a systemic change from a state-controlled command economy to a market system. A market economy is not a free-for-all but needs laws and regulations. For a market to work, it needs a competitive banking system, capital markets, and numerous laws guaranteeing property rights and fair business practices. States need to maintain the rule of law and uphold contracts and the rights to private property. "The quality of market economies is largely [a] function of the characteristics of the state."[42]

It was up to political decision makers to put in place the institutional framework markets require, but this was more forthcoming in some transition countries than in others. The initial phase often was decisive for later development. As the communist regimes disintegrated, this created a chaotic stage that was taken advantage of by economic or political insiders who developed intricate and corrupt schemes to gain ownership or strip the assets of institutions and enterprises entrusted to them. Many factory managers "were quick to spin off valuable assets into special firms under their control, leaving the state with hollow shells and massive debts."[43]

It is beyond the scope of this study to analyze the details of privatization except to point to patterns that set precedents for future illicit behaviors. One pattern emerging in 1987 in the Soviet Union was that state economic managers, administrators, and Komsomol and communist party officials engaged in "spontaneous privatization": the de facto appropriation of state assets for minimal payment or none at all. Steven Solnick has provided this vivid picture of asset grabbing by Komsomol leaders:

> Local agents rushed to appropriate those assets over which their committees could assert control. Local officials took advantage of the new laws on cooperatives to open travel agencies, cafes, and video salons on Komsomol property; they even used money from Komsomol accounts to invest in the first wave of new commercial banks. The bank run that emptied Komsomol's coffers was very real, except the funds withdrawn had come from the dues of other, rank-and-file depositors, accumulated over several decades. . . . By the time of the August 1991 coup, Central Committee staffers and local committees had in effect already plundered and divided the Komsomol's chief assets.[44]

There are no statistics on the extent of spontaneous privatization, but in 1996 two experts on the transition economies noted that the transfer of assets by stealth to enterprise managers and/or to high officials and politicians quite possibly overshadowed most other methods.[45]

The politically connected were the biggest winners, and these usually were the leading cadre of the communist party and its affiliates. The success of the former head of the Hungarian communist youth organization is typical: after creating a one-man company in 1990, he purchased from the old communist party its four newspapers, including Hungary's biggest daily, *Nepszabadadsag*, for a mere 1.5 million forints. In less than a year, this paper alone fetched over one hundred million forints.[46]

A scholar who had been employed by a scientific institute in Latvia recounts more mundane transactions:

[N]omenclature leaders had a priority right to privatize; this was not known to others. They got to privatize the most attractive objects. There was a privatization on all levels. I was a vice-director of [the] institute that time. When the soviet system collapsed we started to "buy out" the institute's property of soviet times, to deal it out among us for very little money. Cars to the bosses, refrigerator[s] to the director, something smaller to the assistants. I got [a] refrigerator and 8 nice soft chairs, and I still have them—and at those times it was a big gain because in shops you could not buy such things.[47]

Some analysts believe that elite groups not only profited from regime collapse, but were a driving force behind it because they saw the opportunities for personal enrichment that it would bring. Marie Mendras argues that the nomenklatura in the republics and the major monopolies of production and distribution claimed autonomy from the central administration to be free to do as they wished.[48] Corrupt elites also needed opportunities to transfer their assets abroad, and this influenced the opening of foreign policy. Established skill at operating in the global arena came in useful: economist Marshall Goldman argues that post-Soviet Russian central bankers followed in the footsteps of their communist-era predecessors who, by funneling illegal funds to foreign communist parties, had become proficient in money laundering.[49]

Steven Solnick sees the opposite causal chain, with officials not initialing but reacting to the decentralization of authority and using the new opportunities to pursue private gains.

Ultimately, at precisely the juncture where the effectiveness of policy reforms depended upon a coherent institutional response, local officials defected en masse and the pillars of the Soviet system crumbled. In effect, Soviet institutions were victimized by the organizational equivalent of a colossal "bank run," in which local officials rushed to claim their assets before the bureaucratic doors shut for good. As in a bank run, the loss of confidence in the institution makes its demise a self-fulfilling prophecy. Unlike a bank run, the defecting officials were not depositors claiming their rightful assets, but employees of the state appropriating assets. . . . [Where] organizational assets were chiefly cash and buildings, hierarchical breakdown was almost total. At both ends of the spectrum, the catalysts of state collapse were the agents of the state itself. Once the bank run was on, the officials were not merely stealing resources *from* the state, they were stealing the state itself.[50]

As these accounts and other sources suggest, the privatization of vast state-owned enterprises and other assets inherited by the post-communist states involved many battles over the spoils of state property. The managers and directors in charge of various assets often emerged as the new owners, at first de facto, and then de jure, often in highly illicit ways.[51] In the former Soviet Union, nomenklatura privatization came to mean the process whereby the wealth of nations was transferred in large part to former communist elites.[52] Privatization proved to be the central mechanism for the acquisition of financial power not only by former communist apparatchiks, but also by organized crime.[53] As a result the term "mafia" came to be commonly used to describe the newly rich and powerful, especially in Russia.

For corruption to occur, there must be both incentives and opportunities. Privatization of the wealth of the communist states provided huge incentives, and opportunities were provided by insufficient regulation. Susan Rose-Ackerman has noted the general rule that "the process of transferring assets to private ownership is fraught with corrupt opportunities."[54] This is even more true if the states in question owned practically everything and where privatization was of historically unique proportions. Yet corrupt opportunities could have been limited by more involvement of pluralist forces and better regulation.

There is a paradox in the privatization process: although it aims at the state being less involved in the economy, the process requires significant public regulation for it to work well and fairly. This means that states in transition have to create new laws and special institutions such as privatization agencies, voucher systems, and much more. Much effort needs to be put into institutionalizing private property rights.[55] Russia was slow in putting such laws in place, which appears to have been a deliberate self-serving act of those profiting from it.[56] Other states in the region took different paths, some more successful and democratic than others, as a comparison of Hungary and Poland demonstrates.

The outcome of privatization was not preordained, and countries differ in the extent to which it was hijacked by the officials in charge. The extent of an institutionalized civic society as well as specific policy decisions made a difference. In his analysis of the Hungarian and Polish institutional settings and elite compositions, Eric Hanley finds that nomenklatura privatization was not a general phenomenon within the former Soviet bloc, but was rather contingent upon certain political factors, namely the implementation of nomenklatura-friendly privatization policies.[57] In Hungary, enterprise directors were remarkably successful in acquiring ownership rights over productive assets, but much less so in Poland. The organized power of Polish workers in employees' councils allowed them to deny managers the capacity to enrich themselves.[58] Besides the strength of the Solidarity movement at the enterprise level and in policy-making bodies, the electoral victory that Solidarity experienced in the late 1980s and early 1990s contributed to democratizing the transition to the market.

In contrast to Poland, Hungarian workers were denied self-organization rights and the state steered them toward profiting from increased opportunities in a legalized second economy. Unlike their Polish counterparts, Hungarian workers largely responded to economic hardships by adopting individual rather than collective strategies.[59] This is especially problematic if others in society have cooperative networks they rely on, as many of the privatization profiteers did.

Economist Marshall Goldman has favorably compared Poland's approach to privatization to that of Russia. In his view, shared by other observers, in Russia "the move to the market has been tainted by the corruption and emergence of a dishonest oligarchy that probably still controls 50 percent of Russia's economic activity."[60] Poland was slower in starting the privatization process, but used the time to design an innovative program that helped restructure former state industries with a minimum of scandal. A carefully designed public voucher system led to the creation of fifteen National Investment Funds that acted as effective overseers of privatization. Poland also introduced manifold laws and institutions on property rights and market rules to safeguard a more orderly transition to the market.

Another crucial difference from Russia and other post-communist states was that Poland's delay in privatizing larger enterprises allowed local entrepreneurs to develop an independent capital base. When Poland started large-scale privatization in 1995–96, Poles already had set up two million or so new businesses, which created a viable market infrastructure with competition and a form of checks and balances. In contrast, Russia's early large privatization meant that there were few self-made entrepreneurs who could participate in the sell-off and the biggest profiteers were existing managers, officials with access to public funds that they could manipulate in their favor, and some fringe elements who had accumulated capital on the black market.[61]

In the transition from a state-controlled command economy to a market economy privatization means two things: in addition to the privatization of state-owned enterprises and assets, a market economy must make room for the emergence of new private property and enterprises. Compared to its peers in the region, Poland was successful on both counts, but most dramatically so in regard to promoting the flourishing of new businesses. In contrast, other countries, such as Russia, hindered the emergence of new businesses both by their overall policies of over-regulation as well as corrupt extortion by licensing officials and others.

Legacies of the Past

Surveys undertaken in the post-communist region suggest that although the use of personal connections has changed, it survives in various ways.[62] A study of informal networks in St. Petersburg in 1993 and 1996 shows the persistence of blat, especially in regard to medical services and education. Some occupations remain desirable specifically for the opportunities for informal exchanges and rent seeking. For instance, "teaching—together with medicine—are two of the Soviet/Russian professions whose relatively low status and salary is compensated for by their huge clientele cutting across all social classes—and at least potentially offering a wide range of possibilities for the informal exchange of favours."[63] This ignores that networks created by public positions are also a public resource, and developing them beyond professional ties to create private obligations and favors is a corrupt activity.[64]

A later study of Russia notes that instead of the exchange of favors, monetary bribes have become increasingly common. According to one estimate, the practices that used to be associated with blat in Russia amount to at least $2.8 billion a year in bribes paid by private citizens. People spend most money (some $606 million) for various services related to medical care, followed by $449.4 million for admissions to universities.[65]

One reason why blat persists is that scarcities persist. Although free markets have caused a structural change in the availability of consumer goods and services, some of these remain scarce and are likely to be so always. High-quality medical services, access to universities, and certain jobs are prime examples. Thus, informal exchange networks that originated in the dysfunctionalities of the communist system live on due to the inability of the market economy and democratic systems to provide every desired good and service to every individual consumer. Even if it were possible to provide an abundance of goods, people would still care about quality. When searching for the best doctor or university program, the information and contacts received through networks remain crucial and can lead to improper influence.

Reliance on personal connections can be dysfunctional not only at the societal level, but also at the private level. Contexts have changed, yet people often inappropriately rely on their old habits. Many post-communist citizens are reluctant to seek the advice of professionals, and when encountering a problem, turn to friends or acquaintances who may have had similar difficulties, but often give poor advice.[66] This legacy of seeking individualized solutions has consequences on the macro level, since, as argued by a legal scholar in Latvia, "if there is a problem, society prefers not to engage in protests, but rather to seek out people who will know how to deal with issues."[67] Some change occurs over time, as the old patterns of social behavior persist mostly among the older generation.

Networking among power elites has both continued and been transformed. New elite groups have emerged, and the organizational backbone of the traditional communist party structure has changed. A regional expert argues that the nomenklatura networks have been transformed into "clientura" networks: "The clientura way is flexible, hidden and lucrative, and controlled by the invisible hand of the new rulers, therefore neither the decision-making process, nor the mutual benefits can be seen."[68] This same author also outlines the rise of a counter-elite in Hungary, which also is seen as constituting a "clientura."[69] At times it appears that specific networks have "grey cardinals," oligarchic leaders who control major flows of money and power, yet while the local and international media have published numerous speculative accounts, few scholarly studies exist to date and more research is needed.

The emergence of post-communist political "machines" has meant that they are compared to similar structures in American cities. Yet, as Michael Johnston has pointed out, there is a difference between broad patronage systems or political machines that dispense relatively minor favors to relatively many people, and small groups using cronyism and nepotism to enrich themselves. The two types of groupings also differ in that the small oligarchies foster group interests in maintaining secrecy and in excluding outsiders,[70] whereas the urban political machines typically focused on co-opting new electorates from previously excluded ethnic groups.

In their study of transitions to democracy, Juan Linz and Alfred Stepan argue the significance of the institutional character of the state elite. They note how in the formerly communist-ruled countries, ex-communists have tried to achieve new legitimacy through elections and how they have worked to retain key positions within state enterprises and bureaucracies. Typically, these old elites do not aim at overthrowing the new regime, but at profiting from it, and this leaves considerable "room for corruption."[71]

Many analysts have criticized the fateful neglect of the first post-Soviet governments of Russia to engage in a comprehensive reform of state institutions, which had many consequences, especially for the emergence of a distorted market economy. The concentration on radical economic changes without complementary political and administrative reconstruction promoted a rapid recurrence of the pathologies of Soviet governance.[72] The neoliberal Western advisers and policy makers in Russia had the naive expectation that after 1991 Russia would be saved by the invisible hand of the market, and they underestimated the role of democratic institutions, especially the rule of law and effective regulation. At the same time, they underestimated the institutional staying power of the established structures and networks interested in continuing to benefit from them.[73]

The paths taken in the early stages of the transition from communism affected the choices that were available later on. In his outstanding analysis of transitions in the entire post-communist region, Joel Hellman found that those people who profited most from partial reforms in the early stages of privatization were the main opponents of further reform. The earliest and biggest winners have undermined the formation of a viable legal system to support the market economy and have fought to maintain the imbalances of partial reforms over time.[74] And they often have been successful, as they have had huge resources that overshadow the resources available to true reformers.

Conclusion

The political systems of post-communist states are influenced—to a varying extent—by the preceding communist regimes as well as how the transition to democracy and market economies occurred. Similarities in corrupt practices throughout the region are witness to the common political history, whereas differences can be explained by individual regime differences, such as Poland retaining more of a civil society throughout the communist period. Distinct patterns of transition and the decisiveness of establishing new political and economic institutions also make a difference, especially in the process of privatizing state and communal assets.

Besides general legacies of the communist systems, the transition from them has included corruption-prone processes such as the exceptionally extensive privatization of state-owned property that led to the appearance of transition profiteers and political oligarchs. Taken together, the legacy of the communist era and the temptations of transition have created a context of significant levels of corruption.

In the case of Russia, Alena Ledeneva has concluded that popular disregard for the law is coupled with disregard for the state. The state is partly responsible for this attitude. Over the course of the 1990s, the public felt betrayed by the outcome of privatization and placed all blame on state institutions and bureaucrats, who found ways to prosper while abandoning the population at large to its own devices.[75]

Even in those post-communist states where the institutions of democracy and market economies have come a long way, many informal practices persist. Old habits die hard, and established structures and procedures retain influence both through inertia and as a safety net in confusing times. Since the old formal institutions have changed, the need for the old informal mechanisms to compensate for their weaknesses has changed as well. The habit of relying on the old-type networks is in tension with the new political systems and markets. The continuing role of exclusive personal networks is problematic not only because they are dysfunctional in the new contexts, but also because they limit how eager people are to join other groups.[76] The persistence of communist-era exclusive networks impedes the development of a civil society composed of inclusive civic associations. More broadly, the core issue of the good governance agenda in the post-communist region is to make a more decisive break with the past and to create better congruence between formal and informal politics.

6

The Opposites of Corruption

The notion of fidelity in office, as old as Cicero, is inextricably
bound to the concept of public interest distinct from private
advantage. It is beyond debate that officials of the
government are relied upon to act for the public
interest not their own enrichment.

John T. Noonan, Bribes[1]

When people avoid or oppose corrupt acts, they do so not only because they
reject something, but also because they believe in clean politics and good
governance. This raises questions about the sources of non-corrupt politics.
Using political theory writings to outline the values of good citizenship and
public spiritedness, this chapter argues that civic cooperation is a crucial
public good and the opposite of corruption. The links between the legitimacy
of political regimes and corruption, along with the distinction between public and private ethics—including the tension between the two in post-
communist practice—are rehearsed.

Fundamentally, a non-corrupt government is based on a democratic public good. An ideal democracy, in which the citizens represent sovereign power
and entrust authority to public officials to serve their needs, is the foundation
and vision for this government. This vision can be safeguarded by institutional means, but only if the citizens themselves participate in governance.
To ensure public integrity and accountability, a civil society and participatory citizenry are crucial. Civic virtue, public responsibility, and bureaucratic
rationality comprise the remaining building blocks of honest politics.

The term "public good" is used here in several ways. A classic notion is
that public goods are those that are enjoyed by entire communities, rather
than individuals. Thus, "the common good is not the increase in the number
of cows each citizen possesses but an increase in the number of temples and
bridges usable by all."[2] Other concrete goods enjoyed collectively are traffic
safety, avoidance of epidemics, public safety and lawfulness, and the responsible use of taxpayer money and public resources. In addition to such

tangible goods, the public good emerges from the cooperation of citizens in their civic community in the pursuit of overall political goals, in a variety of public institutions. Cooperation arises from common beliefs, mutual trust, and aid, and the emotional and normative identification with one's people and nation. Good citizenship also includes the values of public spiritedness, doing one's duty, sacrificing for the common good, and trusting one's fellow citizens as well as political representatives and the rule of law.

Like civic virtue, regime legitimacy is a value-laden term fundamental to understanding corruption. Officials and citizens are much more likely to observe laws and be public spirited if they believe their government has the right to rule and does so in a way that promotes basic public goals. Not all governments do so, and one needs to draw distinctions between government that on the whole serves the common good, and government that is self-serving and repressive. Western social scientists often deal with corruption as if it constituted individual acts of misguided public officials, yet with this they implicitly assume that the state they are talking about is basically sound and legitimate. Such a projection of a legitimate democratic state into other contexts ignores that many states are constituted differently and have despotic rulers.[3] Definitions of corruption are grounded in conceptions of the state and the legitimacy of political regimes.

The most problematic legacy of communism is a distorted view of the public good and the role of democratic citizens in defining it. Following the collapse of the communist regimes in Eastern Europe and the former Soviet Union, formal institutions of democracy were established in most countries of the region. Yet there remains a gap between formal democracy and informal politics. It is an historical irony that the communist regimes, which claimed above all to serve a collective public good, created elites who instead believed in their own personal good above everything else. The political beliefs and habits that underlie post-communist corruption were outlined in the Chapter 5; the focus here is on defining corruption by discussing its opposites, such as the logic of civic virtue and public ethics.

Political Values and Corruption

Scholars and citizens everywhere think and talk of corruption in many different ways. Ultimately, the controversies over how to define corruption are linked to broader issues of what constitutes good politics. Therefore, it is incumbent on every analyst of political corruption to state clearly what normative framework he or she uses.[4] This study uses the culturally neutral definition of corruption as "the misuse of public power for private gain," but the ideas about how to contain corruption emphasize the normative side of a democratically formed public good. Democratic legitimacy and good governance form the contrast to what is presented here as destructive corruption.

In light of the focus on post-communist states, I relate "the misuse of public power for private gain" to the norms and rules of fundamentally democratic political systems as protesters envisioned them when regime transition started during the revolutionary phase between 1989 and 1992. Democracies are not born overnight and true regime change takes time, yet once the new states formally linked their legitimacy to democracy and the rule of law, this became the normative public good that their populations came to expect. Expectations matter because the meaning of corruption goes way beyond its definition in the official laws of any particular state. In the post-communist region a popular way of avoiding accountability is to assert that certain improprieties are not legally defined as corruption. This view was succinctly repudiated by a high official of the Council of Europe when he argued that it is, in fact, "the non-legalistic notion of corruption that the Council of Europe is interested in fighting. Since it stands for the protection of democracy, the rule of law, and human rights, the Council believes that corruption, in all its forms, constitutes a threat to these values. If corruption, in the wide sense, is allowed to spread, it will decay the foundations of our institutions and jeopardize our societies."[5]

Regime Legitimacy and Links to Corruption

Citizen involvement for the public good is related to the legitimacy of the state and its rules and institutions. There are links among the quality of regimes, public institutions, and public behavior. A core question is that of legitimacy, because officials and the citizenry are much more likely to observe the law and be guided by public spiritedness if they believe that a government has the right to rule and does so in a way that promotes the public interest. If, on the contrary, citizens see the regime or specific institutions as repressive, predatory, or incompetent, their support wanes and they tend to focus on their personal good. If this impulse starts to dominate, a corrupt polity, where most officials and citizens focus on using the state to their advantage and on circumventing its rules, may result. This was very much the case in the last phases of communist regimes. As outlined in Chapter 5, during the final decades of communist rule officials and citizens increasingly engaged in informal and illicit practices. Experience of communist administrative power and corruption led people to see the state as arbitrary and predatory, and they reacted by focusing on their own informal networks and human relationships.[6] This legacy of a negative view of the state tends to persist and undermines the reformation of the new governments.

Any assessment of corruption requires an evaluation of the nature of the state in question, its legitimacy, and its norms and practices in regard to the public good. If citizens view a regime as illegitimate and exploitative, they are less likely to feel obligated to act as good citizens who pay taxes and obey the law, and instead are much more likely to engage in illicit practices. A core issue is whether compliance with the law and political rules rests on consensus or control. In the words of Carl Friedrich, "it is possible to state a 'law' or general regularity by saying that the degree of corruption varies inversely to the degree that power is consensual. Corruption is a corrective of coercive power and its abuse, when it is functional."[7]

This latter point highlights the difference between illicit or corrupt acts in communist regimes, which are repressive and malfunctioning, and corrupt acts in democracies, which are representative and mostly functional. Although corruption can work as a corrective for a malfunctioning system, it produces the malfunctioning of an efficient system. The quality of corruption differs depending on institutional and regime quality. There is an explicit difference between corruption that undermines a legitimate democratic system and corruption that people feel forced to use in order to circumvent a repressive, dysfunctional, and illegitimate system. An important way of analyzing the role of regime legitimacy is to ask about the acceptability of corruption in the eyes of the citizenry. Political relationships are based on reciprocity. If citizens perceive that public institutions do not serve them, they themselves do less in terms of public service, paying taxes, and observing laws. A vicious circle can evolve where such popular attitudes lead to even worse government.

Linking corruption to regime legitimacy helps avoid misunderstandings in contexts where total integrity is inappropriate or even counterproductive. When analyzing corruption, one needs to look beyond the corrupt act itself and examine the political context. To reformulate the famous saying by Gertrude Stein, "a bribe is not a bribe is not a bribe," by which I mean that bribing a policeman guarding a hospital against thieves is not the same as bribing the guard of a Stalinist prison camp; corrupt acts differ within specific contexts. The same thought of corruption playing a just role under an unjust regime is expressed by Mother Courage in Bertolt Brecht's play: "Corruption is our only hope. As long as there's corruption, there'll be merciful judges and even the innocent may get off."[8] A similar point has been made by an anthropologist who notes that some Arabs see bribery as a vehicle of democracy inasmuch as the capacity to undercut what a person in power commands by bribing an underling constitutes a check on the power of the dominant figure.[9] The ethos of limitations on unjust state power is crucial. An even larger issue that goes beyond the scope of this study revolves around the ethical discussion of what legal norms can and even should be broken if a political regime is despotic and violates human rights.

Corrupt acts differ in their meaning and consequences and need to be assessed within their contexts. The main contextual line of difference is between legitimate and illegitimate government. Another contextual determinant is whether laws are rational and serve a public good, such as traffic safety, quality education and opportunity, legal security and fairness. Often rules and laws are broken because their purpose is unclear or unacceptable. A comparative study of several post-communist countries found that on average 44 percent of respondents said that people "should ignore or avoid" the law if they considered it to be "very unreasonable or unjust."[10] Other survey data indicate that people do differentiate among public institutions according to their trustworthiness and feel that it is more acceptable for them to engage in petty illicit acts in interactions with poor performers. This illustrates the reciprocal relationship of corrupt behavior and institutional legitimacy as well as the importance of public perceptions of the state.

If a state or specific leadership is seen as illegitimate, a wide gap emerges between the way people evaluate the corruption of the political elite and the petty corruption that average citizens are liable to engage in. Elite corruption is despised and may lead to revolution and system change, as happened in communist Poland in the 1980s. In contrast, petty corruption is more easily excused as a means of daily survival, or is seen even positively as a way to undermine the power of the oppressor state. If corruption is widespread, this means that in the eyes of many, illicit informal practices have become legitimate in place of the formal laws and rules. Similar conclusions emerge from a comparative study of Russia and China: "the main legacy of the communist era . . . is the widespread prevalence of informal societal arrangements and moral understandings for 'getting by' under formal institutions perceived to be self-serving and distant."[11] The legitimacy of the informal systems is typically argued to be a response to the rigidity, repressiveness, and ineffectiveness of the formal system. But what if the system is flexible, responsive to public needs, and effective? Then such illicit behavior undermines the ability of the responsive system to work, which is a core problem for those states in the post-communist region struggling to become real democracies. People tend to transfer their patterns of behavior and belief from one political regime to another, yet this undermines the consolidation of democracy in those cases where there is genuine regime change. This will be discussed at greater length in subsequent chapters.

The Logic of Civic Virtue and Cooperation for the Public Good

To understand corruption and how to motivate people to contain it, it helps to outline its opposite. If corruption is defined as "the misuse of public power for private gain," then the opposite is "the use of public power for the common good." This envisions an ideal democracy in which the citizenry represents sovereign power and its representatives serve the public good. But what is the "public good"? In this study I use the term in two ways: (1) principally, to describe concrete goods that serve all of society, such as traffic safety, avoidance of epidemics, lawfulness, and the responsible use of public resources; and (2) in a less tangible way, to refer to good democratic politics, especially civic republicanism.

The conception of civic republicanism was revived in the 1970s by political theorists and historians of the English-speaking world. The British political philosopher Philip Pettit has called republicanism "a new vision of what public life might be."[12] It has many roots, however, starting with Aristotle, who discussed what constituted an ideal, healthy polity. It is, first of all, a polity in which citizens share in the administration of justice and where politics is a moral activity that makes people realize what is distinctively human about them.[13] Thus the public good is based on good citizenship, understood as active participation in a political community. Sharing in the operation of common affairs creates a sense of belonging and an incentive for concern about the common good.[14] Yet, although all citizens should be committed to the common good, "politics exists only when individuals see that good through different eyes."[15] Aristotle saw strength in pluralism of views. He felt that a healthy polity is also based on equality and the subordination of private interests or associations to more inclusive public interests and associations. Economic life should strengthen communal life.[16]

Besides emerging in the Greek city-state, notions of good citizenship also appeared in the Roman Empire, the medieval and Renaissance city, and the nation-state since the late eighteenth century.[17] Intriguingly, Machiavelli had much to say not just about corruption, but also about its mirror-image concept of a healthy republic guided by civic virtue and the love of liberty. As summarized by one author, "one dimension of political corruption is the privatization both of the average citizen and those in office. In the corrupt state, men locate their values wholly within the private sphere and they use the public sphere only to promote private interests."[18] For Machiavelli, this descent into privatism signaled the onset of corruption. Furthermore, "a thoroughly anti-political, privatized people are incapable of achieving or maintaining free politics."[19] Privatizing politics also undermines people's judgment, leading them to fail to see that poor governance threatens their own long-term interests.

Many in the post-communist region are aware of such arguments and values. When a focus group of public officials in Hungary was asked in the late 1990s to discuss the concept of corruption, the discussion was introduced with the point that the Latin verb *corrumpere* means to break, and the question to be answered was what is "broken" by the act of corruption. Besides answers that the law, or a legal rule is broken, it was emphasized that a duty and a moral norm is broken. Several participants argued that the autonomy and integrity of a human personality is broken, and they stressed that this may be the greatest social damage resulting from corruption.[20]

The revival of the republican ideal since the 1970s has been due to dissatisfaction with an economic model of politics, which is seen to have collapsed public interests into private interests and interest-group pluralism. In contrast, the republican understanding is that "good government should aim at a public good beyond the sum of private interests";[21] a good government is "one which selects all that is best in divided interests and distills them in the name of the public interest or the common good."[22] But to a large extent government entails self-government and the involvement of citizens in deliberating about the common good on the basis of concern for the whole. This on its part presupposes a sense of community and belonging.[23]

The proponents of civic republicanism see it as being in tension with liberalism, which is depicted as being opposed to explicit public value commitments except for an emphasis on the rights of individuals. The critics of liberalism see it as being unable to imagine politics as anything other than interest-group pluralism. Although this too is a form of political participation, sharing in self-rule as idealized by republicanism involves more than the capacity to choose one's goals and to respect others' right to do the same. "It requires a knowledge of public affairs and also a sense of belonging, a concern for the whole, a moral bond with the community whose fate is at stake."[24]

The central idea of liberalism is that government should be neutral toward the moral and religious views of its citizens. Therefore, government should not affirm in law any particular vision of the good life, but focus on providing the legal framework for people to choose their own values. Liberalism asserts the priority of fair procedures over particular ends, but its critics argue that a purely procedural democracy cannot sustain the moral energies vital to democratic life. Liberty requires a cohesive political community as well as civic engagement that envisions a common good.[25] Parallel to this thought, this study argues that procedural containment of corruption is insufficient to safeguard political integrity; it needs to be anchored in a commitment to a public good that extends beyond the sum of individual goods.

There are many variants of republican thought, but they all articulate the importance of commitment to an active civic life, self-fulfillment through political participation, and qualitative links between the private and the public good. Although a democratic republic depends on civic virtue, engaging in it also profits the individual citizen. In the eighteenth century the pursuit of the public interest was deemed to lead to "public happiness."[26] Political scientists such as Robert Putnam emphasize the significance of social capital for individuals as well as the democratic state.[27] The writings on social capital further suggest that the networks of civic engagement create public spiritedness and thus protect against corruption. Political participation is crucial for implementing the common good. Michael Walzer emphasizes that republicanism "is a form of collective self-government" that requires that many citizens vote, join parties and movements, and participate in other forms of political activity. This is virtuous activity, and "interest in public issues and devotion to public causes are the key signs of civic virtue."[28] Similarly, Pettit sees participation in social movements as enabling people to give voice to relevant concerns.[29] One concrete link between the republican ideal of law and political participation is the jury in the American judicial system.

Another source of the revival of "civic republicanism" in the 1970s were the debates among historians about the founding values of American democracy. Republicanism emerged as a new paradigm for interpreting history, and many identified it as the core impulse of the American Revolution, which was seen as having focused on the common good.[30] But as *The Federalist Papers* note, men are not angels; they tend to be self-serving and therefore democracies rely on checks and balances.[31] The founders of American democracy were guided by the suspicion of power and emphasized the counterchecking device of separation and balance of powers.[32] Related political thought includes Montesquieu's notions of the rule of law and separation of powers[33] and recent writings on democratization that ask for vertical and horizontal accountability.[34] A polity can be made more honest by institutional structures and procedures. Yet institutions alone cannot safeguard good politics: that also requires public spiritedness and commitment to the common good. As the political philosopher Michael J. Sandel has argued in defense of civic republicanism, "the procedural republic cannot secure the liberty it promises, because it cannot sustain the kind of political community and civic engagement that liberty requires."[35]

Even the best rules can be circumvented, and thus a non-corrupt polity relies most of all on the quality of the behavior of its citizens and their representatives. It is important to try to select officials who are public spirited and believe in civic virtue. But beliefs matter in other ways as well. They have a self-fulfilling nature in that the belief that people can and do act for the common good is a precondition for anyone engaging in activities that may promote it. Similarly, the expectation that everyone is out only to get the most for themselves will lead to acting in a like manner. How one tries to contain corruption also depends on how a society views human nature, the difference being whether people—and especially politicians—are seen as inherently corrupt, or just as corruptible. If the latter is true, corruption can be contained by public vigilance and institutional means, but it is a hopeless task if politicians are seen as inherently corrupt.

Pettit summarizes the two different assumptions that determine these contrasting approaches to politics.

> [One view is] that people in power are inevitably corrupt: that is, in republican terms, that such people inevitably make their decisions by reference not to considerations of the common good but rather to more sectional or private concerns. This attitude represents a general cynicism about people, in particular about those individuals who seek and get power. The other interpretation is that people in power are not inevitably corrupt but are inherently corruptible: while they may actually make their decisions on a proper, impartial basis, they cannot be relied upon to continue to do so if there are no blocks or checks on the abuse of their power. This attitude is not so much cynicism about those who happen to have power as a realism about what power can do to anyone who gets it.[36]

He adds that the dominant assumption determines how to design institutional checks on power. If one assumes that officials are inherently corrupt, the approach will be centered on how best to subdue deviance. This approach may work in part with truly corrupt individuals, but it is likely to be counterproductive with those officials who start out being public spirited. Their morale is going to be undercut by an overemphasis on controls and sanctions rather than trust that they will do the best they possibly can in specific situations.

In other words, citizens or officials who are "naturally compliant" to public laws and are concerned about the public good feel insulted and become defensive and hostile in the face of too much regulation and oversight. Pettit cites the empirical literature on regulation that supports this logic and refers to the often demoralizing effect of having clerks clock in and out of the office, which undermines the spirit of those committed to their work.[37] Pettit broadens his point about the importance of morale when he identifies the role of ordinary citizens in containing corruption by "virtuous vigilance." This is a form of citizen oversight that goes hand in hand with public acceptance of norms of civility and engagement: "It is only if ordinary members of the community are prepared to complain about petty theft, or littering, or vandalism, that there is any hope of legal sanctions to be effective."[38] He notes that citizens need to be ready to blow the whistle on bribery, corruption, and other forms of malfeasance such as environmental pollution, an area where green movements have proven to be effective watchdogs. The police and other law enforcement agencies can do only so much to induce compliance with the laws; the citizenry has to participate.[39] We will return to these issues later in the book when discussing the most effective anti-corruption strategies.

Basic views of the state also matter in perceptions of its role and value. A private and instrumental view of the state as an institution to be used to promote one's personal good undermines any vision of personal duty to the state as well as the value of civic engagement for the public good.

Communist ideology was based on the Leninist mistrust of the people and the destruction of autonomous civil society. The communist party was the sole source of defining the public good for supposedly voluntary labor in its support and actively mobilized subject citizens, often with highly repressive measures. Directly opposite to this notion of power from above are democracies, where the people are sovereign and therefore define the public interest and delegate power to their representatives. Although it is a civic duty to vote and otherwise participate in public life, this participation is voluntary. It has been a major problem of the transition from communism that popular understanding of this civic side of democracy has been only sporadic, such as in the early activities of movements like Solidarity, the Democratic Movement in Russia, and the popular fronts in the Baltic states and elsewhere. On occasion, individual civic groups work for the common good, but most people have been preoccupied with their private lives. Similarly, one can see few prominent political leaders who, like Vaclav Havel, have consistently encouraged civil society and have advocated civic virtues.[40]

Public versus Private Ethics

Corruption in the post-communist region—and elsewhere—can in part be explained by a confusion of public and private morality. We can speak about political corruption only if a society distinguishes between public and private domains. In the words of Samuel Huntington, "corruption requires some recognition of the difference between public role and private interest."[41] Whether or not this distinction is made depends on each country's prevalent political thought as well as regime and cultural contexts.

The idea that the public and the private are two separate normative spheres has been at the heart of much thinking about modern democracy. The public domain has its own rules about appropriate behavior based on specific legal and ethical norms as well as administrative codes. In the early twentieth century these notions were developed by political thinkers such as Max Weber and Woodrow Wilson, and at times new political leaders or movements—for example, the Progressive movement in the United States in the early part of the twentieth century—have tried to make them work. Led by middle-class

Americans, Progressivism initiated institutional changes to promote more direct democracy, break up economic monopolies and so-called political machines, delegate authority to boards of technical experts, and pass the first pure food and drug legislation.[42]

There is a distinction between each official's public and personal roles. The modern democratic state mandates its representatives to serve the general public and not give preferential treatment to friends and relatives; in fact, most officials take an oath that they will serve the public good and uphold the laws of the country. Public morality is distinct from private morality: it is the glue that holds together a rule-of-law state. At times there is a direct clash between the imperatives of private ethics and public ethics. A judge cannot declare innocent a thief just because he is his brother—in fact, any judge put in that situation should recuse himself and turn the case over to colleagues who have no personal stake in it.

But some conflicts of interest are more complex, and one needs to think of them carefully when aiming at establishing a state that is governed by laws and the political norms espoused in constitutions. A classic illustration is the scandal involving Helmut Kohl, the former German chancellor. After it was proven that he had taken illegal contributions for the electoral campaigns of his party, he refused to release the names of the people who had donated the money by saying that he had "given his word" not to reveal their names. Keeping one's word is a principle of personal ethics, but public ethics demanded that he not undermine the constitution of the Federal Republic of Germany, which stipulates that the financial sources of political parties must be revealed. The fact that a considerable segment of public opinion found Kohl's attitude to be justified illustrates that the separation between the private and public spheres has been significantly eroded in German political consciousness.[43] As Wolfgang Seibel notes: "The allusion to this promise contained an appeal to the moral sentiment in support of unethical behavior. In a constitutional democracy political leaders are obligated to help strengthen public respect for the constitution and the law. The core of Kohl's unethical behavior consists in his doing just the opposite. The gravity of this unethical behavior lies in the fact that he attempted to mobilize good motive[s]—virtues like integrity, trustworthiness, honor, loyalty—to justify wrongful behavior and disregard the constitution and his violation of the law."[44] Kohl undermined the political trust in the constitution of millions of his co-citizens.

As argued by Walzer, political corruption is worse than dishonesty in the private sphere, because it breaks the oath to serve the laws of the state and the good of the people. The republican view is that officials have a normative duty that they promise to serve and are trusted to serve by the people whom they represent. Breaking this public trust is therefore heinous.[45]

Human perceptions and actions are shaped by competing moral imperatives, and much confusion about corruption arises from unclear boundaries
or misplaced references. Private morality focuses on support and loyalty to
one's family, kin, friends, and ascriptive communities such as an ethnic or
religious group. These traditional social ties play a huge role in premodern
societies and take on special meanings under repressive and predatory regimes such communism, where people cannot rely on public institutions for
basic needs and therefore rely on private networks and exclusive communities. But in the context of a modern democracy there is a specific public
morality of the officeholder who, when taking office, typically swears an
oath to serve loyally the entire citizenry of a specific nation, its constitution,
and its laws. Corruption occurs when this oath is broken and the public power
entrusted to an official is misused for personal gain, including that of friends
or relatives. This distinction between public and private domains, loyalties,
and moralities is crucial in the thinking undergirding modern states. This is
true for all strands of democratic thinking, be they oriented more toward the
liberal or republican perspectives.[46]

The constitutional state depends on a variety of institutional mechanisms
to safeguard the observance of the rule of law and public morality. Although it
is desirable that individuals be personally moral and ethical, the system is
based on a different set of principles from personal morality. One can say that
"the success of the constitutional state is founded on its ability to separate the
exercise of power from the moral character of the power holders."[47] Besides
institutional checks and balances that deter the misuse of power, public morality is grounded in the political culture of a society that consists of common
norms and attitudes about appropriate behavior in the public realm, and these
institutional and cultural rules reinforce each other. Notions of difference between the public and private realms are at the heart of democratic thought
about political corruption. This includes the notion of the separation of social
roles, in particular that one should keep one's official or professional role
separate from the personal and familiar. As Max Weber emphasized, the modern bureaucrat is loyal to his boss as the holder of a position, not as a person.
The emphasis is on loyalty to the public role and purpose of the office, which
is evaluated on the basis of professional standards.[48]

The division between the public and the private underlies the concept of
the modern state, which institutionalizes this division. The state and public
domain are based on "norms and values that are part of what we call the civic
culture, the bureaucratic ethos, the ethos of public responsibility, and so on.
These sets of norms and values create expectations and regulate individual
behavior in public roles. Corruption occurs when these cultural standards are
perverted or abandoned. Thus, corruption denotes the process of penetration

of private criteria into the public domain."[49] Interestingly, communist ideology took this principle to the extreme, and the communist regimes radically suppressed the private domain. Political, economic, social, and civic life were all controlled by the state and the communist party, and most private and voluntary activity in these spheres was criminalized. This overemphasis on the public domain and its repressive control by the communist party and the state bureaucracy eventually led to a backlash by private society, which started to extend its domain unofficially during the final stages of communism, and did so officially once the regime changed.

Pluralism and Civil Society as Barriers against Corruption

Pluralism envisages a polity and society that are structured by many autonomous groups and groupings. This is in direct contrast to monopolies, which are the institutional basis of corruption. Pluralism is anti-statist and proposes a state in which power and administrative capacity are diffused to autonomous functional and territorial bodies, to self-governing associations, and to local authorities.[50] Pluralist thinkers have focused on protecting the individual "against the corrupting influence of monolithic power."[51] They also hold that politics is based on groups and that people develop through contributing to associations aimed at definite purposes. Society is composed of associations freely formed by citizens. Pluralists also claim that there is no single common good. This can be linked to the ideals of the American Revolution, which Gale Stokes has subsumed in the statement that it aimed "to abandon the ideal of the general will, the single representation of the popular sovereignty, and to replace it with the idea of limited government in which sovereignty was apportioned among various public entities."[52] In other words, increasing pluralism in the course of building democracy in Eastern Europe bears promise in itself and as a means to contain corruption.

These days social scientists talk less about pluralism and more about the importance of civil society, which at its core is a pluralist idea. Voluntary associations undergird democracy as they provide arenas for civic engagement.[53] Aside from arguments about social capital, analysts note that even limited social pluralism is crucial for the consolidation of democracy, because it creates grassroots institutions and new leaders.[54] But most important for our context, civil society is defined as groups independent of state tutelage and control.[55] The fact that true civic associations work independently of government is a foundation of democracy and a key distinction from communist regimes, which control all social organizations. Democracy differs from communism precisely because it is built on the cooperation of autonomous institutions, in particular civic ones.

Conclusion

Looking at the opposite of a phenomenon can help one understand it. This chapter examines democratic legitimacy and commitment to the public good as the opposites of corruption. Most corrupt actors indirectly recognize this by hiding their acts: corrupt dealings are hidden precisely because the perpetrators realize that their actions are illicit, illegitimate, and often illegal. Another way of analyzing the issue involves the acceptability or even legitimacy of corruption in the eyes of the citizenry. If a regime is perceived as illegitimate and exploitative, its inhabitants are unlikely to feel the obligations of good citizens to pay taxes and obey the law, and they themselves are much more likely to engage in illicit practices. The opposite of corruption includes concepts such as integrity, accountability, transparency, and good governance. Although laws address corruption in the narrower criminal law sense, these general principles play a role in public perceptions.

Corruption has many political costs, a core one being that it undermines public spiritedness and commitment to serving the public good. This is especially costly in democracies, since they rely on the involvement and support of their citizens. Paul Heywood has argued that political corruption—particularly at high levels—is more serious in democracies than in other political systems. Corruption does more damage to democracies because it is more undermining of their basic principles in a way that is not true for non-democracies.[56] Corruption attacks the equality of citizens before institutions, undermines the openness of decision making, and contributes to the government's de-legitimization in numerous ways.[57] Since "the people" are the ultimate authority in democratic states, the meaning of corruption is also defined by public opinion.

The prevalent public understanding of corruption is crucial for the success of any containment program. Since corruption revolves around the use and misuse of public power, a core question concerns the legitimacy of the rulers, that is, their right to rule. This raises the issue of regime type. Simply put, if a political regime is based on the despotic rule of a dictator, or the monopoly of power by an ideological party, or control by a colonial or occupying power, then most of the citizens are likely to see that regime as illegitimate. If, on the other hand, the sovereign in fact is the citizens, or "the people," as is the case in democracies, then most citizens are likely to accept it as legitimate.

A related issue is whether compliance with laws and regulations rests on consensus or control. The argument here is that democracy rests primarily on consensus and therefore needs to rely on enforcement only occasionally. In contrast, any regime that relies on political control tends to trigger noncompliance and therefore needs more police activity. One way to think of this is in terms of reciprocity between the state and its citizens: if the state is seen as exploitative and unjust, citizens reciprocate by withdrawing their support and evading their duties. In repressive systems noncompliance with laws and what looks like corruption may also constitute a form of resistance. As argued by James C. Scott, there is a type of corruption that "represents a kind of subversive effort by a host of individuals and groups to bend the political system to their wishes. Those who feel that their essential interests are ignored or considered illegitimate in the formal political system will gravitate to the informal channel of influence represented by corruption."[58]

7

The Role of Institutions

> Corruption is, of course, one measure of the absence
> of effective institutionalization.
>
> *Samuel Huntington*, Political Order in Changing Societies[1]

Ineffective institutions, many scholars believe, breed corruption. This means that effective institutions can help prevent it. Indeed, the cardinal message of corruption analysts and policy handbooks is that one can deter corruption by creating appropriate institutional structures, procedures, and incentives. The list of suggested mechanisms is long, but a particular emphasis is put on effective checks and balances by a multitude of countervailing powers. An independent and effective judiciary is crucial, and additional balancing measures can be designed to ensure the accountability of public officials. It is a basic principle of democracies that decision makers are accountable to other branches of government and the electorate.[2]

Institutional checks and balances are the hallmark of democracy. They arise from core political processes such as elections, competition between political parties, the power of parliaments, oversight boards, and an independent judiciary. Since the time of Montesquieu, the separation of power has been a defining principle of democracies. Next to the three classic branches of government, the media constitute the "fourth pillar of democracy," with a mandate to promote public debate and watchfulness. Most of all, democracy means that "the people" are the sovereign source of all political power. For the prevention of corruption, this means that individual citizens and their associations can and should participate in politics and watch over how their representatives use the authority entrusted to them. Or, to restate the core idea of the democratic public mandate, institutions and rules are designed to ensure that public officials work for the good of the public rather than to advance their own private interests.

This chapter uses the three levels of analysis outlined in the introduction to present universal, regional, and context-specific arguments about how institutional structures and processes can work against corruption. First, it draws on the large store of anti-corruption handbooks for an overview of the main institutional means of containing corruption. Next, it examines a specific institutional context—a post-communist public health-care system—to identify risk zones for corruption and what can be done about them. Finally, it discusses how the instruments of corruption containment can be adjusted to the needs of post-communist states.

The Institutional Means of Corruption Containment

Political corruption is behavior that takes place within public institutions. Susan Rose-Ackerman has urged that anti-corruption research focus on examining "the institutional incentives facing officials and citizens to accept and to pay bribes."[3] Neo-institutional thinkers emphasize that institutions shape behavior; it follows that changes in their structures and procedures can galvanize new incentives and ways of acting. Institutional changes can help replace the habits and belief patterns of corruption and collusion with those of accountability. Anti-corruption handbooks provide an extensive inventory of laws, structures, and procedures for containing corruption. Transparency International has devised a detailed "integrity system" that is a useful benchmark for evaluating individual polities.[4]

A common thread running through anti-corruption advice is the importance of eliminating monopolies of decision making, since they are the institutional basis of corruption. Social scientists who have theorized about corruption have made the point especially poignantly. Susan Rose-Ackerman has applied the economic principle of the market by saying that bureaucrats tend to behave like monopolists, who profit from increasing prices created by scarcity.[5] Robert Klitgaard has devised a simple but powerful formula suggesting that the key to containing corruption is to limit the monopoly power of any public official:[6]

corruption = monopoly + discretion – accountability

One can rephrase Klitgaard's proposition so that it focuses less on explaining corruption, but on ways to deter it. Reformulated, the proposition states that the three cornerstones of corruption control are:

**de-monopolize decision making + limit discretion +
strengthen accountability**

These three principles are used below to outline institutional tools to decrease the likelihood that public officials will act in illicit ways.

De-monopolize Decision Making

At all levels of governance and within each institution, the structural principle of deterring corruption is the same: no one should have a monopoly of power to make important decisions. Several people, each with a distinct role, need to be involved in all tasks that invite corruption and should have autonomous power bases. At the policy-making level, democracies safeguard the sharing and balancing of power by compelling the executive branch to interact with the legislature and other branches of government. Executive power is limited by the constitution and laws of a country, and the judiciary has the power and duty to review executive decisions. The administrative structures of the state also are subject to numerous rules, oversight, and power sharing.

The de-monopolization of decision making in democratic institutions is implemented both internally and externally. For example, the procurement committee of a ministry needs to divide responsibilities among its members; it should also provide firms participating in tenders with access to external grievance committees. If independent actors can effectively influence and reverse decisions, a system of checks and balances comes into play.

For this to work, the way in which officials implement the law must be transparent. Openness of proceedings and accessibility of information are effective ways to discourage illicit acts, and so is the participatory role of civic associations. Besides administrative review bodies within the governmental structure, the media and civic associations act as external watchdogs to monitor how well public officials do their job of serving the public interest rather than their own private gain.

The structural principle of having more than one person or institution make and review decisions can be realized in many ways. One way to prevent judicial corruption is to use several judges when important cases are decided and to guarantee the right of appeal to higher courts. Decisions on privatization, procurement, and other allocations of valued goods constitute crucial risk zones for corruption and therefore authority for them should be shared. In addition, there must be effective oversight and the possibility of appeal.

The same rules apply to daily interaction between state officials and citizens where money or other important goods are involved. A traffic cop has the authority to issue tickets, yet he should be bound by clear rules and procedures and subject to effective oversight by his superiors. In this case, too, it is important that power be limited structurally: opportunities for corruption are limited if a policeman can only issue traffic tickets and must leave the job of collecting fines to a bank or separate financial office. Poland for one has abolished cash tickets for traffic offenses.[7]

Job rotation and limited tenure of officials are other structural means of limiting power, and so is the geographic or institutional decentralization of decision making and administration. Grassroots corruption can be contained by accountable local self-government. In Russia, experience shows that local highway police supervised by the elected bodies of municipalities are less corrupt than their counterpart that reports to the Ministry of Internal Affairs.[8] Yet these instruments should be used with caution. They can backfire and have an effect opposite to the one desired, for example if decentralization results in less oversight and more unchecked discretion of lower level officials. The de-monopolization of the power to make significant public decisions is not enough in itself; it needs to be combined with effective ways to oversee, check, and review decisions. On the financial side, this means that institutional reforms should include the introduction of transparent accounting standards and the strengthening of the auditor general's office. In addition to regular reviews, auditors should develop a system of random checks, since these can reveal weaknesses in the system and deter illicit acts by raising the risk of exposure.

The logic of the separation and sharing of power is twofold: if there is no monopoly of decision making, the likelihood of corrupt decisions decreases because more people participate in the process and because it is more difficult to hide illicit influences. Oversight and review have a similar impact. An effective review process has both a participatory and preventative role. If decisions can be reversed by another body, this means that decision making is demonopolized. In addition, the very notion that wrongful decisions can be reversed tends to have a prophylactic effect and prevent such decisions from being made to begin with, even more so if the initial decision makers face penalties.

As discussed at more length below, accountability has the crucial role of not only punishing illicit acts, but of preventing them. Deterrence can be made tangible by institutional means, but it has to be complemented by the perception that corruption carries high risks.[9] The credibility of risks is crucial, as has been pointed out both by theorists and people living in the region.[10] An anthropological study conducted in Latvia reports respondent Anna saying about political corruption: "I see that the situation is hopeless. A real, big sentence has not been given to anyone yet. Thus you see that to breach the law is not risky. I do not think people would break the law so much if they knew they could get punished for that."[11] In sum, besides securing the institutional framework for increasing the risk of corruption, actual experience must show that discovery and punishment are likely. With this, many corrupt acts might be prevented.

To increase the riskiness of illicit acts should be the goal of all administrative and judicial oversight bodies. They should not only allow for speedy and effective review of contentious decisions in their regular course of work,[12] they should also engage in random checks and inspections. Individuals contemplating unlawful acts must know that there is a high certainty that review will take place combined with uncertainty about its timing. Deterrence is most effective when detection and prosecution work expeditiously. The law enforcement and judicial systems need to have the capacity to work quickly and well, and to be seen doing so, to deter malefactors.

Perceptions are influenced by institutional track records as well as by knowledge of the actual risk of detection. The latter can be raised by confronting the fact that it is very difficult to prove corruption due to its hidden nature, and that therefore special means of detection and documentation must be used. One means is to establish effective whistleblower protection. People who have direct knowledge or proof of corruption by having witnessed it need to be assured that they will not lose their jobs or otherwise become a target of retribution.[13] Protecting whistleblowers is complicated. A somewhat simpler approach has been adopted in Poland: civil servants who are given an order that is unlawful or wastes resources may request the order in writing and then refuse to carry it out.[14] Another way to counteract the difficulty of gathering proof is to use special investigatory tools such as sting operations and random inspections using sophisticated technology.[15]

The public too has a crucial preventative role in regard to corruption. In a democracy, people have many ways of participating in decisions that affect their lives. Anti-corruption experts consistently emphasize the importance of the media and nongovernmental associations in monitoring public integrity and in acting as its main advocates.[16] Democratic theory recognizes the role of independent media to act as the "fourth pillar" of the democratic system of checks and balances on public power, and this role is crucial to preventing corruption. Free media monitor governmental decisions on a daily basis, they can investigate and expose corrupt acts, and they can inform citizens about effective ways to stop them. Research shows that there is a strong correlation between press freedom and reduced corruption.[17]

The media can illuminate the role of citizen associations, both those that directly work for integrity in public life, such as local branches of Transparency International, as well as those that target issues indirectly related to it, for example taxpayer associations watching over how taxes are used or environmental groups working to protect public goods such as nature. If corruption is entrenched in higher levels of government, citizen associations can form a civic coalition for clean government. Such a coalition can be a forum for demonstrating the ills of corruption, it can provide solidarity and practical support to activists, and it can engage in public-interest lawsuits or electoral mobilization.

Some institutions straddle the borderline between the public and private realms, professional associations being a prime example. All professional organizations, but especially those that are constituted by public officials such as auditors, judges, or doctors, have a duty to engage in self-regulation and self-policing. They need procedures for review of grievances and disciplinary hearings. By tradition, and because they live in comparatively small societies, East European professionals are reluctant to monitor their peers and instead emphasize corporate solidarity. This ignores their duty to the larger public and undermines the status of their profession if they help cover up the malfeasance of colleagues.

Business and professional associations need to be involved in championing professional standards and integrity, both internally among their peers and externally by checking on other players in the public realm. Internal review and oversight bodies should be complemented by external institutions keeping a watchful eye on how decisions involving the public interest are made and implemented. Oversight and review work best when they form a network of bodies participating in the process from the inside as well as from the outside, and when there is both a vertical and horizontal flow of decision-making power.

Limit Discretion

In order to do their jobs, public officials need authority to make decisions. These decisions must be made according to the public interest as defined by laws, rules, and policy instructions. Not every situation can be anticipated, however, so officials also need some freedom to decide how to proceed. The dilemma of discretion is that rules must be flexible, but this opens the door to arbitrariness and administrative corruption. The art of good administration is to avoid micromanagement while keeping discretion within bounds. Carefully balanced rules and codes of behavior can clarify the criteria according to which civil servants should make decisions, illuminating the difference between being flexible in serving the citizenry and being arbitrary or favoring someone for private gain. The appropriate application of rules and regulations is a core aspect of the training of good administrators.

A fundamental way to limit the potential misuse of discretion is to institute an efficient and nonpolitical system of public administration as outlined by Woodrow Wilson, Max Weber, and contemporary theorists of good governance. The ideal bureaucracy stipulates explicit professional rules of conduct and decision making that emphasize merit, impartiality, impersonality, and adherence to transparent procedures. Public administrators should be protected from direct political intervention. A professional and

merit-based civil service helps to protect against the many forms of administrative malfeasance, including nepotism, favoritism, and other partisan or
political influences.[18]

The quality of laws and regulations also makes a big difference. They
need to be clear and avoid being turned into red tape. For administrative
rules to be observed, they need to be legitimate in the eyes of most officials
and citizens. Rules are not followed unless they are in harmony with popular
values and backed up by credible enforcement. When codes of ethics or rules
about conflicts of interest are promulgated, the logic behind them should be
spelled out. This is where professional training as well as publicity campaigns come in. In the post-communist context it is especially important to
explain the civic rationale behind the erection of boundaries between public
and private behaviors.

Transparency of decision making and openness about how public affairs
are handled are additional cornerstones of preventing administrative arbitrariness. Rules, regulations, and decisions should be transparent and information
about them should be easily available to the public. Procedures and fees for
public services as well as information about the right to ask for a review of a
decision with which a citizen may disagree should be posted at administrative
offices. Information, publicity, and transparency are crucial tools to discourage arbitrary and corrupt decision making on all levels of public office.

In the case of procurement, for example, an initial step is to publicize public
tenders and to provide citizens and firms with the information needed to participate. This should be accompanied by transparency about how bids will be
evaluated. There should be clear rules how officials should act in case of conflicts of interest and how to prevent other corruption-prone situations, such as
obscure subsequent "renegotiation" possibilities of accepted bids and contracts.

Transparency about how officials make decisions and use their discretion
can help prevent misuse, and the same is true for information about all aspects of public administration. Some concrete examples of how these principles have been applied in the new Central and East European members of
the European Union will be provided in the following chapter. Modern tech-
nologies can enhance access to information. Estonia is especially advanced
in using the Internet to publicize government information, including the wages
of high-level civil servants and members of the boards and supervisory councils of state-owned enterprises.[19]

Strengthen Accountability

Accountability is a crucial albeit multidimensional concept. It suggests the
importance of "accounting for" an action in the sense of laying it out in a

transparent way, allowing others to understand and react. Another dimension involves the previously discussed review process conducted by independent oversight bodies acting both routinely as well as randomly to maximize their deterrent impact on questionable acts. In addition, the people responsible must face consequences in cases of wrongdoing.[20] The purpose of exposure and punishment is mainly to prevent future malfeasance, but it also strengthens the public's trust in their institutions. The latter can be greatly enhanced if accountability involves restitution to the victims of corrupt acts, be they individuals or the public at large.

Chapter 8 will examine how accountability has been implemented in the post-communist states. Here the focus is on the main instruments by which it can be ensured.

A fundamental precondition for accountability is that there be reliable information about the performance of public officials. As noted by Paul Heywood, "accountability can be enforced only if government activity is transparent: citizens cannot hold their elected leaders to account for activities they are unaware of having taken place."[21] Consequently, much anti-corruption work has focused on passing and implementing "freedom-of-information" acts and on strengthening the quality of investigative reporting. Freedom-of-information laws are the basis for granting access to information about decisions of government and public institutions. Yet these laws are just tools; individual citizens and civic groups have to work to activate them. Governments are reluctant to release information and tend to put obstacles in the path of people asking for it. Litigation is often necessary to secure access to documents. Experience in Bulgaria, Georgia, and Slovakia, for example, shows that the more the laws are used, the more often public-interest litigators win cases, and the more the media publicize such occurrences, the easier it becomes to secure documents.[22]

The de-monopolizing of how decisions are made is a cornerstone of the prevention of corruption, but it also is crucial for accountability. In democracies, citizens hold their representatives accountable by elections, debates, and other modes of political participation such as petitions or protest. Other institutional means to ensure accountability at all levels of governance involve the process of review by oversight bodies, audits, independent and effective judiciaries, and monitoring by the media and civil society. One can speak of both vertical and horizontal accountability as well as the joint efforts of networks of agencies (up to and including high courts) committed to upholding the rule of law.[23]

Police and the judiciary are the core institutions charged with ensuring legal accountability. Unfortunately, they often do their work poorly. Where the regular law enforcement structures work ineffectively, it may be useful to create a special prosecutor or a corruption-prevention office. Anti-corruption bureaus are recommended by most experts, yet Daniel Kaufmann adds a sobering perspective. A survey of elites in developing countries reveals that most respondents are skeptical about such bodies. To be credible, such institutions have to follow the example set by an honest leadership and be independent from political interference. Otherwise, they are easily rendered useless, or, worse, are misused for political gain.[24] This underlines that institutional solutions must be based on a careful assessment of the political context of a specific state.

When corruption is endemic in the judiciary itself, innovative approaches may be needed, such as alternative dispute-resolution mechanisms and more systematic NGO involvement in monitoring.[25] Another technique if accountability works poorly at the local or national level is for institutions at the next higher level of governance to step in. An example from the American context shows how this can work. The city of Chicago has been notorious for political corruption, in part because it has for decades been dominated by a single political party. In the 1980s Chicago saw a ten-year federal investigation into its court system. Operation Greylord led to the conviction of more than one hundred judges, attorneys, and courtroom staff for various forms of corruption. Federal investigators and prosecutors stepped in, investing enormous resources in the operation, because local authorities had proven themselves unwilling or unable to pursue the many allegations of corruption and the voters did not react.[26]

Outside intervention is one way to reach a breakthrough in the fight against corruption if internal solutions fail. For small countries without federal institutions, international bodies may substitute. Since law enforcement touches on the sensitive issue of sovereignty, only time will tell whether international courts will develop a role beyond human-rights issues. To date, international institutions have mostly served as monitoring bodies that have commented on the need to curb corruption. Some institutions, such as the World Bank and the European Union, have also begun to link the provision of international funds to the implementation of effective integrity programs, and there have been recent efforts to expand the role of all-European law enforcement institutions.[27]

One way to mobilize legal institutions to do their job is to allow individual citizens or groups to initiate lawsuits that lead to the review of specific illicit deals and seek financial compensation. Worldwide there are legal and practical precedents when the state or individual victims of corruption file a civil law suit for the value of a transaction. In Europe many countries—including increasingly many from Eastern Europe—have signed the Council of Europe's 1999 Civil Law Convention on Corruption, which requires them to enact domestic laws allowing "persons who have suffered damage as a result of corruption" to sue for damages.[28] Since initiating a civil suit tends to be easier than ensuring that law enforcement pursues a potential criminal act, the option of filing lawsuits should be secured for individuals, firms, and civic groups wishing to do so. Although this can be undertaken by common-cause groups, aggrieved clients of public services (for example, someone who is illegally denied an operation in a state hospital) have more of a direct incentive to do so. Until recently there has been little action in this regard in the post-communist region, but this may be changing.[29]

Lawbreaking can also be deterred by a host of other legal provisions, for example those that allow law enforcement agencies to freeze or seize illegally acquired assets. Besides providing disincentives for potentially corrupt actors, it is important to provide positive incentives for honest people to fight corruption. One possibility is to reward officials and citizens who provide information leading to the successful recovery of embezzled public funds. In the United States, some citizens have received sizable rewards for filing information on corrupt dealings known to them.[30]

An alternative approach is to reward entire institutions. In the early 1980s Ghana established revenue targets and then gave the National Revenue Service a bonus of 3.5 percent of tax revenue and 2.5 percent of customs revenue. As a result, tax and customs revenue rose from 6.6 percent to 12.3 percent of GDP between 1984 and 1988.[31] A similar precedent has been set in South Africa, where a special investigating unit and tribunal were established to target the malpractice of state institutions, and in particular to recover stolen state property. Within a year this commission had uncovered theft of government assets, including land, cars, office computers, and cash of more than $1.5 billion.[32]

The citizenry can discourage corruption in other ways. Public pressure can prevent politicians who have engaged in shady deals from running for office again. Citizens and opposition groups can demand that parliamentary investigative committees be formed, that there be public hearings, and that representatives in parliament pass censure resolutions. Individual citizens as well as groups can organize question-asking in the press and at public meetings, which can be especially effective during election time. To decrease risks and increase payoffs to anti-corruption activists, people can organize support groups and defense funds and lobby for the effective protection of whistleblowers and witnesses. The latter activities are especially important in cases where simple citizens have the courage to challenge grand corruption and malfeasance by prominent politicians or officials. Although it is inspiring to observe a David challenging a Goliath, the public has a duty to assist and protect its heroes.

In sum, there are numerous institutional ways to contain corruption. In each country or context one or the other instrument will have better results. Since impunity is a core issue in the post-communist region, the enforcement of laws should have high priority. Besides increasing overall law enforcement capacities, some special approaches appear promising. Effective means of protecting whistleblowers and witnesses can go a long way in helping to document and prosecute cases of corruption. Law enforcement agencies can become more proactive and initiate investigations by using sting operations and similar means. Where investigatory and judicial institutions have proven themselves inept at prosecuting corruption, one may need to bring in specialized corruption-fighting units and prosecutors. Where illegal activities cross international borders, the cooperation of foreign law enforcement units can tip the balance.

Institutional Corruption and Its Control: Public Health Care

To determine what will work in the post-communist countries, one needs to consider corruption in that specific environment. Because corruption "always takes place in an institutional context,"[33] any good anti-corruption strategy begins by distinguishing the various types of corruption, and then highlights structural and incentive failures within specific institutions. The public health sector is useful as a case study for mapping major differences between types of corruption, providing illustrations of concrete corrupt acts, and then showing how anti-corruption measures might work.

The former communist states inherited an extensive public health system that in most countries has been reformed much more slowly than other public institutions.[34] It is an important sector to analyze because fair and effective health services represent a public good that concerns everyone, and individual access to good medical care is a critical private good to which people go to great lengths to attain. Surveys show, however, that this is a sector where many people have personally experienced corruption.

Many studies from the region report bribes or "gratitude payments" to doctors and other medical staff. When asked about their behavior, respondents often acknowledge that they participate in illicit acts, yet most do not feel responsible for their behavior. Sixty-four percent of a Polish sample said in 1999 that the then-current situation forced people to give bribes.[35] A common belief is that corruption is due less to individual malfeasance than to institutional failings. The institutional arguments presented here in part support such a conclusion, which does not mean that people have no choice in how they act and are not responsible for their actions.

As explained in Chapter 2, post-communist corruption comes in many forms that vary in their political consequences and at times differ from corrupt practices in other parts of the world. In countries with developed economic or social markets, private business or individuals tend to take the initiative in corrupting public officials. In the case of the ex-communist systems making the transition from regimes that monopolized all institutions, the initiative for corrupt acts typically has come from officials in charge of these institutions. The core issue has not been the corruption of the state by outside forces, but corruption by public officials and employees representing the state.[36] Although all corruption is politically detrimental, it is especially devastating if public officials abuse their positions for blatantly self-serving and even extortionist actions. In addition to the damage it does to the public good, in the post-communist region this type of corruption undermines the citizenry's trust in public institutions and even the democratic system itself.[37]

Table 7.1 maps corrupt acts typically encountered within the health-care system. Besides providing an overview and illustrative examples of specific acts, Table 7.1 highlights some of the analytical points made in Chapter 2. Column 1 lists various means of corruption besides monetary bribery, which is all too often taken to be corruption's synonym. Besides money, the currency of corruption also consists of favors, influence, collusion, and extortion. Column 2 illustrates the different goals of corruption, which again extend beyond monetary gain and include access to services and power. In the case of the passive participants and witnesses of corruption, the goal is to be exposed to less stress. Yet, as noted in Chapter 2, dereliction of duty promotes corruption. This has been recognized in Estonia, where it is now a punishable offense for officials who learn of an offer of a bribe or actual bribe to fail to report it to their superiors.[38]

The arrows show that the initiative for a specific act can come from a private or an official entity. Most importantly, Table 7.1 reiterates that corruption occurs at different levels of public life: everyday interaction between citizens and officials, at the administrative level within public institutions, and at the policy-making level. As argued in Chapter 2, the three levels of corruption are a crucial way of differentiating between types of corrupt acts and their varying political consequences.

In each institution and country, anti-corruption strategists need to determine which types of corruption are most harmful to society and the state. The everyday encounter between an individual citizen and official that involves bending a rule appears to be the most innocuous, but not if it involves a surgeon in a public clinic extorting an illicit payment by refusing to operate without it.[39] This example also illustrates a case where a state employee rather than a citizen initiates a corrupt act. Another type of corruption is passive, as when someone ignores his or her duty to stop illicit practices, the example in

Table 7.1

Map of Corruption: Public Health Services

1. Means	2. Goal	3. Illustrative example

Level I. Everyday Interaction between Officials and Citizens

money	bend rule ────────>	patient asks surgeon for
gift	access	preferential treatment
favor ───────>	speed	
contact	quality	
extortion <────	enrichment <────	surgeon extorts illicit payment
ignore duty <────	less stress <────	administrator ignores corrupt act

Level II. Interaction within Public Institutions

money <────>	bend rule <────>	Medical Academy sells diplomas
nepotism		
favoritism <────	profiteering from	clinic director buys supplies
collusion	procurement <────	from wife's company
asset-stripping <────	enrichment <────	deliberate bankrupting of hospital
		to privatize for in-group

Level III. Influence over Political Institutions

position	laws favoring in-group <────	elite cartel of doctors "capture"
party financing <────		health ministry
influence	illicit privatization <────	legislator transforms state
money		sanatorium into private hotel
secret deals		
blackmail		

Note: Arrows indicate direction of initiative.

Table 7.1 being that of a clinic administrator who fails to intervene when extortion occurs.

Much of post-communist corruption occurs within institutions without the involvement of external actors and involves the stripping of public assets by self-serving officials who at times transform entire public institutions into private fiefdoms. At the institutional level, officials may take the initiative in designing schemes such as a medical academy selling admissions, high grades, or even phony diplomas. Other scenarios illustrated in Table 7.1 involve clinic administrators ignoring conflicts of interest and profiteering from procurement, or deliberately bankrupting a hospital in order to privatize it to an in-group.[40]

Conflicts of interest also are at the heart of much policy-level corruption, as when a legislator arranges to transform a state sanatorium into a private hotel owned by himself or his affiliates. Most damagingly, policy-making corruption can include institutional capture by an elite cartel, for example a group of hospital directors taking charge of the ministry of health in order to foster rule-making that safeguards their influence and enrichment. As shown in Table 7.1, this type of corruption involves the misuse of position and party financing to "purchase" laws favoring a narrow group at the expense of the public. Such state capture is often accompanied by blackmail or secret agreements.

One also needs to differentiate between incidental and systemic corruption. It is much easier to control occasional corrupt acts by individuals than acts that are widely engaged in and have a systemic basis, such as illicit payments to state-employed doctors. To change the latter practice, fundamental reforms must be introduced on the policy-making level, yet few post-communist governments have ventured to undertake such reforms because they involve unpopular decisions on insurance and undermine the vested interests of a powerful segment of the medical establishment that has vigorously defended its privileged position.[41] This example also illustrates how corrupt acts on various levels are interconnected and therefore must be addressed together. Piecemeal reforms can have only limited success. Ideally, reforms aiming at the containment of corruption would take a systemic approach to an institution such as the public health system and undertake a fundamental transformation. Nevertheless, the instruments of corruption control listed in the first part of this chapter can trigger partial and gradual reforms.

Table 7.2 again focuses on health services to illustrate some of the internal and external institutional structures and mechanisms that can deter corruption. Parallel to the analytical schema used in Table 7.1, the means of corruption control are subdivided by the three levels of interaction at which they operate. In addition, Table 7.2 differentiates between means of corruption control that are internal and those that are external to a specific institution. The left column of Table 7.2 lists the internal provisions, and the right column lists examples of how external actors can contribute to a more open and honest system.

At the level of daily interaction, even simple measures such as the open posting of fees for specific services can discourage corruption. If the public institution—in our case a clinic—is lax in making such information available, the media or patients' rights organizations can step in. Openly available information about rules and procedures is crucial at the administrative level also, especially in regard to public-property management, procurement, and privatization. At all levels there must be mechanisms for oversight and review; examples are listed in both columns. The table also lists positive incentives that promote integrity, such as rewards and public honors for exemplary

Table 7.2

Map of Anti-Corruption: Public Health Services

Internal Anti-Corruption Instruments	External Anti-Corruption Instruments
I. Everyday Interaction between Officials and Citizens	
Post information on fees	Media publicize fee structure
Patients' advocate in clinic	Patients' Rights Association
Accessible grievance procedure	Legal assistance for victims of medical corruption
Oversight by supervisors, board	Public hearing/forum on clinic rules
Reward/promote exemplary staff	Public honor for surgeon operating on poor patients without fee
II. Interaction within Public Institutions	
Merit system for hiring/promotion	
Rotation of administrative personnel	Whistleblower protection
Publicize rules about procurement	Audit by procurement oversight office
Laws on public property	Monitoring by media, watchdog groups, and law-enforcement
Strengthen esprit de corps	Civil liability for misconduct
III. Influence over Political Institutions	
Lobby political candidates for reform	Electoral accountability
Protests by nurses, doctors, patients	Citizen coalition for better government
Reform group of medical professionals	Limit libel laws
Publicize ethics codes	Pressure by international institutions
Financial disclosure	Investigative reporting

staff. Negative incentives cited include civil liability for officials engaging in misconduct and exposure by investigative reports.

At the policy-making level, protests and reform activities by insiders of health-care facilities can contribute to creating better rules and institutions. Reform-minded groups of medical professionals can publicize ethics codes and promote better financial accounting. External actors such as the media and individual citizens and their associations also have a role to play. They can act as watchdogs that monitor decisions and ask questions, lend support to victims of corruption, protest, and even file lawsuits. The media can publish investigative reports and lobby for libel laws that permit unintimidated public review of politicians' performance. International institutions such as the European Union can put pressure on governments and ministries of health to develop more honest procurement systems for medical supplies.

Recent experience in the post-communist region illustrates how some of these instruments can work in practice. Recognizing that it costs time, money, and courage for clients of public services to use grievance and appeal procedures, "citizen advocacy offices" in the Russian cities of Tomsk and Samara provide support to victims of corruption. The offices first investigate grievances and determine whether they qualify as likely instances of corruption. If so—for example, an official asking for a bribe or people being victimized by non-enforcement of court decisions—the office steps in, taking legal action if necessary.[42] In Latvia, patients of state hospitals were brought together to share experiences and discuss reform proposals. Besides providing information and transparency, such forums increase the risk of public shame to those who engage in illicit practices.[43]

These examples highlight the importance not only of proper institutional procedures, but of a participatory approach involving many citizens. Increasingly, anti-corruption analysts are putting emphasis on civil society and social-action coalitions, rather than a top-down approach.[44] Even for bottom-up solutions, however, the goal is to change policy making and to alter the public environment in which elites operate and to which they are accountable.[45] Such activity can even expand into the formation of electoral coalitions for clean government, as was the case in Slovakia 1998 and Bulgaria 2001.

Adjusting to the Post-Communist Context

Corruption control works only if it takes into account country-specific contexts. All too often, international donors promote holistic strategies that ignore the history and institutional development in different countries.[46] Care must be taken to fashion institutional safeguards against corruption so that they work as intended rather than simply becoming burdensome new bureaucratic strictures. More offices and rules do not necessarily lead to less corruption. They may even have the opposite effect if officials misuse them to hide corruption. As noted in Chapter 2, the misuse of audits and prosecuting powers to hide corruption rather than fight it is especially pernicious. Thorough procedures and documentation were a mainstay of communist state administration,[47] but they were cumbersome and officials developed ways to neutralize them in case they had to defend themselves against charges of mismanagement.

Many contemporary officials who were socialized in that administrative tradition brought these skills to their current jobs.[48] A favored approach is to hide behind the letter of the law and ignore its spirit. This suggests that reformers should focus less on rewriting laws than on fostering a new legal culture. Reformers also should take care to avoid a well-known problem in public administration whereby officials become more concerned about how their decisions will look under ex post facto scrutiny by auditors, law enforcement investigators, and the media than about what they actually accomplish on the job.[49]

Regulation must be carefully directed to where it is most needed, for example the behavior of officials rather than citizens. An analyst reports that, "paradoxically, Russia today, like the Soviet Union, promotes corruption by having too much regulation by government but too little regulation of public officials in the service of that government."[50] Too many laws can be part of the problem as they lead to excessive formalism and vexatious procedures that provoke people to try to get around them.[51] Excessive regulation and oversight result in added costs and sometimes insufferably cumbersome processes. Two critics observe sadly, "the irony of corruption control is that the more anti-corruption control we create, the more we create bureaucratic pathology and red tape."[52]

For example, the Czech Republic instituted an appeals process for procurement tenders, yet appeals typically delay tenders for six to twelve months, hurting both honest and dishonest bidders.[53] The process could be adjusted by building in disincentives for filing baseless appeals. A more fruitful step would be to ensure that procurement officials who make inappropriate decisions are penalized. Regulation works best if it serves to deter wrongful acts, so that appeal procedures need rarely be used.

Anti-corruption measures must be carefully calibrated so they cannot be turned against honest players and corruption fighters. Mechanisms intended to prevent corruption, such as rotation of personnel, can be misused by supervisors to get rid of more honest personnel and potential whistleblowers. As noted by Susan Rose-Ackerman, solutions that work in other contexts can backfire when corruption is systemic.[54] Samuel Huntington has gone further, arguing that in a society where corruption is widespread, the passage of strict laws against corruption serves only to multiply the opportunities for corruption.[55]

Similarly, the frequently mentioned remedy of raising salaries of poorly paid public servants to fortify them against the temptation to "earn something on the side," can backfire unless it is carefully targeted. Increasing the salaries of already corrupt officials is unlikely to make them less corrupt, whereas raising the salaries of sorely underpaid honest public servants can indeed help deter malfeasance. Therefore increases in pay should focus on strengthening the position of the most honest officials as well as those demonstrably involved in efforts to prevent corruption. Changes in salary structures should go hand in hand with a comprehensive review of risk zones for corruption and establishing new safeguards against them.

Of course, once a preventive system is put in place, corrupt officials work hard to find new ways to circumvent it, often quite successfully. In the case of procurement, one popular ruse is to set tender criteria that effectively exclude all but one possible winner. Another is to increase prices for the execution of a contract after it has been granted.[56] But most of all, there is the insidious impact of collusion among various officials and firms. It has been reported that in the Czech Republic "the practice of fixing tenders through collusion is generally felt to be widespread,"[57] and the same has been said for most other post-communist countries.

A broader problem is the influence of informal institutions. As noted by neo-institutional theorists such as Douglass North, informal rules have a powerful modifying impact on formal rules.[58] Institutional checks and balances are a mainstay of anti-corruption policies, and they need to be put in place, but they can be undermined by informal structures and processes. Corruption may initially be contained by limiting formal decision-making monopolies, but informal power monopolies—corrupt networks spanning several branches of government and colluding to protect each other—can arise to replace them. Informal networks and rules constitute an influential legacy of the communist era, as pointed out in Chapter 5. The reliance on personal networks rather than public institutions is exacerbated by other factors as well. In the case of Slovenia, the small size of the country plays a role, as does a long history of close interaction between the public and private sectors.[59]

Informal corrupt networking and collusion are subtle and hard to check. A core difficulty in dealing with collusion is that it can be both active and passive, the latter being expressed through a culture of mutual protection and anticipation of negative consequences even without explicit threats. Clearly, to restrain corrupt actors in post-communist countries, both formal and informal checks and balances are needed.

Another legacy of the communist era outlined in Chapter 5 is that many people learned to ignore or passively support illicit and illegitimate acts. Today this tendency is expressed in several forms. Police and other law enforcement agencies are often still viewed as a repressive part of the state administration and not as crime fighters and protectors of citizens. Moreover, many private citizens and civil servants use collegiality to defend illicit actions, as revealed in a Bulgarian parliamentary committee's interviews.[60] Many citizens, not only the elites, assist each other in small illicit acts considered necessary for daily survival, and so the mutual covering up learned during the communist era persists.[61]

Misplaced notions of collegiality, corporatism, and actual peer pressure undermine oversight procedures in many institutional contexts. This is also true for professional groups that present a monolithic front to outsiders but rarely have effective internal procedures to monitor professional performance and potential malfeasance. Since corruption control is more difficult if an entire professional group feels under attack, it is important to promote reform groups within established professions who understand that everyone wins in the long run if corruption is contained.

Unfortunately, research suggests that anti-corruption agencies work best where they are needed least—that is, in countries with lower levels of corruption. The main reason is that the success of anti-corruption mechanisms is linked to the quality of overall governance structures, especially the legal system.[62] Similarly, research on the success of anti-corruption efforts in the post-communist transition countries shows that these efforts are most likely to succeed in countries with low levels of administrative corruption, since established administrative structures have less power to block reforms.[63] Success is also much more likely if anti-corruption programs incorporate civil society and the "third sector" more broadly, such as in Lithuania. In countries such as Azerbaijan, where reform measures have been largely "top down," based on presidential decree, implementation has been severely lacking.[64]

Conclusion

The basic institutional formula for containing corruption is to de-monopolize decision making, limit discretion, and institute and enforce mechanisms of accountability. This is especially important to post-communist states, since the preceding communist regimes were characterized by monopolies of all kinds, extreme discretion for both communist party and state officials, and little accountability. In contrast, the institutional design of democracies emphasizes countervailing powers that balance each other. The common thread in all corruption-prevention advice is to secure institutional checks and balances, oversight, audits, independent and effective judiciaries, and monitoring by the media and civic society. Anti-corruption handbooks provide an extensive inventory of specific institutions, laws, and procedures. This inventory is a useful guide to what an ideal non-corrupt polity looks like and what it should aim for. But no single law or institution is a silver bullet. Analysts often speak of an "anti-corruption infrastructure" that combines many measures.   .

The institutional agenda is clear, but one needs to adapt it carefully to local contexts. In the post-communist region, the insidious role of informal networks that can undermine formal mechanisms of accountability must be kept in mind. Informal power monopolies often act like political cartels and work through collusion. Institutional checks and balances that allow for accountability are necessary, but not sufficient to ensure implementation. The actors within institutions must be both able and motivated to enforce the anti-corruption measures. In other words, procedural democracy is not enough; an infusion of democratic spirit is also needed.[65]

Yet public-spiritedness is not sufficient either. The public must be convinced that complying with the formal rules pays off both individually and collectively. This is where neo-institutional thinking about incentives, the calculus of how others in society act, and the adjustment of informal rules become helpful in gaining insight about "how the system really works" and how to develop appropriate strategies for dealing with it. The following chapters will explore these questions further.

8

Implementing Institutional Accountability

Inconsequential accountability is no accountability at all.

Andreas Schedler, "Conceptualizing Accountability"[1]

Once one recognizes that corruption is a serious problem, the core issue is how to contain it. This is a democratic concern: how can one make accountable those holding public office, and how can one measure success? As argued in Chapter 7, institutional frameworks for creating checks and balances are the foundation of accountability. The common thread in all advice about institutional solutions for containing corruption is an emphasis on countervailing powers and monitoring by media and civic society. Especially relevant to the post-communist region is a clarification of the boundaries between public and private interests. Official conduct can be regulated by laws, rules, and ethics codes. The institutional inventory is useful for outlining what an ideal non-corrupt polity looks like and what one should aim for. However, even though by late 2003 many states in the region had adopted most of the recommended anti-corruption laws and institutions, this appears to have had little effect.

Institutions in post-communist states that look like those found in developed democracies nevertheless function differently, mostly due to informal processes. This confirms Douglass C. North's argument about the huge modifying impact of informal rules on formal rules.[2] This chapter therefore probes more deeply into the implementation of accountability. What are the results of all the structures, laws, and procedures? How have various democratic institutions implemented their mandate? How effective have they been in promoting accountability? If some instruments have been more effective than others, what can one learn from that?

"Accountability" is a crucial concept defining the limits of corruption, and it has several meanings. One is "accounting for" an action by laying it out in a transparent way for others to know about it. A second aspect is that a review process is triggered if anything is questionable. If wrongdoing is found, the perpetrators face consequences, including punishment.[3] Accountability refers to responsiveness to many constituencies, including both one's own public as well as international actors. Andreas Schedler emphasizes "answerability" and "enforcement" as well as the positive power of dialogue, which others have referred to as the deliberative side of democracy.[4] "Accountability is antithetical to monologic power. It establishes a dialogic relationship between accountable and accounting actors. It makes both parties speak and engages them both in public debate."[5] Accountability in modern democracies goes beyond restraint and oversight by public agencies and the electorate. It calls for multiple forms of self-restraint,[6] and a culture of public-spiritedness.

In assessing the concrete implementation of accountability, this chapter first outlines its various dimensions, be they electoral, public, legal, financial, or other. It then assesses how effectively accountability has been ensured along each dimension in the ex-communist members of the European Union. These include Poland, the Czech Republic, Slovakia, Hungary, Slovenia, and the three Baltic states, all of which joined the EU in May 2004. Bulgaria and Romania, also considered, hope to join in 2007.

Effective accountability can be measured by indicators such as electoral upsets, resignations of officials, the impact of media reporting and parliamentary hearings, reversals of corrupt arrangements, and the frequency of corruption investigations and convictions. An analysis of these indicators in the ten countries named above shows that among the systems that work, the watchdog role of the press and NGOs stands out. The most effective promoters of cleaner politics are the print media, the electorate, and civic associations. The main laggards are the formal administrative control structures and the judicial system. This points to some theoretical and practical conclusions about the democratic role of civil society in comparison to formal political institutions.

The balance sheet of accountability is less an inventory of institutions that foster low levels of corruption than an attempt to go behind the facades of institutions to assess their actual workings. Clearly a single chapter cannot compare all cases on all scores; instead this chapter presents typical cases for each dimension of accountability. In an effort to focus less on problems and more on solutions, it also highlights instances of progress. Unfortunately, good data often are unavailable and much more in-depth research is needed. What is presented here is a balance sheet for the period up to early 2004 as well as a template of issues for additional research and analysis.

A Balance Sheet of Accountability

Institutions matter greatly in preventing illicit behaviors, but they can be Potemkin villages and therefore one needs to establish a balance sheet of real accountability. Here a multidimensional approach is taken to measure the effectiveness of accountability mechanisms:

Electoral accountability: How free and fair are elections and campaign financing? Has corruption been a major theme in election debates and has it led to electoral upsets? Did actual policy change follow?

Governmental accountability: Do scandals lead to high-level resignations, a change of government, parliamentary investigations? What is the final resolution of cases?

Legal accountability: To the extent that corruption-control laws exist, do they have enforcement provisions? If enforcement provisions exist, are they actually used, and against what type of corruption? How many cases have been investigated and what proportion end up in trials and sentences? Is there legal recourse for victims of corruption?

Administrative accountability: What is the effect of internal oversight and disciplinary procedures? Is whistleblower protection in place and working? What is the impact of external watchdog groups and citizen appeal rights?

Financial accountability: Is the use of public moneys transparent? How often are audits undertaken and what is their quality and result? What is the enforcement record in terms of fines and repayments of misused funds?

Public accountability: How effective is "the court of public opinion"? What is the effect of investigative reporting and commentary? Has monitoring by civic groups been successful and have individual protests been influential?

Professional accountability (by disciplinary and licensing boards, professional associations, and similar organizations): How could these mechanisms be improved?

International accountability: Has there been responsiveness to local associations of foreign businesspeople and to monitoring by international actors?

The analysis of these dimensions is mostly qualitative, with some quantitative indicators as summarized in Table 8.1. Country reports are the main sources, most importantly the monitoring reports sponsored by the European Union during the process of new member accession.[7] As the summary of these reports notes, however, "because the European Union itself lacks a clear anti-corruption framework," there has been a tendency to assess corruption only as defined by criminal law and with a bias of focusing on bribery alone. "This perspective misses some of the most important aspects of corruption-related problems in these States, ranging from societal tolerance of corruption to more-or-less deep-rooted traditions of allocating resources on the basis of patronage networks."[8] To this one can add that the reports say little about other aspects of corruption identified in Chapter 2, such as state or institutional capture and asset-stripping schemes. Yet these are the forms of corruption that most concern local populations and that most tarnish the reputation of governments and individual politicians.

Electoral Accountability

Since the collapse of communism, the states of the Baltic and East European region have held multiparty elections recognized as having been free and fair. Nevertheless, the competition for public office has been rendered unequal by the flow of large sums of money to some parties in return for the promise of political payback. In the case of Bulgaria, the 2002 EU monitoring report speaks of "extremely weak" regulation and supervision of party finances and suggests that this may be linked to high-level corruption. Romania is evaluated in a similar vein. Comments about Hungary and other countries emphasize the widespread covert and unchecked funding of political parties.[9]

Despite relatively advanced laws on party finance, in Lithuania the "supervision of party finances appears to be largely formal . . . and there is evidence of strong ties between parties and business groups."[10] Throughout the region, party and campaign finance reform have increasingly moved to the forefront of discussions about political accountability. One remedy is party funding from the state budget, which has made a difference in Poland and the Czech Republic. Poland reformed its law on party financing in 2001; political parties that fail to submit financial reports, or whose reports are rejected by the election commission, face significant sanctions. Individuals responsible for violations are subject to hefty fines and imprisonment of up to two years.[11]

Electoral accountability in the ten accession states has worked in the sense that, with the exception of Slovenia, where governments typically have been re-elected, these countries have experienced significant electoral upsets. Some of these have occurred explicitly under slogans of anti-corruption, but in other cases the theme has been implicit in popular disappointment that has led to an electoral see-saw effect whereby incumbents and the opposition take turns in winning elections. One scholar speaks of the East European states as "protest vote democracies."[12] Often new parties appear on the scene and gather significant support, but the voters tend to get disappointed again and search for another alternative in the next electoral round.

The EU monitoring report notes how politicians use promises of cleaner politics as a way to topple governments, "but post-election anti-corruption drives lack competence or real political will, or even worse are used mainly to attack or undermine political opponents."[13] This was most notable in Poland in 2001, where elections were fought mostly on the issue of corruption, but the resulting government made few changes. A similar pattern occurred in the Czech Republic, where the Social Democratic Party won the 1998 elections on a promise to implement a "Clean Hands" anti-corruption program, but then nothing was done. The poor performance of this program drew scathing reviews from opposition parties as well as the media, and it was declared a failure in 2000. Subsequently, however, no new anti-corruption policy emerged. To the contrary, an unspoken agreement seemed to be in effect between the leading political parties to maintain silence on suspected corruption in each other's ranks until the June 2002 elections.[14] These elections brought into office a more standard coalition government, one of whose main promises again was to fight corruption.[15]

In Bulgaria the containment of corruption has been major issue since 1997, when a new government came to power on a platform prioritizing it. Yet the subsequent national anti-corruption strategy remained focused on low-level malfeasance. Virtually no progress was made toward fighting corruption at the policy-making level.[16] Bulgaria's elections in June 2001 brought another major upset when a new party founded by Bulgaria's former king scored a huge victory, mostly due to promises of a politics of morality and corruption cleanups.[17]

Latvia too has followed the regional pattern of see-saw electoral upturns reflecting voter dissatisfaction. Most recently the parliamentary election in fall 2002 led to the formation of a coalition government whose core was constituted by two newly formed parties that made anti-corruption their main campaign issue. This government took some significant initiatives to contain corruption, but had made no major inroads when it fell apart fifteen months later in spring 2004.[18]

As the numbers in Table 8.1 illustrate, opposition forces promising to institute corruption-free governance have won electoral victories in most of the new EU member countries. Throughout the region, corruption increasingly became an issue in electoral battles.[19] Some changes typically are made after elections, yet by early 2004 no true breakthroughs were visible.

Governmental Accountability

Although they often allege malfeasance of others, politicians and public officials in the post-communist region have shown little concern for ethics in their own actions. Latvia is quite typical in that as of early 2003 there was no practice of officials voluntarily recusing themselves in cases of conflict of interest.[20] Moreover, legislatures have been notably slow in passing appropriate laws. When laws on conflict of interest and transparency in the financial affairs of high officials do exist, they are weak, lack provisions for sanctions in case of violation, and prove to be ineffective in practice.

Table 8.1

Numerical Indicators of Accountability

	Estonia	Latvia	Lithuania	Poland	Czech R.	Slovakia	Hungary	Romania	Bulgaria	Slovenia
1. TI-Corruption Score 2003	5.5	3.8	4.7	3.6	3.9	3.7	4.8	2.8	3.9	5.9
2. Election upset	?	2002	?	2001	1998	1998	2002?	2004	1997, 2001	?
3. Annual average of bribery convictions, 1997(98)–2001	35	18	48	325	117	28	279*	270	23	32
4. Bribery convictions per one million inhabitants	25	7.8	13.7	8.4	11.3	5.1	27.6	12	2.9	16
5. Special anti-corruption unit	no	yes	yes	no	no	no	no	no	no	no

Sources: Author's calculations and summary from Open Society Institute, *Monitoring the EU Accession Process: Corruption and Anti-corruption Policy* (Budapest, 2002), and Report on the Fight Against Corruption in Slovakia, October 2001, www.government.gov.sk., and Transparency International website www.transparency.org.

Notes: Row 1. Transparency International Corruption Perception Index: 10 = low, 0 = high corruption.
Row 2. Corruption is a leading issue in election, new government promises cleanup.
Row 5. Autonomous institution with investigatory authority, as of 2003.
*Includes trafficking in influence.

In Bulgaria, for example, many legislators have had external business interests. Conflict of interest regulation is minimal. Since 2000, senior officials have had to submit declarations of assets and income, "but supervision and enforcement is inadequate and there are no sanctions for violation."[21] In Estonia, the Parliamentary Special Committee on Anti-Corruption Activities is supposed to check declarations of economic interests of deputies and high government officials, yet this (in mid-2001) was seen by many as purely formal and in need of improvement. The situation is similar in Slovenia, where the Conflict of Interest Act passed in 1995 is largely ineffective and imposes no sanctions; attempts to amend the act have been rejected.[22]

Whenever corruption scandals involve high-level politicians, a core difficulty is to prove malfeasance. Parliamentary investigatory committees have rarely been established, and conclusive findings have been even rarer. In Hungary, the procedures of setting up inquiries are complicated and the practice has been politicized. Four investigatory committees suggested by the governing parties between 1998 and 2002 were established, but twenty-one others suggested by the opposition during the same period were not approved.[23] This deficient self-policing has left to the media and civic groups the task of demanding integrity and bringing issues to light. Media investigations of conflicts of interest of Lithuanian members of government forced the resignation of three senior politicians in 2002 and led to the creation of the Principles of Governmental Ethics and Code of Conduct for Governmental Offices. A former Estonian prime minister resigned after press revelations concerning misallocation of apartments while he was mayor of Tallinn. In Slovakia as well, several ministers who had disregarded conflicts of interest resigned under media pressure during 1998–2002. In contrast, the Hungarian government became increasingly unresponsive to external monitoring during the same period.[24]

In the Czech Republic several ministers have been the subject of corruption scandals. In early 2001 the minister of finance resigned, but other cases have petered out. Politicians and governments strongly resist the initiation of inquiries. At times they attack the accusers, as when the Czech government in 2001 and 2003 tried to sweep several serious cases under the carpet and tried to punish the journalists who uncovered them. One of the scandals involving the Ministry of Foreign Affairs led to a general secretary leaving office, only to be later arrested and charged with planning the murder of the journalist who had investigated the affair. The subsequent investigation indicated widespread corruption in the allocation of public contracts by the ministry.[25]

Resignations do not necessarily mean investigations, and investigations do not necessarily lead to a conclusive finding by law enforcement agencies.

The first criminal investigations of high-level corruption started only around 2001–2, at the end of the first decade of post-communist rule.

Legal Accountability

A study of the justice system in Latvia illustrates that during the first decade of post-communist rule corrupt persons could act with impunity. Even when the press raised serious allegations, procurators were strikingly hesitant to open investigations. In a notorious case where three million lats (about $5 million) disappeared in a transaction intended to salvage the funds of a bankrupt bank that was itself under criminal investigation, the procuracy started its work only after six weeks of public uproar and only after a formal complaint had been filed. Of those cases that are investigated, only a small fraction reach the courts, and of these only a fraction lead to convictions. The study reports that the number of people convicted for bribery and other crimes while in office decreased from 89 in 1997 to 33 in 2000. This is in contrast to the much higher incidence of bribery reported by respondents in various surveys.[26]

Several dimensions of legal accountability have to be in place for it to be effective: (a) laws must be passed and they must have enforcement provisions; (b) there must be a sustained effort to enforce the laws by investigating allegations and launching prosecutions where appropriate; (c) perpetrators must be convicted and sentenced by more than a slap on the wrist. Only if these criteria are met is the public likely to feel that justice is being done, and only then can one expect deterrence of corrupt acts to become effective.

(a) By early 2004 most of the countries examined here had made progress in passing laws, but the legal and institutional provisions for enforcement were surprisingly poor. Lithuania was the first country to break this mold by creating a specialized anti-corruption agency in 1997. The Special Investigation Service has helped to fine-tune the legal framework, has launched numerous investigations, and has detained a relatively high number of public officials.[27]

Most other states in the region lack independent anti-corruption units, with Latvia being the other exception (see Table 8.1). The complications Latvia experienced in establishing its Corruption-Prevention Office, however, in themselves illustrate the many obstacles in the path to the effective implementation of anti-corruption programs. The law establishing the office was passed in early 2002, but there were numerous delays in authorizing funds and starting to set up the institutional structure. From the start, intense political and legislative battles were fought over who the director should be and how he—or she—should be selected. By May 2004 the search for a director had been launched on four occasions, triggering new controversies each time. This troubled history has limited the productivity of the office. It has had some successes, however, in tightening adherence to campaign finance laws, initiating several corruption investigations, and initiating its own undercover work.[28]

(b) For legal accountability to work, formal inquiries first have to be launched. As noted by Susan Rose-Ackerman, "the effectiveness of the judiciary will be low if no one brings cases."[29] Police and other law enforcement agencies need to be active, yet throughout the region investigators have been slow in opening investigations and ineffective in conducting them. A September 2001 report on Latvia by international experts noted that "to date there appears to be no evidence of any successful investigations originating from police intelligence. The notable cases all seem to stem from disenchanted third party involvement in the incident. This suggests insufficient intelligence gathering activity in the area of corruption, plus a lack of proactive investigative techniques."[30] Latvia's creation of the specialized Corruption-Prevention Office and its intensification of investigatory efforts since late 2002 in large part came in response to such criticism.

In Latvia and elsewhere the procuracy holds the strategic position in the battle against corruption and it is there that judicial reforms need to be focused. Procurators decide whether or not to open investigations, how to formulate cases, how to present them to a court, and whether to appeal to higher courts if an outcome appears unsatisfactory.[31] If the regular procuracy is passive, it helps to form special subunits. The Czech attorney general in 2000 established special teams of prosecutors and a separate department to supervise investigations of serious financial crimes. As a result, fifteen investigations were completed by mid-May 2001 in which 410 million euros in damages were identified. Similarly, sting operations had proven themselves on three occasions in Slovenia by early 2002.[32]

(c) The effectiveness of legal accountability can be measured by how many cases are brought before the courts, and how they are handled. Getting good data on investigations and conviction is very difficult throughout the region, and this in itself is an indicator of poor performance. When statistics are available, their meaning is often unclear. This is true even for Estonia, which tends to have the best records, yet even those records speak only vaguely about crimes involving the "misuse of official position" and the "abuse of authority." The most precise data exist on bribery: in Estonia during 1999 twelve people were convicted for accepting a bribe, six for giving a bribe, and one for arranging a bribe. In most cases the sentences were conditional or consisted of fines.[33]

Data on sentences again are difficult to obtain. Sentences have mostly been light, but this began to change around 2003 when Poland, for example, increased penalties for corruption from three to eight and from five to twelve years of imprisonment.[34] In May 2004 a Latvian court passed its most severe corruption penalty ever when it sentenced a procurator to ten years in jail. The most serious charge against him was the extortion of a $40,000 bribe for closing a case against a corrupt policeman.[35] In a similar case half a year earlier, a tax inspector was given a three-year suspended sentence for extorting a $80,000 bribe from a firm.[36]

Since anti-corruption laws of most post-communist countries have focused on active and passive bribery, and some data exist on convictions in these cases, bribery statistics help to get a quantitative assessment of the scale of legal consequences for corrupt acts. Summary data for bribery convictions in Estonia and other states for the years 1998–2001 are given in Table 8.1. Since the populations of the countries differ, the table also includes conviction rates per one million inhabitants per year. As the numbers illustrate, very few people have been convicted. Bulgaria has the lowest number, with only 2.9 convictions per one million inhabitants, whereas in Estonia the rate is nearly ten times as high.

Data like these lend support to the argument that there is an inverse correlation between the level of corruption and the number of reports to the police.[37] Similarly, a higher level of convictions per capita often is less an indicator of high corruption than of a more determined fight against it. Lithuania's relatively high conviction rate suggests that its special investigatory unit has been successful. Many of those brought to justice have been police officers, and a judge was convicted in 2000 after having been caught through a sting operation.[38]

The EU monitoring report comments on low conviction rates by saying that "these figures provide very little information about the real extent of corruption, but rather indicate the lack of enforcement of the existing provisions."[39] As implied, the quality of legal accountability is best measured by relating the number of prosecutions to the number of crimes committed. Unfortunately, this ratio is very difficult to ascertain, but future innovative research strategies may provide insights. One approach would be to count the number of corrupt acts as alleged in the press and compare that to the numbers of cases investigated, those actually prosecuted, and convictions reached. The size of the gap between each pair of numbers provides a rough measure of legal accountability. One could also calculate probabilities of investigations or criminal cases being launched as well as probabilities of convictions. An attempt to do this was made for Russia in 1995, with the conclusion being that "the probability that a defendant will end up behind bars after a case is begun by the prosecutor's office does not exceed 0.08."[40]

Corruption investigations against higher-level officials and politicians have been rare, but their number has been on the rise in recent years. Estonia has led the way. In 2001 the former chairman of the board of a major bank was convicted for misuse of funds from the American Foreign Aid Foundation. He was sentenced to eighteen months in prison for transferring 1.9 million euros to his own bank. Another major case involved the director of the Estonian Traffic Insurance Foundation, who was convicted of corruption and misuse of official position and had to return more than 1.2 million euros to the state.[41] Intriguingly, such convictions correlate with Estonia's low score on various corruption perception indexes, whereas in Romania "strong perceptions of high-level corruption are in stark contrast to the complete absence of convictions at that level."[42]

In Slovakia, Hungary, and Bulgaria several high-level corruption investigations, mostly related to privatization, were initiated in 2002. In Bulgaria thirty-four senior public officials were charged, including nine former ministers.[43] As noted in Chapter 3, the Lew Rywin scandal in Poland between 2002 and 2004 implicated many leading politicians, but only Rywin was convicted. The year 2004 also brought the impeachment of Lithuania's president, resulting in his removal from office. Two of three charges were for corrupt acts: influencing the outcome of privatization and making a political decision in exchange for campaign funds.[44]

On balance, legal accountability has been weak throughout the region, mostly because enforcement of relatively comprehensive anti-corruption laws has been anemic.[45] One reason is poor funding of the judiciary. In Bulgaria, the funding allocated to the judiciary amounts to less than 1 percent of GDP, compared to a European norm of 3 to 4 percent.[46] Some observers believe that such underfunding is deliberate. At a conference on the judicial system in Latvia in May 2002 there was broad consensus that the judicial system has not been a priority for political leaders. Several former justice ministers complained that finance and prime ministers usually allocate little more than half the amount the Justice Ministry requests.[47] Throughout the region one notes neglect of the needs of the judicial branch. This can hardly be justified in economic or budgetary terms, since in addition to its political costs, corruption carries a high financial price. As noted in Chapter 1, a rough calculation suggests that between 1 and 2 percent of GDP is lost to corruption in procurement alone. These losses are up to twice as large as the amount Bulgaria now spends on its judicial system.

Administrative Accountability

Systems of public administration need to be based on professionalism, and officials must be accountable to oversight bodies. In Slovenia internal administrative controls are rarely put to work. Romania is characterized by broad executive discretion "stemming from the widespread use of ordinances, excessive immunity provisions for both current and former members of the Government, poorly defined civil servant responsibilities, patronage at all levels and the ineffectiveness of procedures for redress against administrative decisions."[48]

Lithuania has done better. It has undertaken a fundamental civil service reform, passed a code of ethics for civil servants, and established a merit system of hiring that is working relatively well. Citizens can appeal to administrative courts against both the legality and substance of official actions. As of mid-2002, however, the public was insufficiently aware of these rights. An ombuds office staffed by five people who review grievances was not working as well as it might. Its main contribution was its deterrent effect, but because its recommendations were not always being enforced, even this was diminished. Lithuania also offered only limited protection to whistleblowers.[49]

In comparison, Bulgaria was doing significantly worse on all measures of administrative accountability. As of July 2002 a law providing for an ombudsperson was only being drafted. Civil-service reforms were said to be "largely cosmetic" and "mechanisms for redress against administrative actions are burdensome and ineffective."[50] The Code of Conduct for Civil Servants was vague and did not provide clear rules on conflicts of interest. By imposing a duty of loyalty to the employing institution, the code may encourage the withholding of public information. This also discourages whistleblowing, a situation exacerbated by the absence of mechanisms or legal provisions protecting whistleblowers.[51] Latvia has signed the EU Criminal Law Convention, which includes provisions for whistleblower protection, but in fact very little is in place and people reporting on malfeasance often end up losing their jobs.[52]

Administrative accountability also involves effective disciplinary proceedings for civil servants. Data on this are scarce, probably because little is done in this area. In Latvia only eight civil servants were disciplined between January 2001 and October 2003.[53]

Financial Accountability

Corrupt impulses can be triggered by a thirst for power, prestige, and influence, but money is often at the core. Fortunately, many instruments are available to ensure financial accountability. A basic one is the legislature's control of the state budget. Unfortunately, the communist-era tradition that the bureaucracy decides on much of its budget persists, and this creates a nontransparent maze of sub-accounts. In 2001, twenty-one extra-budgetary accounts were under the sole purview of the Bulgarian government. Although it had expended many resources on internal audits, external financial controls remained weak and the impact of the National Audit Office's findings was said to be almost zero.[54] The situation is similarly ambiguous in Hungary, where the State Audit Office has wide-ranging powers to investigate, but no power to impose corrective measures.[55]

In contrast, Lithuania responded to EU requirements by introducing a three-tier system of financial control: state control, municipal control, and internal audits. In 2000, audits performed by the state control office led to thirty cases being turned over to the prosecutor's office with twelve more being submitted in the first nine months of 2001. Poland's Supreme Audit Chamber also is highly effective, but as of mid-2002 the same could not be said for follow-up by the procuracy. On the other hand, parliamentary committees often use the audit reports to pass motions demanding that specific ministers undertake corrective measures.[56] In sum, the new member states of the EU have made progress in putting the mechanisms of routine audits in place, but the implementation of corrective measures and sanctions for malfeasance tends to be lacking.

Little attention has been paid to monitoring less routine financial affairs that invite corruption. Most states in the region have problematic and contradictory regulations about state subsidies and guarantees for big business as well as for erasing tax debts. As the local branch of Transparency International has noted in the case of Latvia, this is an area where "political corruption and lobbying have every opportunity to flourish."[57] Future research would do well to examine the circumstances under which specific enterprises have received financial advantages from the state.

Public procurement too illustrates the blatant as well as subtle ways in which financial accountability is undermined. State procurement everywhere involves huge amounts of public money, and malfeasance is difficult to prevent. A finding about Estonia characterizes the entire region, in that "local observers believe tender fixing is common, and corruption in procurement at [the] local government level is believed to be more-or-less widespread." This is due less to weaknesses of the law than to the strength of personal networks and the fact that "everybody knows everybody," resulting in "widespread collusion."[58] Similar reports have been made about other countries. There is agreement that despite legislative progress the regulation of public procurement remains ineffective, in particular with regard to supervision and redress. The EU monitoring report speaks of a system of contract allocation that has allowed widespread collusion and probably major high-level corruption.[59]

Nevertheless, some differences can be observed in the effectiveness of redress and sanctions for violations of procurement regulations. Although

Bulgaria's Public Procurement Act, as of mid-2002, did not provide for the annulment of contracts awarded in cases where its provisions were violated, Slovakia in 2000 had already created an office of public procurement that reviews appeals. Irregular agreements are legally null and void; appeals have become more frequent, and hundreds of contracts have been partially or entirely annulled. In one instance the office canceled two tenders where the technical requirements for the purchase of small buses clearly were rigged in favor of one specific company.[60]

Lithuania does allow for grievances and lawsuits, but they are cumbersome and little is known about the results. Auditors have suggested that the procurement office assess the terms of important procurements in advance rather than reviewing them after the fact. They also recommended that the names of officials who approve the conditions for tenders be published.[61] An international assessment of the situation in Latvia in 2001 noted that "although officials involved in public procurement are viewed as a high-risk group," very few cases were brought before the courts.[62] Another study, in 2002, reported that higher bids often won tenders and that violations of regulations were common. When the State Comptroller's Office in 2000 examined forty-five procurement cases, it found that in most cases legal requirements had been disregarded. Some violators were fined, but usually consequences were negligible even when cases were brought to court. Valts Kalniņš cites a firm going to court and being declared the legitimate winner of a tender, yet still being denied the contract in question.[63] Again, enforcement of the law clearly is the core issue.

Experts from the World Bank have made recommendations for improving the system. The law that is in force since January 2002 has adopted them in part, but research by Transparency International–Latvia suggests that accountability has hardly improved. Cooperation between the audit office and procuracy is poor, and audits rarely lead to revision of contracts. The procurement oversight office has little power and "until now no dubious case has been taken to trial and nobody has received any real punishment. The procuracy does not understand the importance of investigating these cases and is inactive."[64] Reports on Hungary note a tendency to violate the spirit if not the letter of public procurement regulations.[65] In sum, financial accountability in public procurement is feebly enforced throughout the region.

Public Accountability

In a democracy, public officials are accountable to the citizenry, which in turn has a duty to be informed and to participate in activities that help form a better polity. Public accountability depends on the work of responsible media and the involvement of civil society in monitoring public affairs. What is the overall balance on this score?

As noted in Chapter 7, citizens can hold their elected leaders to account only if they are informed about their activities. Legislation providing access to public information has been passed in most of the ten countries under review, and has made a difference to both journalists and the public. In Slovakia the passing of a Freedom of Information Act in 2001 was effective in that the state audit office started to publish its reports. The media have also used the act to monitor state institutions more closely, for example by reporting on the allocation of subsidies by the Ministries of Economy and Agriculture.[66] Nevertheless, an analysis of governmental transparency in 2002 found that legal provisions have been incomplete and have led to few actual changes in public access to information.[67]

Throughout the region, the media, and the press in particular, have been leaders in putting corruption issues on the public agenda and calling for accountability. Yet the media at times are pressured to promote particular political or business interests. An additional concern is corruption in the media itself, specifically hidden advertising and politically motivated campaigns such as one against a project to reform customs offices in Bulgaria.[68] Good, in-depth investigative reports are scarce, in part because several countries retain comparatively strict libel laws that protect public officials more than private citizens. Bulgarian as well as Latvian journalists have faced high fines for "publicly insulting a public official." Recently there has been some change in Latvia, where the leading newspaper, *Diena*, appealed a libel conviction and in late 2003 won on appeal.[69]

Despite limitations and pressures, the media have been active in uncovering corruption. Their reports and questions have triggered many investigations, caused the dismissals or resignation of officials and politicians, and contributed to the downfall of governments.[70] The media often take the role of de facto enforcer of the many laws and regulations that have no other enforcement mechanism. The media allow the "court of public opinion" to penalize improprieties and limit the misuse of office.

Nongovernmental associations are the other pillar of public accountability, and they have played a key role in the development of anti-corruption policy. Local branches of Transparency International and similar associations have engaged in a variety of initiatives to promote accountability. There are many examples of this. In Poland several civic organizations joined together in fall 2002 to monitor the follow-up to election promises about fighting corruption.[71] Bulgaria's "Coalition 2000" is an umbrella organization of civic groups that since 1997 has engaged in a variety of anti-corruption initiatives: it has been a forum for public awareness raising and program development; and it has cooperated closely with reformers in the government, but has also monitored governmental performance on all levels. Partners of the coalition set up "public-private councils" to facilitate citizens' appeals against arbitrary treatment; others initiated civic observers and public mediators in several municipalities. Its comprehensive approach to corruption extends to the launching of research to allow more informed policy making.[72]

The public's right to governmental accountability means more than a review of official acts: it includes its participation in the making of policy. This can mean discussions at open meetings and hearings whenever a major project is launched. Such consultations in fact are increasingly required by law. Yet here again, stipulations written into law do not automatically translate into practice. A study of the restructuring of the regional passenger transport system in Latvia found that even though the law provides for public hearings, this did little to influence outcomes. People who were affected by changes in railway routes were halfhearted in their attempts to influence decisions, and officials in charge were unresponsive to the suggestions that were made. It was proven that the Latvian Railway, in spite of being a state-owned joint stock company, sees itself "solely as a business entity rather than a socially responsible institution, which works for the public good."[73]

Although some experiences dishearten further civic activism, successes lend it renewed vigor. In Latvia both the local branch of Transparency International and the Council of Foreign Investors have succeeded in causing corruption prevention to be taken seriously. The council has argued forcefully that investment requires a lawful business environment. Since the late 1990s it has repeatedly met with the prime minister and other officials and put forth specific demands for reforms, some of which have been implemented. Transparency International–Latvia, like Coalition 2000 in Bulgaria, has engaged in more comprehensive programs, among them campaigns to stop illicit deals before they are completed and it is more difficult to reverse them. An example is a campaign to save a youth recreation park from privatization, which will be discussed in Chapter 9.[74]

Recently party and campaign finance reform has become a new focus for civic activism. Existing systems give unfair advantages to parties with hidden financial resources. Furthermore, nontransparent party financing is linked to state capture in that political parties and individual politicians become subservient to the economic forces that finance them.

Transparency International–Latvia has spearheaded several successful actions for election campaign finance reform. TI–Latvia first succeeded in getting new laws passed, including a law that as of August 15, 2002, all campaign donations have to be registered on the Internet within ten days, and parties must file reports about the moneys spent for advertising both before and after an election.[75] The director of TI–Latvia believes that this success was related to the political parties' being sensitive to publicity and wanting to show themselves in a positive light, even more so as during election time they tend to be especially aware of the very low trust the public places in them. In Latvia, as elsewhere in the post-communist region, political parties rank at the bottom of the institutional trust scales.[76]

But TI–Latvia and its allies encountered more resistance when they moved to their next target, the use of hidden media advertisements in elections. Copying the tactic of the Argentine group "The Power of Citizens," the activists calculated the cost of advertisements in the media and compared them with the officially declared expenses of the political parties, revealing discrepancies of about 60 percent. Publicity about this finding too was a step toward reform.[77]

The project started several months before Latvia's parliamentary elections in October 2002. Besides trying to limit the influence of hidden campaign finance, organizers aimed to mobilize the public against the widespread journalistic practice of publishing glowing material about political parties and their leaders without clarifying that the material had been bought. From the start, this initiative encountered tremendous opposition, especially from the media. Informally, journalists and newspaper owners often granted the existence of hidden ads, but they were outraged about the threat to their income and reputation.

The campaign revealed that many newspapers, especially the smaller regional ones, financially depend on these hidden ads. As the hidden payments were revealed, the affected media reacted angrily and self-righteously with statements such as "we need that to survive." Instead of feelings of guilt, there were aggressive countermoves,[78] both by threats of lawsuits and an intense media campaign against the sponsors of the project, the Soros Foundation–Latvia, which was accused of itself being corrupt.[79] Counterattacks also argued that "everyone uses hidden moneys," and it thus is illegitimate to focus on media and political parties.[80]

Despite such confrontations, the project documented a dramatic increase in campaign outlays that were underreported by political parties. This forced the Anti-Corruption Bureau to investigate party declarations, which revealed illegal donations, falsified signatures, and other transgressions. Some cases were turned over to law enforcement agencies and twenty-five parties were required to cede illegal donations to the state. These events were widely reported in the media.[81] The increased political sensitivity of the issue encouraged civic groups to initiate a more radical campaign finance law, which was unexpectedly passed by the legislature in February 2004. This law strictly limits campaign expenses and arguably is the most progressive in the entire region. Although a great success, more skeptical analysts point to loopholes in the law and the likelihood that it will be changed as important elections approach.[82]

Civic monitoring can be a powerful tool, especially if nongovernmental organizations focus on one or several particular issues on a long-term basis. In Slovakia too the local branch of Transparency International and the Fair Play Alliance since 2002 have sought to serve as permanent civic watchdogs over the performance and finance of political parties. Since Slovakia has a ban on political advertising on the radio and television as well as strict limitations on print media and outdoor advertising, a quantitative approach to measuring advertising expenses was inappropriate. Instead the Fair Play Alliance focused on a qualitative analysis of pre-election campaigns: it laid out the weaknesses of existing laws and state control mechanisms, shed light on hidden donations and conflicts of interest, collected proof about the lack of disclosure and two dozen companies that did not fulfill their legal duties and were not penalized. It also analyzed the financial situation of political parties and suggested necessary changes. All this was done in the expectation of long-term rather than short-terms results.[83]

Professional Accountability

At its core, civil society and democratic accountability rely on individuals and groups voluntarily to comply with laws and monitor themselves. Self-monitoring is especially important in the case of associations representing professionals with a public mandate, such as lawyers, notaries, and doctors. A democratic citizenry wants to minimize state regulation and supervision of its affairs, but this means that it has to engage in credible self-monitoring. Professional associations need to establish performance standards and codes of behavior, even more so if they have been ceded certain rights by the state, for example the issuing of licenses. They must establish oversight and disciplinary boards to review the activities of their members. It is also incumbent on them to participate in policy making to assure that the sphere they work in is as corruption-free as possible. Anti-corruption activists in the post-communist region have paid insufficient attention to this dimension of their work. Professional review bodies often do not exist, and existing ones rarely challenge illicit practices of colleagues. There are some exceptions: in 2002 Poland reformed the functioning of its disciplinary courts for judges by creating several levels of hearings and making them public.[84]

Ideally, changes within professional associations come from the inside, for example from the activities of internal reform caucuses. People working within established professions know best where cleanups are needed, and are best able to mobilize their peers to carry them out. If they do not perform this function, they invite public scrutiny and demands for external monitors. When this has happened, for example in regard to doctors working in the public health-care system, the doctors argued that they are not public officials as defined by law and therefore the restrictions on public officials do not apply to them. Poland has solved this difficulty by defining as a public official "any person who performs a function within the public sector and administers, disposes of or participates in decision-making concerning public assets."[85]

International Accountability

Corruption in the post-communist region has been addressed by several international actors. Some individual governments have raised the issue in bilateral talks and have spoken out publicly. For example, on April 15, 2003, U.S. ambassador Michael Guest urged the Romanian government to take direct action against corruption. In a strongly worded speech, Guest called corruption "a shame" for Romania and said that the situation was grave. His remarks were echoed by the head of the American Chamber of Commerce in Bucharest, who said that corruption could hamper Romania's efforts to join the EU in 2007. The European Commission's representative also said he agreed with the Guest's remarks.[86]

Besides individual admonitions to institute a cleaner government, major initiatives have been undertaken by the World Bank, OECD, and various European institutions.[87] The Council of Europe, which has close ties to the EU, has developed several anti-corruption conventions, a set of "Guiding Principles," and a framework to monitor adherence to these principles—the Group of States Against Corruption (GRECO). The EU has urged candidate states to ratify the conventions and has made corruption clean-up efforts a key issue for accession. Assessments of progress in containing corruption have been part of the annual country reports on accession. In its November 2001 summary of individual country assessments, the EU Commission concluded that corruption was a "serious" problem or "source of concern" in five of ten accession states (Bulgaria, Czech Republic, Poland, Romania, and Slovakia) and a continuing problem in three countries (Hungary, Latvia, and Lithuania); it refrained from criticizing only two countries (Estonia and Slovenia). The implication was that progress in containing corruption was a requirement for accession, and some progress was indeed made, in particular in the passing of laws and the creation of more anti-corruption mechanisms. More comprehensive assessments of progress were hampered by the EU's lack of clear benchmarks for assessing corruption in member states, including older members.[88]

Accession negotiations involved the harmonization of laws in a number of areas that are crucial to a sound anti-corruption policy. This has included civil service reform, judicial reforms, and state financial control and audit. The last focuses on adopting international audit standards and establishing independent and effective internal control systems for government branches. The EU has also urged reforms in public procurement, specifically compliance with EU Commission directives on procurement. As a result of all this pressure by the EU, the new member states have passed important laws in all these areas and partly upgraded their enforcement. The progress achieved in the Czech Republic in increasing the effectiveness of enforcement bodies and the courts in tackling corruption was to a large extent made possible by EU assistance. The Bulgarian government too has explicitly cited EU accession as a major motive for the adoption of its national anti-corruption policy. Others have made similar statements. Czech Ministry of Justice officials said that the justice reform program of 2002 would never have been conceived or funded without pressure from Brussels. In the case of the Polish police, the EU has had a threefold impact: it has provided financial and training assistance, it has worked with Polish teams to include them in EUROPOL, and it has helped harmonize police standards and legislation with EU requirements.[89]

International accountability has fostered judicial and police cooperation within the EU, including cross-border cooperation in prosecuting high-level corruption. In 2001–2 the EU set up a judicial cooperation network that among other things targets transborder cases of fraud and corruption. It has also extended the mandate of the European police network EUROPOL, and is working on new legislation to strengthen law enforcement.[90] This is likely to develop further once the Western and Eastern parts of Europe become more integrated. The EU's anti-corruption agency, OLAF, which has a mandate to get involved in cases where the financial interests of the EU as an organization are at stake, is also likely to expand. An important precedent was set in April 2004 when OLAF asked Estonia to investigate a suspicious procurement deal involving moneys spent on a PHARE project. An Estonian court found one of the members of the procurement commission guilty of misconduct, and it appeared that the EU would demand repayment of the misappropriated funds.[91] Another important precedent was set in June 2004 when an American court found former Ukrainian prime minister Pavlo Lazarenko guilty of money laundering, wire fraud, and extortion.[92] Legal accountability is beginning to be internationalized.

Besides promoting corruption containment directly, international institutions have complemented the work of national institutions, especially as sponsors of high-quality research and in outlining agendas for policy initiatives. International concern has also served as a powerful argument in internal political debates, permitting proponents of more decisive cleanup efforts to point to these prestigious sources of information and pressure. Such arguments often have been successful.[93]

Increasingly, embattled journalists and the relatively small groups of transparency activists forming civil society networks against political corruption have received support from transnational civil society. Groups such as the "International Consortium of Investigative Journalists," and the global office of Transparency International can provide concrete support as well as international visibility.[94] This is an anti-corruption tool that could make even more of a difference in the future.

Conclusion

This chapter has examined the effectiveness of various instruments for curtailing corruption in the transition countries, with a focus on how well accountability has been ensured. Many laws and mechanisms have been put in place, but the big challenge is to make institutional accountability measures work. This means that the capacity of relevant state and civil society actors needs to be built up and the focus of reducing corruption must be on implementation.[95]

When international donors and experts urge the new democracies to put in place a host of anti-corruption institutions and laws, they do so with the implicit assumption that the existence of institutions in itself guarantees their functioning. This cannot be taken for granted. One needs to see how these instruments actually work in specific political, regional, and national contexts. Similar institutions can function quite differently in different contexts. Comparative political analysis needs to integrate theories and findings drawn from worldwide experience with those grounded in regional contexts. One has to look closely at how the generic ways of containing corruption work within the post-communist states. Or, as is the practice of the national integrity surveys devised by Transparency International, one needs to differentiate between measures that are in place de jure and de facto.[96]

The balance sheet of accountability for the ten new members of the EU reveals that the media and public pressure have proven to be most effective in fostering reforms. Administrative monitoring, law enforcement, and the judicial system have been much less effective in bringing corruption under control.

9

The Role of the Right
Anti-Corruption Strategy

> The greatest enemy of corruption is the people. This is why
> almost every new government—elected or not—justifies itself
> by promising to combat the corruption of the previous regime.
> Even though individual citizens participate in corruption, the
> people as a whole despise it and understand the warping of
> incentives that it entails.
>
> *Robert Klitgaard, "Strategies for Reform"* [1]

As it has increasingly become recognized that corruption in the post-communist region causes governance failures and popular distrust of the state, national as well as international policy makers have searched for remedies. Since the late 1990s, many anti-corruption strategies and programs have been written and new laws and structures created, but with limited success. There continues to be strong popular and scholarly skepticism about the efficacy of institutional reforms, and population surveys continue to show broad distrust of public institutions, including corruption prevention councils.[2] Clearly, institutions set in place to fight corruption are not enough in and of themselves; the people working in them need to do their job, but for that they must be motivated. This chapter analyzes what motivates people to oppose corruption along with their reasons for participating in corruption, either passively or actively. Only if one understands the incentives for being a part of corruption or for fighting it, can one arrive at promising strategies to bring about change.

While the two preceding chapters have outlined institutional means and incentives for containing corruption, the focus of this chapter is on corrupt behaviors and what affects them. Political corruption is a deliberate act, the "misuse of public power for private gain." The corrupt act takes many forms, but as a purposive action, it involves decision making and assessments of costs and benefits. Therefore, to prevent corruption, one needs to influence the calculus of what can be gained. If corruption involves "low risk, high profit," it needs to be changed to a situation where people see it as carrying "high risk, low profit."[3] As noted in the preceding chapters, the reality of risk can be increased by various institutional means, especially regular as well as random reviews of the decisions public officials make in regard to public goods. In addition to real risk, it is important to ensure that people perceive corruption as risky. The perception of risk is crucial for deterrence to work; raising this credibility is a core goal of corruption prevention.

Understanding and Targeting the Structure of Motivation

The strategic goal of any anti-corruption effort is to change the behavior of people who misuse public power for private gain. In addition to reshaping incentives by institutional change, strategies must focus on changing the perceptions and expectations of the people involved. As a first step one needs to analyze who the actors are and what their incentive structure is. This chapter presents an analytical schema showing that in every corrupt act there are three basic actors: the person initiating the corrupt act, a second person who participates actively or passively, and the "third actor." The third actor is an individual or a larger group of people who pay the costs of corruption, although they may not always be aware of it. For any anti-corruption strategy to work, it must consider all three actors, understand the logic of their motivation, and change it in a way that prevents future corrupt acts. Effective corruption control needs to address how the actors involved calculate their risks and benefits, and this chapter examines this calculus in both theoretical and practical terms.

In analyzing the structure of motivation, it again helps to apply neo-institutional thinking that goes beyond focusing on formal political rules and structures and also examines "the logic of strategic situations."[4] Basic notions of rational choice institutionalism help to outline the calculus of people as they decide whether to engage in corruption or participate in its control. Neo-institutionalists emphasize that the choices of actors are constrained not only by institutional structures, but also by how other people act. Rules of the game are both formal and informal, and include assessments of the balance of power among political actors. This approach clarifies how choices are structured when people decide how to behave.

People calculate their preferred ways of acting both by thinking about personal preferences and by trying to estimate how other actors are likely to behave. There is an interactive dynamic in that decisions revolve around both how a specific individual acts and how other people act. This chapter presents this interaction in several ways. It lays out a schematic table listing all possible variants of how the three actors can be related to each other and then analyzes what changes anti-corruption policies should focus on.

As emphasized throughout this study, corruption is a deliberate action in the public realm, the misuse of power for private gain. As an action that takes place in the public sphere, it affects other people in that sphere, and these other people—or actors—have choices in how they respond. The main choice is whether they will work toward the prevention of corruption—trying to make sure that public power is used for the public good, as intended in democracy—or whether they will allow corruption to occur and even participate in it. Action is dynamic, and each act by one person or group of persons influences future decisions of other individuals or groups.[5] Here one can differentiate between the logic of decision making at the individual level and at the institutional level.

Individual-Level Calculus

Corruption scholars Susan Rose-Ackerman and Robert Klitgaard have used a principal-agent-client model to analyze the incentive structure for potentially corrupt acts. In his use of the model, Klitgaard establishes the principal as the head of a government agency distributing public goods such as pensions. The principal needs to employ agents to work with the clients who are supposed to benefit. Yet an agent also has personal interests and is able to sacrifice the interests of the principal. All of the actors weigh how to act based on a cost-benefit analysis, which includes calculations of economic payoffs as well as moral rewards, career prospects, and the probability of punishment.[6]

Since anti-corruption strategists want to influence what decisions are made, this model is very useful. It identifies the actors in a potentially corrupt context as well as their expected payoffs for different choices. Each participant—the person initiating a corrupt act, the person deciding whether to take part, and the third actor, deciding whether to try to prevent it—calculates the costs and benefits of specific behavior. This approach stipulates that corruption involves three actors, each of whom can be an individual or a group of people. The corrupt act itself involves a minimum of two actors: a person who initiates it, and a second person who decides whether to take part. For the purposes of the analysis here, the initiator is called the corrupter and the second person the corruptee. The involvement of the corruptee is crucial in order to qualify an act as corruption rather than some other crime. If an official embezzles funds, it is simply embezzlement; it becomes corruption if the same agent misuses his power to involve another person, for example a cashier. This second actor becomes corrupt the moment that actor decides for his or her "personal gain" by taking a share of the embezzled funds or ignoring the duty to intervene. Avoiding intervention is tempting if it involves complex procedures of reporting and investigation, possible retribution by the embezzler, or other costs, as is often the case in post-communist countries. The second actor participating in the "misuse of public power" experiences a twofold pressure: in addition to the temptation to take money, there is the difficult decision of how to react to the corrupter, who in this example is a colleague or supervisor and as such is embedded in the same institutional context. Thus, the corrupter is misusing public power in a dual sense, both by engaging in a criminal act and by putting undue pressure on a subordinate or colleague. Recognizing that second actors often are coerced into taking part in a corrupt act suggests that anti-corruption strategists should provide the means of resistance. Strong whistleblower protection and civil service review boards are two instruments that can help.

Besides focusing on the corruptee as someone who is pulled into a corrupt act by a corrupter, anti-corruption tactics need to address the third actor, who represents an immediate victim or the general public that a public institution is supposed to serve. The third actor—or principal—can be an individual citizen in need of a service, a societal group, or a supervisor. In contrast to Klitgaard's model, which identifies the principal as the head of a public agency, this study defines the principal on a more fundamental level as the sovereign in a political system whose rights are infringed upon by corruption. In a democracy, the citizenry forms the source of legitimate public power; "the people" is the sovereign who mandates policy and entrusts its representatives to act on its behalf to secure a common good such as public health. If its representatives abuse this trust, it is up to the citizens to make clear that democratic governance is a public good that cannot be privatized. Thus the actions of an organized citizenry are essential to effective corruption control; it is they who have to enforce accountability through elections, the law, and a variety of civic actions as outlined in Chapter 8.

The third actor is the key to effective corruption control. This is obvious if that actor is identified as a supervisor or auditor, but the stake of other people becomes clearer as one considers the mandate of public institutions to serve common goods such as health. The corruption of public power carries costs, and specifying them is one way to motivate third actors to get involved. Since corruption is hidden, however, the victims are often unaware of it, or they underestimate its costs, especially in the short term. Anti-corruption messages, therefore, need to outline concrete short-term costs, such as a patient waiting for an operation being pushed aside if a bribe allows someone to jump the queue, as well as long-term costs, such as the rise of a lawless society. Policies need to try to change established patterns of thinking. One such pattern revolves around the notion of "good" corruption that is func-

Table 9.1

Corruption Winners and Losers

	Corrupter (A)	Corruptee (B)	Third Actor (C)
1.	win	win	win
2.	win	win	lose
3.	win	lose	win
4.	win	lose	lose
5.	lose	win	win (anti-corruption goal)
6.	lose	lose	win (anti-corruption goal)
7.	lose	win	lose
8.	lose	lose	lose

A and B can be either a citizen or an official
C can be another citizen, competitor, supervisor, or the public at large

Examples:
1. Cut red tape
2. A bribes B to jump queue
3. A and C conduct sting operation against B
4. A extorts bribe from B by over-regulation
5. A tries to extort B, B refuses and reports to C, who penalizes A
6. A and B collude in procurement fraud, C penalizes A and B
7. A tries to extort B, who refuses and blackmails A
8. A bribes B to ignore sanitation law, epidemic results

tional in the sense of overcoming the oppressive red tape for which the communist regimes were notorious.[7] Another widely held view, based on experiences during the communist era and confirmed during the last decade, is that established elites are able to act with impunity no matter what. In addition, there is little recognition that in a democracy police and other public institutions can in fact serve the public good and that the citizenry has a stake in them not being undermined by corruption.[8]

Each corrupt interaction results in winning and losing sides, and there are many scenarios where the citizenry, defined here as the third actor, loses out. This is illustrated by the analytical schema in Table 9.1, which shows the winners and losers of corruption in all configurations. Theoretically, there are eight possible scenarios. Considering each scenario, with an illustrative case, helps us understand the interactive patterns of corrupt acts, an understanding that is crucial for designing a good anti-corruption strategy.

The first scenario listed shows all three actors to be winners and exemplifies functional corruption, for example when a bribe cuts through red tape. Yet why is there red tape to begin with? This scenario has long-term negative effects in that it fosters the belief that the state and its rules are a hindrance rather than a means to promote public interests. If this is true, then the rules need to be changed, but if the rules have a legitimate purpose, then undermining them results in scenario number eight, where all three actors lose. An example is the corrupt bending of sanitation rules, which can result in a health epidemic that affects everyone in society, including the corrupt players themselves or people close to them. Due to the legacy of communist-era red tape, convincing potential anti-corruption constituencies that scenario number one is not in their best interests due to long-term consequences is one of the biggest challenges in their mobilization.

Scenario number two most clearly pinpoints the third actor as the loser and is thus likely to trigger counteraction, especially by evident losers when a winner jumps ahead of them in the queue or gets a job or contract through favoritism. Examples are disappointed bidders, patients and other consumers of public services, and taxpayers. As Table 9.1 illustrates, there are other scenarios as well where the citizenry (the "third actor") loses out, namely, in scenarios four, seven, and eight. Scenario four involves a case where the initial corrupter is the only winner, for example if a bureaucrat deliberately over-regulates a public issue in order to extort bribes. This is also a good illustration of the fact that corruption often involves other pathologies than bribe taking.

Scenario seven depicts an interactive sequence, where the corrupter as well as the public end up as losers because the second actor turns the tables on the initial corrupter and blackmails him over the initial approach. The goal of any anti-corruption policy is to arrive at the situations shown in scenarios five or six, where the citizenry wins by preventing or penalizing corruption. The public or other third actors also win in scenario number three, but only if the initiator of corruption pretends to try to corrupt someone else (such as in a sting operation); otherwise it is unsatisfactory if the corrupter is among the winners.

Today all too many third actors still participate in corruption, either actively or passively. In part this is due to a systemic contagion effect; that is, the experience of widespread corruption by high- and low-level officials lowers the threshold for others to participate in the same behavior, even more so if there are evident instances of corruption but no consequences for the perpetrators. Impunity has the opposite effect of deterrence and undermines compliance with the law by even more people. Impunity leads corruption to feed on itself, a situation that will be elaborated upon below. If the opposite is the goal, and society aims at a downward spiral of corrupt behavior, then its high price must become more evident both to perpetrators and to society at large. In the case of corrupt actors, prevention will work only if there are credible risks, including experiencing the reality of a significant group of them paying the price for their actions by going to jail, having their property confiscated, and losing their reputations. But this will only happen if other powerful actors in the polity—including a participatory citizenry—understand the costs of corruption to the extent that they will move to counteract it. Or, talking in terms of incentives, society at large needs to believe both in the normative value of a low-corruption polity and in the concrete benefits that it brings.

Although the third actor is key in the containment of corruption, strategies need to focus on the two other actors as well and on ways to increase their risks and uncertainty. Much can be gained by convincing second actors—the corruptees—to refuse to become part of an illicit scheme. Better yet, one must try to convert the second actors into third actors who actively oppose corruption. People have a choice whether they are "the ones who by their complacency and their collusion may contribute to corruption taking place or who by their vigilance and integrity may assist authorities in monitoring public officials."[9] Or, in the words of this study, citizens have a choice whether they will be accomplices and victims of corruption, or whether they become part of a counterforce.

If institutions provide checks and balances, corruption can be contained. People must be motivated to take the necessary steps but cannot be expected to pay extraordinary costs. Positive motivation involves a host of material and nonmaterial considerations that include tangible benefits, position, prestige, moral satisfaction, and the respect of friends and colleagues. A good anti-corruption strategy considers such payoffs. A simple way is to honor and reward honest public servants and outstanding activists. But tangible rewards are insufficient; one also needs to highlight the intrinsic values of civic virtue and the pursuit of the public interest, as outlined in Chapter 6. This can be accomplished by a comprehensive public education campaign.

Group-Level Calculus: The Spiral of Corruption

How a person decides to act is influenced not only by the decisions of other individual actors with whom the decision maker is interacting, but also by the decisions of the surrounding critical mass of people. Typically, the critical mass means the majority of actors at the institutional, or system, level. Simply put, if most or all people within an institution engage in corrupt acts, the pressure on any individual to do the same increases dramatically. Speaking of society at large, Klitgaard has stated that "at some point there is a spiral of increasing corruption, [and] even honest citizens may need to be corrupt to get by."[10] This is very much what people in the post-communist region mean when they say that they are forced to participate in corruption. Why, exactly?

The pressures on an individual actor are manifold: for one, as the quote by Klitgaard implies, if corrupt deals are the norm, people feel they must engage in them to get what they need, for example, a service at a public clinic or a bonus at a place of work. This often happens in post-communist countries, especially when colleagues or peers exert direct pressure on hesitant "corruptees" to participate in a group scheme or to otherwise go along with illicit acts. Besides this direct coercion by associates, there is the pressure of perceptions and expectations, and this too has several ways of coming into play. One effect was already alluded to in the discussion of the calculus of the third actor and the role of contagion. The perception or knowledge that one's peers engage in corrupt acts lowers one's own psychological threshold to engage in the same behavior. Claus Offe calls this a "mechanism of corruption feeding on itself."[11]

Citizens who are honest taxpayers and consumers of public services are a basic constituency for reform, but many in fact participate in everyday corruption, which they justify in various ways.[12] In many parts of the post-communist region, one can speak of a self-sustaining system of corruption in which officials seek bribes, and citizens are willing to pay and even offer them to get what they need.[13] This system is built on an interactive pattern of expectations in that people act based on what they believe others in society expect or how others will act. A good anti-corruption strategy tries to influence this pattern so that people increasingly anticipate that others in society will act with integrity.

Perceptions and expectations can create a spiral of self-fulfilling prophecies. In the words of Peter Eigen, "a self-perpetuating cycle can develop, with a broad expectation of corruption causing an increase in its incidence. Such a system rewards the unscrupulous and demoralizes the honest. A 'brain drain' often follows, as people who reject the system emigrate to countries in which they will be rewarded for their skills and productivity."[14] Even if the people with more integrity do not leave the country, they are likely to leave public service if the institution they have been working in has crossed the threshold to systemic corruption. This again strengthens the influence of corrupt agents remaining in the institution and others flocking to it. The spiral of corruption affects businesses as well as individuals: if many firms that engage in procurement tenders do so with illicit methods, other firms either lose out or feel "compelled" to engage in the same practices.

Another systemic way in which corruption spreads is linked to the flow of information. Since corrupt acts are illicit and people try to hide them, those involved in corrupt interactions have poor information about what they can get away with and how. Once corruption is pervasive, uncertainty over who will accept a bribe is reduced and the citizen's dominant strategy will always be to offer a bribe. This behavior leads to even further corruption, since the officials' opportunities to accept bribes inevitably increase.[15] Social networks frequently act as the promoters of corruption by providing information about whom to approach if one intends to give or take a bribe and what the prices are.[16] The same conclusion emerges from Chapter 3 and Chapter 4, which cited various sources indicating that information about corrupt practices most often comes from relatives, friends, or acquaintances. As one of the sources cited showed, many people also say "this is a tradition, everyone does that,"[17] thereby indicating an environment that invites illicit behaviors by various signals.

The dynamics of reciprocity offer another way self-perpetuating mechanisms play a role in the spread of corruption. Honest persons, defined as those who are concerned about contributing to the public good, expect that others share this concern and will reciprocate. If this belief turns out to be false, the public-spirited actor is demoralized. An example involves this author's own changing behavior during a stay in Moscow in 1988 when she initially always held the door for the person following her into the metro station, but soon gave up on that practice since hardly anyone reciprocated. Similarly, people say that they feel justified in cheating on taxes because the government cheats them on benefits. The links between lower- and higher-level corruption have been noted by Louise Shelley: "With impunity for those at the top, those at the lower levels feel no incentive to trim their excesses."[18] Experiences and attitudes like these create a chain of reciprocal noncooperation for a common good.

The negative side of reciprocity also comes into play in promoting more unlawfulness among corrupt actors. As noted, post-communist societies have inherited the habit of the corrupt and powerful engaging in mutual blackmail by threatening each other with the revelation of compromising material.[19] Moreover, corrupt networks tend to expand and self-perpetuate. Their members have a strong motive to keep non-corrupt individuals out of politics, or to try to co-opt anyone who gains power nevertheless. Fear of disclosure adds another strong motive for perpetuating both the network and its corrupt dealings, and thus many political decisions are made to protect implicated officials, be they in one's own network or in another one that is protected on the basis of a collusive quid pro quo.[20]

Corruption perpetuates itself for other reasons as well. Fear of exposure of previous corrupt dealings leads to new corrupt acts to prevent investigations. Aside from blackmail, this often involves other criminal acts such as threats, physical violence, and murder. If a certain threshold is crossed, a vicious circle that is difficult to break comes into play. Yet, although it appears that the system is perpetuated by its own dynamics rather than human agency, people still do make decisions and can engage in strategic action to generate a downward spiral. In fact, this is the core goal of a good anti-corruption policy.

Anti-Corruption Strategies: Changing the Calculus

If one wants to contain corruption on the systemic level, the goal should be clearly defined as such and each measure taken should be analyzed as to the degree to which it promotes systemic change, even if individuals are the immediate target. Some strategies were already mentioned when discussing the individual-level calculus about corruption; here the focus will be on how one can strategize to achieve a downward spiral in regard to the institutional level of corruption. As the discussion of the scenarios in Table 9.1 demonstrates, there are three types of actors who need to be considered in any anti-corruption strategy: the corrupter, the corruptee, and the third actor. Although the main goal is to deter people from initiating corrupt acts to begin with, a narrow focus on the first actor can limit results. Corrupters rely on the passive or active collaboration of second actors, and in many situations it is easier to deter corruption by focusing on this second link in the process of "misuse of public power." If potential victims and other third actors become galvanized to work to prevent corruption, it is possible to limit or even reverse the spiral of corruption.

Most analysts of corruption cleanups advocate a multipronged approach to produce substantial and enduring results, yet they differ in their emphasis on targets, methods, and who should constitute the initial driving force. The last depends on the level of corruption that is targeted; thus high-level corruption requires national attention and civic organizations to push for change, while eliminating low-level bureaucratic corruption is often in the interest of top officials.[21] Where post-communist governments have initiated anti-corruption programs, they typically have focused on petty rather than grand corruption, and international assessments highlight their lack of political will to be more decisive. As noted by analysts at the World Bank, "combating corruption requires strong and credible political leadership. Yet this is precisely the aspect of the political system that is most seriously undermined by administrative corruption and state capture."[22]

How to put to use existing political institutions is a major dilemma in a situation where the local populations believe that high-level political corruption is the core problem. Therefore, an initial move is to examine how state capture and other forms of high-level corruption can be contained by sustained action on the part of the citizenry. This involves what has been called a "community justice strategy," the mobilization of democratic forces from below and the forging of anti-corruption coalitions by galvanizing a plurality of civic and nonprofit organizations to act as direct checks on state power.[23]

The first step in designing a strategy is to identify who might participate in such a coalition and to examine their incentives. A crucial group includes people who bear the immediate costs of corrupt acts, such as individuals who are extorted by officials and firms losing contracts due to corrupt procurement practices. They have an obvious interest in making use of institutional means of recourse such as grievance procedures, independent review boards, and the legal process. Yet as outlined in the preceding chapters, institutional means of accountability may prove to be insufficient since the implementation of laws is often handicapped. At this point, the enforcement of the law needs to be demanded by a larger coalition consisting of anti-corruption activists, associations of businesspeople, reform politicians, and the media. Although these groups, with the exception of the anti-corruption activists, may promote their own goals by such activity, what are the incentives for civic activists and common-cause groups? For one, they represent the public and thus the "major victim" of corruption.[24] Second, every society includes some members who are altruistic and work for the common good for its own sake,[25] and as the social movement literature has shown, civic activists also benefit from social capital, trust, and camaraderie. Nevertheless, galvanizing civic groups for sustained activity is not easy, with one theorist arguing that reform networks need to develop especially strong emotive ties and frequency of contact to be able to make a difference.[26]

Reform groups also have to overcome the classic free rider problem, where the success of an activity depends on other people joining in. Taking an active stance against corruption is a typical social dilemma of individual motivation in an interdependent situation in which the short-term costs are quite high, and the long-term payoff is a common good enjoyed by many. There is a tension between individual and group incentives that can lead to zero cooperation. As formulated by Elinor Ostrom: "in a public-good dilemma . . . all those who would benefit from the provision of a public good—such as pollution control, radio broadcasts, or weather forecasting—find it costly to contribute and would prefer others to pay for the good instead. If everyone follows the equilibrium strategy, then the good is not provided."[27] One way to solve this problem is to think in terms of an assurance game involving demonstration effects and tipping points. As the East European protests in 1989 revealed, the decisions of individuals whether or not to participate in joint activity are influenced by a set of assurance games that involve their own and other social groups. When the majority of members of one social group become active, this becomes known as a "tipping point." Tipping points can then act to trigger the involvement of other societal groups. As this happens, regime actors go through the reverse process of de-assurance as their instruments of power are gradually undermined by the grassroots movement.[28] A variant of this solution to the collective action problem is to point to the role of organizations, since they help overcome suboptimal collective outcomes by providing information about the behavior of other actors. Besides spreading information, organizations and other institutions also help enforce commitments, which allow individuals to cooperate.[29]

The success of this or any other anti-corruption strategy depends on its ability to gain momentum and achieve a spiraling effect where corrupt acts become less and less feasible. In addition, any strategy needs to specify long- and short-term goals, how best to accomplish them, and when to implement them. Timing is very important and windows of opportunity for new initiatives need to be taken advantage of, especially when a new government has been elected, public outrage over scandals rises, or there is new external pressure.[30] All these conditions are currently present in the East European and Baltic regions, and as public anger has risen, corruption has triggered electoral upsets in Slovakia, Poland, Bulgaria, and elsewhere. Both NATO and the European Union have made it an issue for accession. A window of opportunity, a crisis, or what strategic action theorists call a "focal point" can be decisive. In Hong Kong such a focal point emerged after a corrupt police official's escape from prison touched off mass outrage. The anti-corruption program's first success in the struggle to win public confidence was when he was brought back to Hong Kong for trial and imprisonment.[31] As more high-level scandals break in the post-communist region, they can trigger a similar focal point for change.

If the timing is opportune, what should be the initial target of the campaign? It appears to be a mistake to start by targeting the everyday survival strategies of citizens, such as gratitude payments to doctors. The populations need to support reforms, and in the countries surveyed, people are far more angry about corruption among top government officials than among officials who deal with ordinary people.[32] Yet anti-corruption experts differ on the effects of "frying some big fish." Supporters of this approach argue the importance of demonstrating that nobody is above the law and that the program is serious about consequences.[33] In light of the widespread sense of immunity among post-communist elites, this approach is intuitively attractive. When investigators have raised questions about possible malfeasance, members of the elite have been stunningly shameless in refusing to reply or offering superficial replies.[34] And they get away with it, because their attitude is bolstered by the tradition of mutual covering up and the servile belief of other actors that the powerful are not to be called to account. As noted in Chapter 4, the population at large feels helpless and has little trust in its political leaders and institutions, yet expresses the vain hope that "the state" will some-how clean up its own act. A breakthrough is needed to change these atti-tudes, and proving some corruption cases against high-level officials and punishing them appears to be the key. If those responsible for grand corrup-tion are called to account, this can significantly raise the credibility of any anti-corruption program and galvanize public support. Once this happens, there will be increased support for the more fundamental reforms that need to follow individual prosecutions.[35]

The focus on bringing some high officials to account is contradicted by the Transparency International approach, which is based on including politi-cal leaders in the building of broad coalitions against corruption. This coali-tion "seeks to minimize confrontation and political wrangling, preferring to work cooperatively with government and citizens' groups. . . . It is not intent on investigating individual cases, exposing villains, or casting blame. It seeks to strengthen anti-corruption systems."[36] Transparency International focuses on long-term successes and holistic strategies, since a piecemeal approach can falter and bring about an even more defeatist attitude. Any strategy needs to consider the nature and consequences of likely counteractions. Anti-corruption activities do not take place in a vacuum. There are significant power groups that have a palpable interest in the vagueness of law or that profit from the routine failure to implement court decisions and administra-tive rulings. Stephen Holmes calls these "anti–rule-of-law constituencies."[37]

Much of the high-level corruption in the post-communist region involves powerful elite cartels that support each other and, when challenged, are apt to mobilize their supporters to cry that they are the target of political manipu-lations, a witch-hunt, or a Stalinist-type show trial. Elite cartels are also likely to coerce investigators. To date, few high-level scandals in the region have been investigated, and convictions have been rare. If any attempt is made to enforce the law against elite members, the case has to be prepared very care-fully to secure proof and conviction. If "big fish" are accused, yet cannot be convicted in a court of law, the attempt backfires, confirming popular opin-ion that the powerful are untouchable.

Since it is important to signal to corrupt actors and the public that corrup-tion control works, an alternative is to aim at a quick success on the institu-tional level. A careful analysis should pinpoint a public sector where corruption has been costly, yet where institutional reforms and activist involvement prom-ise success. Once a sector is pinpointed, it is crucial to mobilize the constitu-encies that have a stake, for example patients' rights associations and groups of reformist doctors.

An example of radical reform of a specific institution "from above" was set by Georgia's new president, Mikhail Saakashvili, who in summer 2004 created an entirely new traffic police force after concluding that the old one had become a major source and symbol of corruption. He first dismissed the old traffic police, then replaced them with a new force modeled after Western examples. A new police force was recruited, trained, given a new name and new equipment. This force is smaller and therefore can be paid more.[38]

Securing "islands of integrity" can jump-start public confidence in reform and can trigger the subsequent improvement of other institutions. The likelihood of such a demonstration effect is supported by the findings of William L. Miller and his collaborators that popular criticism is focused on specific institutions and scandalous events.[39] Similarly, the research of William Mishler and Richard Rose shows that citizen trust in political institutions is linked less to overall personal or cultural dispositions than to experience with these institutions and micro-level performance evaluations.[40]

Even small, initial successes are important to signal that corruption can be stopped. An example from Latvia shows how civic groups defending the public good can succeed with a broadly based effort. In spring 2002, Transparency International–Latvia led a grassroots campaign against a suspect effort to privatize a youth sports and recreation facility, the Sun-Park. The park had been donated to the public by a private benefactor in 1913, and it served its function through all of Latvia's political ups and downs until 2000, when the Ministry of Education as its institutional caretaker started a behind-the-scenes move to privatize it to a financial oligarch, former KGB director Indriksons and his firm, Skonto. When this became public knowledge, TI–Latvia started a protest campaign that combined appeals to legislators and government figures with civic mobilization. They adeptly organized public meetings of activists and the people living in the area, highlighted both the concrete and symbolic value of the Sun-Park to the public, and gained sympathetic media coverage. The breakthrough came when TI–Latvia garnered the support of fifty-eight other nongovernmental groups and thousands of individuals who signed appeals. In April 2002, the government took the Sun-Park off the list of objects to be privatized, in part because the public campaign allowed more reformist forces in the government to take the upper hand by arguing that they had to make concessions to public opinion. This points to an important link between successful grassroots and elite reform movements. As the organizers note, "this is the first time that the representatives of society have put so much pressure on the government that it was forced to review a previous decision and to change it."[41]

An initial success in containing corruption can encourage "third actors" in other sectors and lead to a snowball effect. Yet there can also be the opposite result if several small snowballs—so to speak—prevent the avalanche that is needed to clear the field. In this scenario, corrupt power brokers use the apparent small successes as a facade for showing that they are doing something against corruption, while actually continuing pernicious practices. Since this negative outcome conforms with historical experience and the often cynical outlook of the people in the post-communist region, serious efforts must be made to demonstrate that this is not the case.

The core goal of any anti-corruption strategy is to send a clear signal that corrupt practices will be curtailed. Credibility is of special importance in societies such as those in the post-communist region, where irresponsibility and inefficiency have been widespread and the citizenry has arrived at the sad point of simply not believing or trusting the government. To change such a situation "the involvement of the people is crucial."[42] There are many ways to activate such involvement, but one always must consider the morale and perceptions of participants. Anti-corruption handbooks emphasize that publicity and higher awareness of the costs of corruption are positive first steps toward popular mobilization against it,[43] yet the perception of high levels of corruption can backfire if it promotes the idea that corruption is so pervasive that its containment is impossible. An even more negative outcome is that the remaining honest officials and citizens conclude that they have been foolish not to get involved themselves and share in the spoils. This is one more reason for any anti-corruption strategy to balance raising awareness with enforcement.[44]

In the final analysis it all comes down to effective deterrence. Corrupt acts can be deterred if it is highly probable that people who engage in them will be called to account and will pay a significant price. Exposure alone can have high costs for people in the public realm, but so can other ways of having to answer for one's actions, not least if the questioning occurs before oversight or legal bodies with the power to impose real sanctions. There are some findings that in Central and Eastern Europe social networks and reputation are a substitute for effective courts,[45] which again underlines the importance of societal involvement in any effort to control corruption. Or, to phrase it differently, although it is crucial that formal courts deal with corruption more decisively, a large part of corruption control also involves the court of public opinion. If societies become much less tolerant of corruption, exposure alone can go a long way to prevent further acts. Social censure and shame can significantly influence behavior. The reverse is true as well: peer pressure can enable or even encourage corrupt practices; this needs to be changed.

Most anti-corruption experts emphasize the importance of corruption prevention and that one needs to be careful not to rely too heavily on sanctions. Daniel Kaufmann has argued that overemphasis on enforcement and prosecution is similar to a public health strategy that focuses on dealing with people once they become sick, rather than engaging in prophylactic health measures.[46] This is convincing insofar as in fighting any crime prevention is always better than prosecution, yet without prosecution there cannot be real prevention, because there no longer is any risk in engaging in corrupt acts. The key to an effective anti-corruption strategy is to use sanctions not as an end, but as a means of deterrence by creating an effective level of credibility that sanctions will be forthcoming. If the risk of sanctions is real, the calculus of corruption changes accordingly, and then, paradoxically, fewer actual sanctions are needed. Although one can agree with the statement that "the overall strategy, in other words, must be one of prevention, with prosecution and punishment eventually coming to play supporting rather than leading roles,"[47] the key word in our context is "eventually." At a time when political corruption in the post-communist region remains mostly unpunished, the sequencing of various means of fighting it, starting with raising the credibility of the risk of sanctions, is crucial for preventing a continuing spiral of corruption.

Conclusion: Anti-Corruption Incentives and Strategies

Any anti-corruption strategy that is right for a concrete institution or country needs to be determined on the ground, within the specific context. Rather than trying to provide detailed road maps, this chapter has outlined a framework for analyzing specific situations and thinking strategically about incentives and how to change them. Most of all, one needs to examine how people make decisions in corrupt contexts. Aside from the insights provided by studying dominant attitudes and discourses, it helps to systematically outline the choices that individuals have as they decide whether to engage in corrupt acts or whether to work to counter them. The schema presented in Table 9.1 shows that there are at least three actors in every corrupt interaction: the corrupter, the corruptee, and the third actor. A good anti-corruption strategy tries to influence the decisions of all three of them.

Most fundamentally, strategists want to influence the first actor and deter any potential corrupt act, and for this it is crucial that such acts carry high risks and low benefits. In the post-communist region the opposite has mostly been true, in that benefits have been high and risks low. This has in large part been due to the behavior of second and third actors. All too many second actors have been willing to passively or actively participate in corrupt acts, and all too many third actors have failed to take a strong stand and say that they as individuals, or as groups representing society, are no longer willing to pay the high costs of corruption. Although it is important to encourage second actors to "blow the whistle," or otherwise become third actors who counter corruption, the real key to the effective containment of corruption is to mobilize the third actor. This means that both individuals and groups should become active in the various ways outlined in this and the two immediately preceding chapters: they should monitor how public power is used and demand accountability. Corrupt acts can be prevented only by effective monitoring and credible risks.[48] Although every separate action is important, a strategy is required that aims at galvanizing large-scale and coordinated civic activism from below, because it is crucial to reverse the spiral of corruption at the societal level.

How individuals make decisions is affected by decision processes at the collective level. People look for signals as to what is expected of them and how others in society behave. If a "normalization" of corruption occurs in public opinion, a negative spiral results whereby more and more people feel that they have little choice but to go along with what most others in society are doing.[49] This acceptance includes the perception that little can be done to reverse this spiral, but for corruption control to work the opposite needs to be true: people need to believe that change can be brought about. The material in this and other chapters suggests that specific societies or institutions reach tipping points after which there are upward and downward spirals of corrupt behaviors. Strategists aiming at significant change need to work toward reaching a tipping point after which corruption spirals downward. This can be accomplished if more and more individuals and civic groups become engaged and either use many small successes to trigger more change, or manage to create a focal breakthrough through a major event such as a high-level criminal prosecution, as was the case in Hong Kong. Since impunity at high levels has been a core issue in the perpetuation of both grand and petty corruption in post-communist countries, it is very likely that the successful prosecution of some "big fish" will have a similar effect in these cases. Although in principle it is best to have prophylaxis rather than prosecution, prophylaxis in the post-communist region will only work once the credibility of a high risk of being penalized for corruption is established. As it is, the lack of sanctions and accountability has seriously weakened the prevention of corruption.

In sum, this chapter argues that anti-corruption policies in the post-communist region will only work if they involve real accountability and are based on the active involvement of strategic subgroups of the populace. In addition to civic groups being galvanized, it is important that they are joined by reform groups of professionals in the civil service, law enforcement and the judiciary, and the business community. The media too have a crucial role to play in publicizing anti-corruption initiatives and every success they attain. Anti-corruption work by public administrators and high officials can help, but in the long run the mobilization of democratic forces from below and the forging of civil society is the decisive way to contain corruption in a democracy.

——— 10 ———

Conclusion:
How to Contain Corruption

This study's underlying theme is that democratic consolidation is tied to the degree of success in dealing with corruption. Another core argument is that the pervasiveness of corrupt behavior can be changed by various means. Corruption is not an immutable fact of politics, as fatalists believe, but can be limited by good policy. The three cornerstones of corruption containment are creating institutional checks and balances, assuring that the mechanisms of accountability actually work, and mobilizing the citizenry to participate in enhancing the public good. Yet anti-corruption policies only work if a host of other factors are considered, as discussed throughout this study and summarized in Figure 10.1.

A Model

The first crucial link to lowering levels of corruption involves the legitimacy of the political regime of any particular state and the extent to which it galvanizes virtuous public behavior. Corrupt behavior is linked to negative views of politics and the citizen's role in it. People must believe their system of government works. If they are convinced of the efficacy of the regime, they will be motivated to work for the common good of the nation.

It is insufficient to fight "against" corruption; people must believe in a positive alternative to dirty politics. For this one needs to go beyond the teaching of ethics and outline the logic and value of civic virtue and a state with an engaged citizenry cooperating for common goals. Many post-communist citizens yearn for a political system that works well and that they can support. Building legitimate political regimes is difficult, but as argued in Chapter 6 it is crucial for fostering public spiritedness, which can be defined as the opposite of corruption, namely, "using public power for the public good."

Figure 10.1 Influences on Levels of Corruption

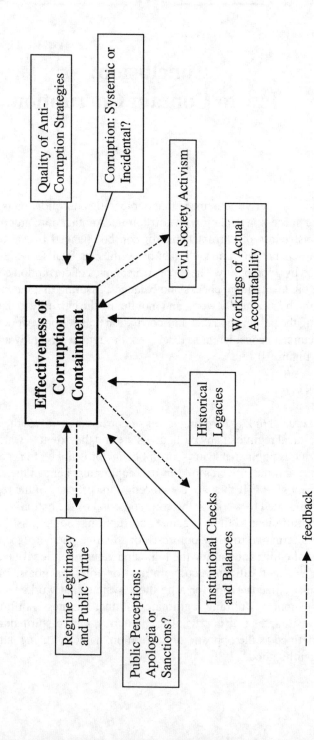

This leads to the second factor shown in Figure 10.1, the extent to which citizens and officials think that certain corrupt acts can be justified or are unacceptable. Public values and views are expressed in discourse, which creates a climate of either corruption apologia or social rejection. Anti-corruption work needs to limit tolerance for both petty and grand corruption. Honest people are the core constituency for reform, but to date all too many post-communist citizens participate in petty corruption and tolerate it in others. Yet many are also angry, especially about high-level corruption. When designing anti-corruption strategies, this ambivalence should be anticipated. A good policy can use the anger to mobilize people against grand corruption and pinpoint the danger of tolerance for petty corruption.

As emphasized throughout this study, the level of corruption can be influenced by democratic institutional checks and balances on power holders, especially as exercised by an independent judiciary, oversight bodies, and free media. Good laws and institutional mechanisms go a long way in inhibiting corrupt impulses. This logic is summarized in the anti-corruption formula that corruption can be contained by de-monopolizing decision making, limiting discretion, and creating accountability.

How well this works is influenced by manifold historical legacies, especially the habits formed under the preceding communist regimes. Old habits die hard, even more so if they are based on informal structures, such as networks of personal exchange of favors at the elite and mass level. As argued in Chapter 5, the communist regimes promoted the emergence of powerful networks of political patronage and personal influence, and this legacy survives in part, most dangerously so in the case of political cartels that engage in state capture. Mutual covering up and the use of kompromat are other habits that subvert the ability of the rule of law to function coherently.[1]

Established patterns of behavior and incentives often undermine political accountability. It is not enough that laws and institutional accountability provisions exist, they must have real consequences. The implementation of effective accountability constitutes the fifth pillar of the corruption-containment edifice. Once the people in the region see that politicians and officials are held accountable for their actions, corruption will decline and trust in public institutions will grow.

The sixth factor depicted in Figure 10.1 is the involvement of civil society in corruption containment. As argued in the Chapter 9, the mobilization of citizens "from below" is a crucial driving force for cleaner government. This can mean civic activism of various kinds, including the forming of electoral coalitions. On a daily basis, nongovernmental associations have an important role in corruption monitoring and promoting various projects that raise awareness and increase political transparency.

The seventh and eighth determinants of the effectiveness of corruption control involve the intensity of corruption and the extent to which an appropriate anti-corruption strategy can be worked out. If corruption is widespread or even systemic, it is much more difficult to contain. Systemic corruption can be institutionalized, or it can be the result of pervasive patterns of popular behavior. Individual behavior is tied to the behavior of others and if "everyone" engages in illicit acts, it is difficult to reverse the trend. Here the media have to walk a fine line: they must expose corruption, yet coverage must be concrete and non-fatalistic. If corrupt acts are projected as being the dominant public behavior of elites and masses, this may become a self-fulfilling prophecy.[2] Good policy must aim at the opposite, that is, triggering a downward spiral, where fewer and fewer such acts occur.

As Figure 10.1 suggests, the influence of the various factors determining the effectiveness of corruption containment is not one-directional and contains feedback processes. Increasing success in controlling corruption, for example, changes public perceptions and encourages more people to resist it. As discussed in Chapter 9, both corruption and corruption fighting can be contagious and can affect the actions of other people in society.

Practical Considerations for Devising an Anti-Corruption Strategy

For any anti-corruption strategy to work, the policy makers first need to consider the meaning of "strategy." Strategy is a plan of action that outlines not only what one wants to achieve and by what basic instruments, but also calculates the sequence of steps that will lead to the goal. It must consider how to avoid structural pitfalls and it needs to anticipate countermoves of the opponent, in our case, people who profit from corruption. Based on such an analysis, policy makers must identify initial priorities, the steps that will have the highest impact on countering existing corruption and the policies that will have the highest deterrent effect on future corrupt acts.

There are many other considerations for identifying initial targets of anti-corruption. How can the largest sum of public money be saved? How can one get quicker and more visible results? What results will have highest impact on overall morale and credibility that the corruption spiral is being reversed? Timing of new initiatives must be considered carefully to enhance their impact, and the same applies to the maximum impact of international support. Above all, one needs to weigh carefully who can be the most effective driving force spearheading initiatives: should these be political leaders, specialized anti-corruption units and bureaus, or civil society and popular mobilization?

If the last is decided on because the political establishment itself is too corrupt to undertake reform, civic society activists must take account of the unequal balance of power confronting them. Officials heading public institutions have a built-in advantage of resources and a network of dependent workers. Individuals challenging "the system" are unlikely to succeed unless they manage to organize one or several groups that can stage a sustained campaign and support each other. Effective solidarity is important because officials have the power of retribution. They can penalize those who challenge the status quo with loss of jobs or stipends and many other means. Institutional corrupt actors have a high stake in protecting themselves and their schemes, and they tend to be very adept and determined at fighting off any challenges.

To counter the strength of this system, anti-corruption groups can apply the lessons of the dissident movements fighting the communist regimes that also looked very powerful. The dissidents were victorious when they based themselves on well-thought-out strategies of lawfulness, the higher moral ground, mutual aid and solidarity, the use of international publicity, and appeals for mass support at decisive moments. It bears remembering that corruption and the self-dealing of officials were major issues raised by Solidarity and similar groups during the end phase of the communist regimes. Where corruption is endemic in post-communist states, similar movements may emerge in time.

The Four Stages of Corruption Containment

The ultimate goal of this study is to understand what it takes to have effective corruption control. The first step is to recognize that corruption is a serious issue, and this also constitutes the first of four phases in the development of anti-corruption policies. Besides acknowledging that corruption has a price, this initial stage involves starting to research the facts about the corruption one is dealing with. The second stage begins to put in place the legal and institutional mechanisms of accountability, and the third stage is where these mechanisms actually start to work as intended. The fourth stage involves the fine-tuning of the corruption-prevention enterprise so that it becomes a normally functioning part of developed democracies.

The twenty-eight post-communist states of Eastern Europe and the former Soviet Union differ considerably in regard to the stage of anti-corruption policy they are in. The avant garde is constituted by the states that became full members of the European Union and NATO. For them, the phase of recognizing the seriousness of corruption started around 1995–96; the second stage of initial laws and institutions to prevent corruption began to be put in place between 1997 and 1998, and was basically completed by early 2004, mostly because an anti-corruption policy was required for accession to the European Union. Whether, and to what extent, these institutional measures have started to work and whether these states have entered the third stage of effective corruption control is discussed in Chapter 8. It is an open question when these states will reach "normal" levels of corruption as encountered in consolidated democracies. For many other states in the post-communist region, an even longer road lies ahead.

Notes

Notes to Chapter 1

1. Michael Johnston, "Corruption as a Process," in *Coping with Corruption in a Borderless World*, ed. Maurice Punch et al. (Deventer: Kluwer Law and Taxation Publishers, 1993), p. 43.

2. John Gardiner, "Defining Corruption," in *Coping with Corruption*, p. 25.

3. Robert Klitgaard, *Controlling Corruption* (Berkeley: University of California Press, 1988), p. xi.

4. James C. Scott, *Comparative Political Corruption* (Englewood Cliffs, NJ: Prentice-Hall, 1972), p. 2.

5. *Webster's International Dictionary*, 2d ed., s.v. "corruption."

6. A similar point in regard to bribery is made by John T. Noonan, *Bribes* (Berkeley: University of California Press, 1984), p. xi.

7. Transparency International–Latvia, *The Face of Corruption in Latvia*, report [in Latvian] (Riga: Apr. 2000), p. 19. The representative survey included 2,001 respondents.

8. Ibid., p. 23.

9. Ibid., p. 25.

10. William L. Miller, Ase B. Grodeland, and Tatyana Y. Koshechkina, "Are the People Victims or Accomplices? The Use of Presents and Bribes to Influence Officials in Eastern Europe," Discussion Paper #6 (Budapest: Open Society Institute, 1998).

11. Transparency International, *Global Corruption Report 2004* (London: Pluto Press, 2004), p. 11.

12. See for example, Seymour Martin Lipset and Gabriel Salman Lenz, "Corruption, Culture, and Markets," in *Culture Matters: How Values Shape Human Progress*, ed. L.E. Harrison and S.P. Huntington (New York: Basic Books, 2000), pp. 112–25.

13. Paul Heywood, "Political Corruption: Problems and Perspectives," *Political Studies* 45 (special issue, 1997), p. 421.

14. Carl J. Friedrich, *The Pathology of Politics: Violence, Betrayal, Corruption, Secrecy and Propaganda* (New York: Harper & Row, 1972), p. 17.

15. Richard Rose, William Mishler, and Christian Haerpfer, *Democracy and Its Alternatives* (Cambridge, UK: Cambridge University Press, 1998), p. 188.

16. A recent example involves the populist military regime in Ghana, which installed popular tribunals for corrupt officials that had people shot. Ghana also put "fast track" courts in place to deal with corruption cases quickly. Seminar presentation by Jennifer Hasty, Institute for Advanced Study, Princeton, Fall 2002.

17. Seth Mydans, "Georgian Leader Agrees to Resign, Ending Standoff," *New York Times*, Nov. 24, 2003, p. 1.

18. Klitgaard, *Controlling Corruption*, p. 1.

19. See several chapters in Stephen Kotkin and Andras Sajo, eds. *Political Corruption in Transition: A Skeptic's Handbook* (Budapest: Central European University Press, 2002).

20. For a good summary, see Gabriel Ben-Dor, "Corruption, Institutionalization, and Political Development: The Revisionist Theses Revisited," *Comparative Political Studies* 7, no. 1 (1974), pp. 63–83.

21. Samuel Huntington, *Political Order in Changing Societies* (New Haven, CT: Yale University Press, 1968), p. 64.

22. William A. Clark, "Soviet Official Corruption under Perestroika: A Balance Sheet," *Current Politics and Economics of Russia* 2, no. 3 (1991), p. 209.

23. Most prominently, Nathaniel H. Leff, "Economic Development Through Bureaucratic Corruption," *American Behavioral Scientist* 8, no. 3 (Nov. 1964), pp. 8–14. Leff's argument presupposes an ineffective bureaucracy; see p. 10.

24. Paolo Mauro, "Corruption and Growth," *Quarterly Journal of Economics* 110 (Aug. 1995), pp. 681–712.

25. Sanjeev Gupta, Hamid Davoodi, and Erwin Tiongson, "Corruption and the Provision of Health and Education Services," in *The Political Economy of Corruption*, ed. Arvind K. Jain (London: Routledge, 2001), pp. 111–41.

26. Commission of the European Communities, *Communication from the Commission to the Council, the European Parliament and the European Economic and Social Committee on a Comprehensive Policy against Corruption*, Brussels, May 28, 2003, p. 12.

27. Ibid., p. 16.

28. This is an approximate average, as outlined in Chapter 2. In some cases it is higher, such as in Bulgaria, where the average cost increase of procurement due to corruption is calculated at 20 percent. Open Society Institute, *Monitoring the EU Accession Process: Corruption and Anti-corruption Policy* (Budapest: 2002), p. 120.

29. Louise Shelley, "Crime and Corruption," in *Developments in Russian Politics*, ed. Stephen White, Alex Pravda, and Zvi Gitelman. (Hampshire: Palgrave, 2001), p. 251.

30. See the Selected Bibliography, especially the volumes edited by Heidenheimer and the works by Susan Rose-Ackerman, Michael Johnston, and Robert Klitgaard.

31. Valerie Bunce, "The Postsocialist Experience and Comparative Politics," *PS: Political Science and Politics* 34, no. 4 (Dec. 2001), p. 793.

32. Ibid., p. 794.

33. World Bank, *Anticorruption in Transition: A Contribution to the Policy Debate* (Washington, D.C., Sept. 2000).

34. The TI Corruption Perceptions Index ranks countries in terms of the degree to which corruption is perceived to exist among public officials and politicians. It is a composite index, drawing on fourteen different polls and surveys from multiple independent institutions carried out among businesspeople and country analysts, including surveys of residents, both local and expatriate.

35. Reports on the new EU members from East Central Europe were published in November 2002 by www.eumap.org, and www.greco.coe.int has published sixteen reports on post-communist countries. Follow-up evaluations and other reports are forthcoming.

36. For example, Agnese Barstad, "Culture of Corruption? Interpreting Corruption in Soviet and Post-Soviet Contexts," M.A. thesis, University of Bergen, Norway (2003).

37. A similar approach is used in Adam Przeworski, *Democracy and the Market:*

Political and Economic Reforms in Eastern Europe and Latin America (Cambridge, UK: Cambridge University Press, 1991).

38. *Webster's New International Dictionary*, 3d ed., s.v. "systemic."

39. Pathbreaking works include James G. March and Johan P. Olsen, "The New Institutionalism: Organizational Factors in Political Life," *American Political Science Review* 78 (1984), pp. 734–49, and Peter B. Evans, Dietrich Rueschmeyer, and Theda Skopcol, eds., *Bringing the State Back In* (Cambridge, UK: Cambridge University Press, 1985). For a good overview of the literature, see Karen L. Remmer, "Theoretical Decay and Theoretical Development: The Resurgence of Institutional Analysis," *World Politics* 50 (Oct. 1997), pp. 34–61.

40. William A. Clark and Philip H. Jos, "Comparative Anti-Corruption Policy: The American, Soviet and Russian Cases," *International Journal of Public Administration* 23 (2000), pp. 101–48.

41. On survey results on mass attitudes compare, for example, William Mishler and Richard Rose, "What Are the Origins of Political Trust? Testing Institutional and Cultural Theories in Post-Communist Societies," *Comparative Political Studies* 34, no. 1 (Feb. 2001), pp. 30–62.

42. A.W. Goudie and David Stasavage, "A Framework for the Analysis of Corruption," *Crime, Law and Social Change* 29 (1998), pp. 113–59, p. 114.

43. Also, Michael Johnston, "The Political Consequences of Corruption: A Reassessment," *Comparative Politics* 18, no. 4 (July 1986), p. 463.

Notes to Chapter 2

1. Robert Klitgaard, *Controlling Corruption* (Berkeley: University of California Press, 1988), p. xi.

2. An article on China differentiates between individual corruption and "collective corruption" where a group of public officials collude in corrupt schemes. Ting Gong, "Dangerous Collusion: Corruption As a Collective Venture in Contemporary China," *Communist and Post-Communist Studies* 35, no. 1 (Mar. 2002), pp. 85–103.

3. William L. Miller, Ase B. Grodeland, and Tatyana Y. Koshechkina, *A Culture of Corruption? Coping with Government in Post-Communist Europe* (Budapest: Central European University Press, 2001), pp. 64–69.

4. This was stated by a researcher of the Hungarian Association of Police in an interview conducted on January 2002, reported in Open Society Institute, *Monitoring the EU Accession Process: Corruption and Anti-corruption Policy* (Budapest, 2002), p. 183.

5. World Bank, *Anticorruption in Transition: A Contribution to the Policy Debate* (Washington, D.C., Sept. 2000), p. 9.

6. Open Society Institute, *Monitoring the EU Accession Process*, p. 183.

7. Ibid., p. 444.

8. Ibid., p. 445. In Poland an audit found that driver's licenses could be obtained for bribes ranging from 19 to 533 euros.

9. Louise Shelley, "Crime and Corruption," in *Developments in Russian Politics*, ed. Stephen White, Alex Pravda, and Zvi Gitelman (Hampshire: Palgrave, 2001), pp. 246–47. There is little research on this side of institutional corruption. A similar phenomenon, and lack of research on it, are noted in the case of China by Xiaobo Lu, *Cadres and Corruption: The Organizational Involution of the Chinese Communist Party* (Stanford, CA: Stanford University Press, 2000), pp. 201–2.

10. Open Society Institute, *Monitoring the EU Accession Process*, p. 439.

11. See also Vadim Radaev, "Corruption and Violence in Russian Business in the Late 1990s," in *Economic Crime in Russia*, ed. Alena V. Ledeneva and Marina Kurkchiyan (The Hague: Kluwer Law International, 2000), p. 66.

12. "For the average enterprise, the senior manager must devote 27 percent of the workweek attending to government regulations or officials from state or local government institutions." James Anderson, *Corruption in Latvia: Survey Evidence* (Washington, D.C.: World Bank, Dec. 16, 1998), p. 24.

13. Susan Rose-Ackerman, *Corruption: A Study in Political Economy* (New York: Academic Press, 1978), p. 90.

14. Klitgaard, *Controlling Corruption*, p. 79.

15. Andras Sajo, "Clientelism and Extortion: Corruption in Transition," in *Political Corruption in Transition: A Skeptic's Handbook*, ed. Stephen Kotkin and Andras Sajo (Budapest: Central European University Press, 2002), p.17.

16. Marshall I. Goldman, *The Piratization of Russia: Russian Reform Goes Awry* (London: Routledge, 2003), p. 213.

17. Radaev, "Corruption and Violence in Russian Business," pp. 67–68.

18. Timothy Frye, "Corruption: The Polish and Russian Experiences," USIA Electronic Journal, *Economic Perspectives* 3, no. 5 (Nov. 1998), p. 2.

19. Inna Pidluska, Ukrainian Center for Independent Research, conference presentation as reported in Robert Lyle, "Ukraine under Corruption Spotlight," *RFE/RL Newsline*, Part II (Feb. 26, 1999).

20. *Diena*, May 30, 2000. A later newspaper report discussing the need for civil servant salary reform cites a representative of the Finance Ministry saying that many state agencies pay about 200 percent more than the "formal" salary, but that other agencies are unable to do so. It also reports that some agency directors are paid 2,000 lats a month. *Dienas bizness*, July 20, 2001. This is a fantastic amount if one considers that state-employed teachers, nurses, and other personnel typically are paid less than 100 lats per month.

21. Open Society Institute, *Monitoring the EU Accession Process*, p. 256. Study visits by officials to foreign countries have often turned out to be expensive pleasure trips. In another case, the mayor of the Estonian city of Voru sent four members of the town government for a week to a seminar in Morocco, exceeding the budget for the trip by 300 percent. In this case, the town council forced the mayor and his assistant to resign. Ibid., p. 200.

22. John M. Kramer, "The Politics of Corruption," *Current History* 97, no. 621 (Oct. 1998), p. 331.

23. *New York Times*, Aug. 24, 2000.

24. *Moscow News* of July 11, 1996 reported that between 1992 and 1996 some 300 generals built dachas in the Moscow region—costing between $200,000 and $3 million each—using embezzled materials and employing military personnel who had been promised early release from service. Cited in Kramer, "The Politics of Corruption," p. 331.

25. Open Society Institute, *Monitoring the EU Accession Process*, p. 422.

26. Ibid., p. 486.

27. Ibid.

28. World Bank Warsaw Office, *Corruption in Poland*, Oct. 11, 1999, p. 16. Retrieved from www.worldbank.org.pl/html/corruption/html.

29. Open Society Institute, *Monitoring the EU Accession Process*, p. 178.

30. Kramer, "The Politics of Corruption," p. 330.

31. Open Society Institute, *Monitoring the EU Accession Process*, p. 120.

32. Ibid., p. 437. The same report says that in Poland the practice of collusion in fixing tenders is endemic.

33. Ivan Miklos, *Corruption Risks in the Privatisation Process* (Bratislava, May 1995). Retrieved from www.internet.sk/mesa10/PRIVAT/CORRUPT.htm.

34. Open Society Institute, *Monitoring the EU Accession Process*, p. 200.

35. World Bank, *Anticorruption in Transition*, p. 32.

36. Open Society Institute, *Monitoring the EU Accession Process*, pp. 441–42.

37. Ibid., p. 501.

38. Ibid., p. 164.

39. World Bank, "New Frontiers in Diagnosing and Combating Corruption," *Notes* no. 7 (Oct. 1998), p. 2.

40. Aviezer Tucker, "Higher Education on Trial," *East European Constitutional Review* 9, no. 3 (Summer 2000), pp. 88–89, speaks of state university corruption by the communist academic nomenklatura.

41. Aviezer Tucker, "Western Academic Aid to Eastern Europe," *Telos* no. 102 (Winter 1995), pp. 149–58.

42. Joel Hellman and Daniel Kaufmann, "Confronting the Challenge of State Capture in Transition Economies," *Finance and Development* (Sept. 2001), pp. 31–32.

43. World Bank, *Anticorruption in Transition*, p. 2.

44. Council of Europe, Group of States Against Corruption, *Evaluation Report on Georgia*, June 15, 2001, p. 10.

45. Open Society Institute, *Monitoring the EU Accession Process*, p. 509.

46. Roustam Kaliyev, "Russia's Organized Crime: A Typology, Part I," *Eurasia Insight* (Feb. 6, 2002), p. 1.

47. Ibid., p. 2.

48. Andras Sajo, "Corruption, Clientelism, and the Future of the Constitutional State in Eastern Europe," *East European Constitutional Review* 7, no. 2 (Spring 1998), p. 38.

49. Shelley, "Crime and Corruption," p. 244.

50. Open Society Institute, *Monitoring the EU Accession Process*, p. 579.

51. Ibid.

52. See the review symposium on David Stark and Laszlo Bruszt, "Postsocialist Pathways: Transforming Politics and Property in East Central Europe" (Cambridge, UK: Cambridge University Press, 1998) in *East European Constitutional Review* 9, no. 1/2 (Winter/Spring 2000), pp. 101–20, especially Venelin I. Ganev, "Notes on Networking in Postcommunist Societies," ibid., pp. 101–7.

53. John Higley, Judith Kullberg, and Jan Pakulski, "The Persistence of Postcommunist Elites," *Journal of Democracy* 7, no. 2 (1996), pp. 133–47. The article summarizes many other studies. See also Olga Kryshtanovskaya and Stephen White, "From Soviet *Nomenklatura* to Russian Elite," *Europe-Asia Studies* 48, no. 5 (1996), pp. 711–33.

54. Heiko Pleines, "Large-scale Corruption and Rent-seeking in the Russian Banking Sector," in *Economic Crime in Russia*, ed. Alena V. Ledeneva and Marina Kurkchiyan (The Hague: Kluwer Law International, 2000), p. 191.

55. Peter Eigen, "Combating Corruption around the World," *Journal of Democracy* 7, no. 1 (Jan. 1996), p. 160.

56. Cited in Vitaly A. Nomokonov, "On Strategies for Combating Corruption in Russia," *Demokratizatsiya* 8, no. 1 (Winter 2000), p. 125.

57. Open Society Institute, *Monitoring the EU Accession Process*, p. 461.

58. James H. Anderson, *Corruption in Slovakia: Results of Diagnostic Surveys* (Washington, D.C.: World Bank, 2000), p. 50.

59. Ibid., pp. 456, 492.

60. Caroline Humphrey, "Dirty Business, 'Normal Life,' and the Dream of Law," in *Economic Crime in Russia*, ed. Ledeneva and Kurkchiyan, p. 178.

61. Grigory Yavlinsky, "Russia's Phony Capitalism," *Foreign Affairs* 77, no. 3 (May/ June 1998), p. 78.

62. Personal communications.

63. Open Society Institute, *Monitoring the EU Accession Process*, p. 454.

64. Louise Shelley, "Crime, Organized Crime and Corruption in the Transitional Period: The Russian Case," paper presented at the Law and Society conference, Budapest, July 4–7, 2001, p. 1.

65. Ibid., p. 9.

66. Pidluska, conference presentation reported in Lyle, "Ukraine under Corruption Spotlight."

67. Sajo, "Clientelism and Extortion," p. 15.

68. Ibid., p. 44.

69. Federico Varese, "The Transition to the Market and Corruption in Post-socialist Russia," *Political Studies* 45 (1997), p. 583.

70. Shelley, "Crime and Corruption," p. 252.

71. Louise I. Shelley, "Corruption in the Post-Yeltsin Era," *East European Constitutional Review* (Winter/Spring 2000), p. 73.

72. *RFL/RL Research Report I* (Aug. 14, 2000). Retrieved from www.rferl.org.

73. *New York Times*, June 17, 2001, p. 12.

74. The notion of "rule through law" has been formulated by Mykola Riabchuk, "Perilous Ways to Freedom: Independent Mass Media in the Blackmail State," paper presented at the special convention of the Association for Nationalities Studies, Forli, Italy, June 4–9, 2002, p. 7.

75. Roman Frydman, Kenneth Murphy, and Andrzej Rapaczynski, *Capitalism with a Comrade's Face: Studies in Postcommunist Transition* (Budapest: Central European University Press, 1998), p. 14.

76. Lack of evidence was the main reason cited why only 1,925 convictions were obtained out of 5,422 cases of administrative misdemeanors relating to corruption sent to trial in Ukraine in 1997. Peter H. Solomon, Jr. and Todd S. Foglesong, "The Two Faces of Crime in Post-Soviet Ukraine," *East European Constitutional Review* (Summer 2000), p. 75.

77. Open Society Institute, *Monitoring the EU Accession Process*, p. 266.

78. Nomokonov, "On Strategies for Combating Corruption in Russia," p. 124.

79. Jens C. Andvig, "Issues of Corruption: A Policy-Oriented Survey of Research," manuscript, 2001, p. 9.

80. *Moscow Times*, Jan. 13, 2000, as reported in *RFL/RL Research Report*, Part I (Jan. 14, 2000).

81. Open Society Institute, *Monitoring the EU Accession Process*, 143; also Lubomir Lizal and Evzen Kocenda, "Corruption and Anticorruption in the Czech Republic," William Davidson Institute Working Paper #345 (Ann Arbor, MI, Oct. 2000), p. 22.

82. Susan Rose-Ackerman, "Reducing Bribery in the Public Sector," in *Corruption and Democracy: Political Institutions, Processes and Corruption in Transition States in East-Central Europe and in the Former Soviet Union*, ed. Duc V. Trang (Budapest: Institute for Constitutional and Legislative Policy, 1994), p. 21.

83. Keith A. Darden, "Blackmail as a Tool of State Domination: Ukraine under Kuchma," *East European Constitutional Review* 10, no. 2/3 (Spring/Summer 2001), pp. 67–71.

84. Ibid., p. 71.

85. Akos Szilagyi, "Kompromat and Corruption in Russia," in *Political Corruption in Transition: A Skeptic's Handbook*, ed. Stephen Kotkin and Andras Sajo (Budapest: Central European University Press, 2002), p. 209.

86. For an exposé how this works in the Czech Republic, see Jeffrey M. Jordan, "Patronage and Corruption in the Czech Republic, Part I," *RFE/RL East European Perspectives* 4, no. 4 (20 Feb. 2002).

87. Leonid Polishchuk, "Decentralization in Russia: Impact for Quality of Governance," paper presented at the IRIS Center Conference on Collective Action and Corruption in Emerging Economies, Washington, D.C., May 1999, p. 20.

88. World Bank, *Anticorruption in Transition*, p. 46.

89. Quentin Peel, "From Glasnost to Gazprom," *Financial Times*, Apr. 30, 2001, p. 13.

Notes to Chapter 3

1. Peter Ford, "Poland Lifts Veil on Corruption," *Christian Science Monitor*, Mar. 7, 2003.

2. For more details, see the end of this chapter.

3. Robert D. Behn, *Rethinking Democratic Accountability* (Washington, D.C.: Brookings Institution, 2001), pp. 83–84.

4. Ivan Krastev, "Corruption, Anti-Corruption Sentiments, and the Rule of Law," in Andrea Krizsan and Violetta Zentai, *Reshaping Globalization: Multilateral Dialogues and New Policy Initiatives* (Budapest: Central European Press, 2003), pp. 135–56.

5. James H. Anderson, *Diagnostic Surveys of Corruption in Romania* (Washington, D.C.: World Bank, 2001), pp. vi, 8.

6. For an elaboration see Chapter 5; see also Wayne DiFranceisco and Zvi Gitelman, "Soviet Political Culture and 'Covert Participation' in Policy Implementation," *American Political Science Review* 78, no. 2 (June 1984), p. 604.

7. Transparency International–Latvia, *The Face of Corruption in Latvia*, report [in Latvian] (Riga: Apr. 2000), pp. 62, 130. The survey had 2,001 respondents and the sample was designed to represent the general population.

8. James H. Anderson, *Corruption in Slovakia: Results of Diagnostic Surveys* (Washington, D.C.: World Bank, 2000), p. 16.

9. William L. Miller, Ase B. Grodeland, and Tatyana Y. Koshechkina, *A Culture of Corruption? Coping with Government in Post-Communist Europe* (Budapest: Central European University Press, 2001), p. 85.

10. Ibid., p. 84.

11. Ibid., p. 83.

12. Anderson, *Corruption in Slovakia*, p. 23.

13. Agnese Barstad, "Culture of Corruption? Interpreting Corruption in Soviet and Post-Soviet Contexts," M.A. thesis, University of Bergen, Norway (2003), p. 149.

14. Ibid., p. 151.

15. Anderson, *Corruption in Slovakia*, p. 7.

16. Ibid.

17. Susan Rose-Ackerman, "Trust and Honesty in Post-Socialist Systems," *Kyklos* 54, nos. 2/3 (2001), p. 424.

18. Transparency International–Latvia, *The Face of Corruption in Latvia*, p. 19.

19. James H. Anderson, *Corruption in Latvia: Survey Evidence* (Washington, D.C.: World Bank, Dec. 16, 1998), p. 10; Anderson, *Diagnostic Surveys of Corruption in Romania*, p. 5.

20. Rebecca Case, *UNDP and Other Anti-Corruption Efforts in Bulgaria*, a case study prepared for the Donor Standards in Anti-Corruption Project (Cambridge, MA, Sept. 2002), p. 15.

21. Miller, Grodeland, and Koshechkina, *A Culture of Corruption?* pp. 100–101.

22. Anderson, *Corruption in Slovakia*, p. 32.

23. William L. Miller, Ase B. Grodeland, and Tatyana Y. Koshechkina, "Are the People Victims or Accomplices? The Use of Presents and Bribes to Influence Officials in Eastern Europe," Discussion Paper #6 (Budapest: Open Society Institute, 1998), p. 5.

24. Miller, Grodeland, and Koshechkina, *A Culture of Corruption?* p. 105.

25. Ibid., p. 106.

26. Ibid., p. 105.

27. Ibid.

28. Ibid., pp. 208–9.

29. Open Society Institute, *Monitoring the EU Accession Process: Corruption and Anti-corruption Policy* (Budapest, 2002), pp. 401–2.

30. Cited in Ingrīda Puce, "Reports about Corruption in Latvia by International Organizations (EU, EC, OECD, WB) and Their Influence on the Political Agenda of Political and Economic Elites, 1992–2001" [in Latvian], M.A. thesis, University of Latvia, Department of Communication, Riga (2002), p. 40.

31. Pyotr Magdashian, "Battling Corruption in Armenia," *Local Government Brief* (Summer 2003), p. 13.

32. Specifically, the indexes are based on the 1999 Business Environment and Enterprise Performance Survey (BEEPS). World Bank, *Anticorruption in Transition: A Contribution to the Policy Debate* (Washington, D.C., Sept. 2000).

33. Ibid., p. xvii.

34. Ibid., p. 3.

35. Ibid., pp. xvi, 89–90.

36. Ibid., p. xix; for details on the methodology, p. 5.

37. Cheryl Gray, Joel Hellman, and Randi Ryterman, *Anticorruption in Transition 2: Corruption in Enterprise-State Interactions in Europe and Central Asia 1999–2002* (Washington, D.C.: World Bank, 2004), p. 50. Retrieved from www.worldbank.org.

38. Ibid., p. xii.

39. Anderson, *Diagnostic Surveys of Corruption in Romania*, pp. 6–7.

40. Klāvs Sedlenieks, "Corruption Close-Up" [in Latvian], unpublished report (Riga: Soros Foundation, 2000–2001), p. 8.

41. Ingrīda Puce, "The Corruption Theme in Agenda Setting and the Journalist's Role in It" [in Latvian], thesis for attainment of a bachelor's degree, Department of Communications, University of Latvia, Riga (1999), p. 29.

42. Ibid., pp. 38–41; Transparency International–Latvia, *The Face of Corruption in Latvia*, pp. 232–36.

43. Open Society Institute, *Monitoring the EU Accession Process*, pp. 476–77.

44. Ibid., p. 488.

45. Ibid., pp. 479–80.

46. Ibid., p. 287.

47. Transparency International, *Global Corruption Report 2003*, p. 168. Retrieved from www.globalcorruptionreport.org.

48. Ivan Krastev and Georgy Ganev, "Do Uncorrupt Governments in Corrupt Countries Have Incentives to Launch Anticorruption Campaigns?" *East European Constitutional Review* 12, no. 2/3 (Spring/Summer 2003), pp. 90–91.

49. Transparency International, *Global Corruption Report 2004* (London: Pluto Press, 2004), p. 243; Ford, "Poland Lifts Veil on Corruption"; "Let the Circus Begin," *Poland Monthly*, Mar. 5, 2003; *World Press Review Online*, Apr. 30, 2004, www.worldpress.org.Europe/1098.cfm.

50. Krastev and Ganev, "Do Uncorrupt Governments in Corrupt Countries Have Incentives to Launch Anticorruption Campaigns?"

51. Ibid., p. 88, and Open Society Institute, *Monitoring the EU Accession Process*, pp. 82–84.

52. Puce, "The Corruption Theme in Agenda Setting," p. 33.

Notes to Chapter 4

1. Michael Johnston, "Corruption as a Process," in *Coping with Corruption in a Borderless World*, ed. Maurice Punch et al. (Deventer: Kluwer Law and Taxation Publishers, 1993), p. 52.

2. Agnese Barstad, "Culture of Corruption? Interpreting Corruption in Soviet and Post-Soviet Contexts," M.A. thesis, University of Bergen, Norway (2003), p. 81.

3. Frederick Stapenhurst and Sahr J. Kpundeh, "Public Participation in the Fight against Corruption," *Canadian Journal of Development Studies* 19 (1998), p. 501.

4. Much of this material was collected during research trips in Latvia. I am grateful for travel grants from the International Research and Exchanges Board (May 2002) and from the University of Illinois at Chicago (Aug. 2002 and May 2003).

5. Alejandro Moreno, "Corruption and Democracy: A Cultural Assessment," *Comparative Sociology* 1, nos. 3/4 (2002), pp. 495–507.

6. Ibid., pp. 500–501.

7. Ibid., p. 496.

8. Rein Taagepera, "Baltic Values and Corruption in Comparative Context," *Journal of Baltic Studies* 33, no. 3 (2002), pp. 243–58.

9. Moreno, "Corruption and Democracy," p. 504.

10. Carole Pateman, "Political Culture, Political Structure and Political Change," *British Journal of Political Science* 1 (July 1971), pp. 291–305.

11. Andras Sajo, "From Corruption to Extortion: Conceptualization of Post-Communist Corruption," *Crime, Law and Social Change* 40 (2003), pp. 171–94, p. 172.

12. James H. Anderson, *Corruption in Latvia: Survey Evidence* (Washington, D.C.: World Bank, Dec. 16, 1998), p. 25.

13. Speech by Latvian politician Vilis Krištopāns, *Valdības Vēstnesis*, Apr. 2, 1999.

14. Open Society Institute, *Monitoring the EU Accession Process: Corruption and Anti-corruption Policy* (Budapest, 2002), p. 586.

15. Ibid., p. 83.

16. Ibid., pp. 439–40.

17. Ibid., p. 443.

18. Ingrīda Puce, "Reports about Corruption in Latvia by International Organizations (EU, EC, OECD, WB) and Their Influence on the Political Agenda of Political and Economic Elites, 1992–2001" [in Latvian], M.A. thesis, University of Latvia, Department of Communication, Riga (2002), p. 24.

19. Lena Kolarska-Bobinska, "The Impact of Corruption on Legitimacy and Authority in New Democracies," in *Political Corruption in Transition: A Skeptic's Handbook*, ed. Stephen Kotkin and Andras Sajo (Budapest: Central European University Press, 2002), p. 324.

20. Cited in Puce, "Reports about Corruption in Latvia," p. 34.

21. Anton Steen, "How Elites View Corruption and Trust in Post-Soviet States," in Transparency International, *Global Corruption Report 2004* (London: Pluto Press, 2004), pp. 323–25.

22. "Corruption in Business—It Pays Off and Is Unavoidable" [in Latvian], *Kapitāls*, no. 10, 1999, pp. 5–9.

23. Ibid., entire.

24. "Bribery" [in Latvian], *Kapitāls*, no. 6 (2001), p. 23.

25. Ibid., p. 25.

26. Ibid., p. 28.

27. *Latvijas Vēstnesis*, Dec. 5, 2000.

28. Interview in *Moskovskie Novosti*, July 29, 2002, cited in V. Shlapentokh, "Russia's Acquiescence to Corruption Makes the State Machine Inept," *Communist and Post-Communist Studies* 36 (2003), p. 156.

29. Radio Free Europe/Radio Liberty Newsline, Mar. 14, 2002, cited in Open Society Institute, *Monitoring the EU Accession Process*, p. 468.

30. Open Society Institute, *Monitoring the EU Accession Process*, p. 241.

31. Seventy-eight percent of respondents said so in 1997, compared to 84 percent in 1999. Kolarska-Bobinska, "The Impact of Corruption," p. 322.

32. Rebecca Case, *UNDP and Other Anti-Corruption Efforts in Bulgaria*, a case study prepared for the Donor Standards in Anti-Corruption Project (Cambridge, MA, Sept. 2002), p. 7.

33. Author's notes while listening to debates about corruption at various events in Latvia, August 2002.

34. Deputy Ilga Kreituse, cited in *Vakara Ziņas*, June 5, 1997.

35. Sandra Steinerte, *Essay for Youth Contest* [in Latvian] (Transparency International–Latvia: Riga, 2002), p. 3.

36. Open Society Institute, *Monitoring the EU Accession Process*, p. 460.

37. Alina Mungiu-Pippidi, "Culture of Corruption or Accountability Deficit?" *East European Constitutional Review* 11/12, nos. 4/1 (Fall 2002/Winter 2003), p. 80.

38. Pyotr Magdashian, "Battling Corruption in Armenia," *Local Government Brief* (Summer 2003), p. 13.

39. Kiva Maidanik, "Corruption, Criminalization, Kleptocracy: 'Transition Phase'? Dead-End Branch? Foundational Structures?" *Russian Politics and Law* 36, no. 1 (Jan./Feb. 1998), p. 23.

40. Peter Ford, "Poland Lifts Veil on Corruption," *Christian Science Monitor*, Mar. 7, 2003.

41. This is a rendition of the difficult-to-translate idiomatic expression "Vārna vārnai acī neknābj."
42. Notes from public discussions and Internet chat rooms.
43. Barstad, "Culture of Corruption?" p. 91.
44. Ibid.
45. Klāvs Sedlenieks, "Corruption Close-Up" [in Latvian], unpublished report (Riga: Soros Fund, 2000–2001), pp. 15–16.
46. Ibid., p. 20.
47. Open Society Institute, *Monitoring the EU Accession Process*, p. 559.
48. Ibid., p. 523.
49. Svetlana P. Glinkina, "The Ominous Landscape of Russian Corruption," *Transitions* (Mar. 1998) (no pagination).
50. Kolarska-Bobinska, "The Impact of Corruption," pp. 323–24. Very similar findings for a survey in November 2000 are reported in Open Society Institute, *Monitoring the EU Accession Process*, p. 402.
51. Transparency International–Latvia, *The Face of Corruption in Latvia*, report [in Latvian] (Riga: Apr. 2000), p. 190.
52. The sample is not intended to be representative; it consists of fifteen men and five women, half of them between thirty to thirty-five years old, and four others between twenty-five and twenty-nine years of age. The author focused on people active in business or public institutions, and used a snowball technique to find his respondents. Sedlenieks, "Corruption Close-Up," pp. 3–8.
53. Ibid., pp. 13–14, 18.
54. Ibid., p. 19.
55. Ibid., p. 22.
56. Magdashian, "Battling Corruption in Armenia," p. 13.
57. See, for example, William Mishler and Richard Rose, "Trust, Distrust and Skepticism: Popular Evaluations of Civil and Political Institutions in Post-Communist Societies," *Journal of Politics* 59, no. 2 (May 1997), pp. 418–51, and Susan Rose-Ackerman, "Trust and Honesty in Post-Socialist Systems," *Kyklos* 54, nos. 2/3 (2001), pp. 415–44.
58. Lubomir Lizal and Evzen Kocenda, "Corruption and Anticorruption in the Czech Republic," William Davidson Institute Working Paper #345 (Ann Arbor, MI, Oct. 2000), p. 8.
59. Mishler and Rose, "Trust, Distrust and Skepticism," p. 429.
60. Sedlenieks, "Corruption Close-Up," p. 39. Similar arguments appear on pp. 19, 41.
61. Alena V. Ledeneva, *Unwritten Rules: How Russia Really Works* (London: Centre for European Reform, 2001), p. 10.
62. See various data and arguments in Cheng Chen and Rudra Sil, "Bringing Legitimacy Back In: The State of the State in 'Democratic' Russia and 'Authoritarian' China," paper presented at the annual meeting of the American Political Science Association, Boston, Aug. 28–Sept. 1, 2002.
63. Data from an early 1998 national representative survey of 1,500 respondents cited in ibid., p. 8.
64. Barstad, "Culture of Corruption?" pp. 175–76.
65. Ibid., p. 82.
66. Delna, p. 198.
67. Istvan Hagelmayer, "Opening Statement," in *Corruption and Democracy:*

Political Institutions, Processes and Corruption in Transition States in East-Central Europe and in the Former Soviet Union, ed. Duc V. Trang (Budapest: Institute for Constitutional and Legislative Policy, 1994), p. 12; for a similar statement see Ivan Miklos, *Corruption Risks in the Privatisation Process* (Bratislava, May 1995), p. 12.

68. Open Society Institute, *Monitoring the EU Accession Process,* p. 140.

69. Anderson, *Corruption in Slovakia,* p. 58. Fewer than 12 percent of the officials surveyed in 1999 indicated that they would certainly report a peer who accepted a bribe.

70..Open Society Institute, *Monitoring the EU Accession Process,* p. 558.

71. World Bank, *Corruption in Georgia: Survey Evidence,* report (Washington, D.C., June 2000), p. 19.

72. In the 1999 survey in Slovakia of public officials, of those who answered, 18 percent said that bribes would be shared with colleagues and 5 percent said they would be shared with superiors. Other surveys note higher rates of bribe sharing in other countries. Anderson, *Corruption in Slovakia,* p. 57.

73. Cited in Federico Varese, *The Russian Mafia: Private Protection in a New Market Economy* (Oxford University Press, 2001), p. 89.

74. Social Correlative Data Survey, "Attitudes Toward Corruption among Residents of Latvia" [in Latvian], unpublished report (Riga: PHARE project, Mar. 2001).

75. Ibid. Since the data are available only in the aggregate percentage form, no tests for significant statistical differences were undertaken. Percentage results suggest that responses differ little by nationality, gender, age, education, and other demographic indicators.

76. William L. Miller, Ase B. Grodeland, and Tatyana Y. Koshechkina, *A Culture of Corruption? Coping with Government in Post-Communist Europe* (Budapest: Central European University Press, 2001), p. 32.

77. James H. Anderson, *Diagnostic Surveys of Corruption in Romania* (Washington, D.C.: World Bank, 2000), p. 60.

78. Ibid., p. 29.

79. Barstad, "Culture of Corruption?" p. 165

80. Seymour Martin Lipset and Gabriel Salman Lenz, "Corruption, Culture, and Markets," in *Culture Matters: How Values Shape Human Progress,* ed. L.E. Harrison and S.P. Huntington (New York: Basic Books, 2000), pp. 112–25.

Notes to Chapter 5

1. As cited in Steven J. Staats, "Corruption in the Soviet System," *Problems of Communism* 21 (Jan./Feb. 1972), p. 43.

2. Valerie Bunce, *Subversive Institutions: The Design and Destruction of Socialism and the State* (Cambridge, UK: Cambridge University Press, 1999), p. xii.

3. For a similar statement, see Michael Johnston, "The Political Consequences of Corruption: A Reassessment," *Comparative Politics* 18, no. 4 (July 1986), p. 463.

4. Allen Kassof, "The Administered Society: Totalitarianism without Terror," *World Politics* 16, no. 4 (July 1964), pp. 558–75.

5. Ken Jowitt, "Soviet Neotraditionalism: The Political Corruption of a Leninist Regime," *Soviet Studies* 35, no. 3 (July 1983), pp. 275–97.

6. John M. Kramer, "Political Corruption in the U.S.S.R.," *Western Political Quarterly* 30, no. 2 (June 1977), p. 218.

7. William A. Clark, "Crime and Punishment in Soviet Officialdom, 1965–90," *Europe-Asia Studies* 45, no. 2 (1993), p. 260.

8. William A. Clark, "Soviet Official Corruption under Perestroika: A Balance Sheet," *Current Politics and Economics of Russia* 2, no. 3 (1992), p. 212.

9. Charles A. Schwartz, "Corruption and Political Development in the USSR," *Comparative Politics* (July 1979), pp. 437–40, quote from p. 431. See also Konstantin M. Simis, *USSR, The Corrupt Society: The Secret World of Soviet Capitalism* (New York: Simon and Schuster, 1982), which provides numerous details about what the author see as a pervasively corrupt political establishment.

10. Leslie Holmes, *The End of Communist Power: Anti-Corruption Campaigns and Legitimation Crisis* (New York: Oxford University Press, 1993), p. 7.

11. Staats, "Corruption in the Soviet System," p. 40.

12. *Pravda*, Aug. 16, 1972, stated that this happens with "astounding frequency." Kramer, "Political Corruption in the U.S.S.R.," p. 222.

13. Kramer, "Political Corruption in the U.S.S.R.," pp. 222–23.

14. Marie Mendras, "Rule by Bureaucracy in Russia," in *Democracy and Corruption in Europe*, ed. Donatella Della Porta and Yves Meny (London: Pinter, 1997), pp. 120.

15. Agnese Barstad, "Culture of Corruption? Interpreting Corruption in Soviet and Post-Soviet Contexts," M.A. thesis, University of Bergen, Norway (2003), p. 52.

16. Alena V. Ledeneva, *Russia's Economy of Favors: Blat, Networking and Informal Exchange* (Cambridge, UK: Cambridge University Press, 1998), p. 1.

17. Ibid., p. 39 and others.

18. James R. Millar, "The Little Deal: Breshnev's Contribution to Acquisitive Socialism," *Slavic Review* 44, no. 4 (1985), p. 702.

19. See Gabriel Ben-Dor, "Corruption, Institutionalization, and Political Development: The Revisionist Theses Revisited," *Comparative Political Studies* 7, no. 1 (1974), pp. 63–83.

20. Clark, "Soviet Official Corruption under Perestroika," p. 209.

21. Millar, "The Little Deal," p. 695.

22. Ibid., pp. 695–96.

23. Ibid., p.700.

24. Ibid., p. 698.

25. Schwartz, "Corruption and Political Development in the USSR," pp. 437–40.

26. Ilja Srubar, "War der reale Sozialismus modern? Versuch einer strukturellen Bestimmung," *Kölner Zeitschrift für Soziologie und Sozialpsychologie* 43, no. 3 (1991), pp. 415–32, especially p. 424.

27. Antoni Z. Kaminski, "Coercion, Corruption, and Reform: State and Society in the Soviet-type Socialist Regime," *Journal of Theoretical Politics* 1, no. 1 (1989), p. 87.

28. Schwartz, "Corruption and Political Development in the USSR," p. 441.

29. Rasma Karklins, "Explaining Regime Change in the USSR," *Europe-Asia Studies* 46 (formerly *Soviet Studies*), no. 1 (Jan. 1994), pp. 29–45.

30. For a view that clientelism was more of an "addendum" to overall social relations, see S.N. Eisenstadt and Luis Roninger, "Clientelism in Communist Systems: A Comparative Perspective," *Studies in Comparative Communism* 14, no. 2 and 3 (Summer/Autumn 1981), pp. 233–45.

31. Jacek Tarkowski, "Patronage in Centralized Socialist Systems," *International Political Science Review* 4 (1983), pp. 495–518; Gyula Józsa, "Politische Seilschaften

in der Sowjetunion," *Berichte des Bundesinstituts für ostwissenschaftliche und internationale Studien*, no. 31, 1981.

32. John P. Willerton, *Patronage and Politics in the USSR* (Cambridge, UK: Cambridge University Press, 1992), p. 5.

33. Ibid., pp. 10–13.

34. Ibid., pp. 12–19.

35. Ibid., pp. 19–20.

36. Ibid., p. 228.

37. Jowitt, "Soviet Neotraditionalism," p. 288.

38. Milovan Djilas, *The New Class: An Analysis of the Communist System* (New York: Praeger, 1957); Michael Voslensky, *Nomenklatura: Anatomy of the Soviet Ruling Class* (London: Bodley Hall, 1984).

39. Jacek Szymanderski, "Moral Order and Corruption in Transition to the Market: Popular Beliefs and Their Underpinnings," *Communist Economies and Economic Transformation* 7, no. 2 (1995), pp. 249–57.

40. Willerton, *Patronage and Politics in the USSR*, p. 20.

41. Kaminski, "Coercion, Corruption, and Reform," p. 87. The article was submitted for publication in January 1988. The timing is important in light of subsequent claims that "nobody" foresaw the collapse of the communist regimes.

42. Laszlo Bruszt, "Market Making as State Making: Constitutions and Economic Development in Post-Communist Eastern Europe," *Constitutional Political Economy* 13 (2002), p. 55.

43. Roman Frydman, Kenneth Murphy, and Andrzej Rapaczynski, *Capitalism with a Comrade's Face: Studies in Postcommunist Transition* (Budapest: Central European University Press,1998), p. 13. Studies of the darker side of market transitions have proliferated in recent years. For a summary review, see Johanna Granville, "'Demokratizatsiya' and 'Prikhvatizatsiya': The Russian Kleptocracy and Rise of Organized Crime," *Demokratizatsiya* 11, no. 3 (Summer 2003), pp. 449–57.

44. Steven L. Solnick, "The Breakdown of Hierarchies in the Soviet Union and China: A Neoinstitutional Perspective," *World Politics* 48 (Jan. 1996), pp. 228–29.

45. Daniel Kaufmann and Paul Siegelbaum, "Privatization and Corruption in Transition Economies," *Journal of International Affairs* 50, no. 2 (Winter 1996), p. 428.

46. Frydman, Murphy, and Rapaczynski, *Capitalism with a Comrade's Face*, p. 13.

47. Barstad, "Culture of Corruption?" p. 71.

48. Mendras, "Rule by Bureaucracy in Russia," pp. 123, 118.

49. Marshall I. Goldman, *The Piratization of Russia: Russian Reform Goes Awry* (London and New York: Routledge, 2003), pp. 156–73.

50. Solnick, "The Breakdown of Hierarchies in the Soviet Union and China," p. 7.

51. John M. Kramer, "The Politics of Corruption," *Current History* 97, no. 621 (Oct. 1998), p. 330. There are many studies of privatization; for example, Edward P. Lazear, *Economic Transition in Eastern Europe and Russia: Realities of Reform* (Stanford, CA: Hoover Institution Press, 1995), and Bartlomiej Kaminiski, ed., *Economic Transition in Russia and the New States of Eurasia* (Armonk, NY: M.E. Sharpe, 1996), pp. 206–19.

52. Kramer, "The Politics of Corruption," p. 330.

53. Louise Shelley, "Crime and Corruption," in *Developments in Russian Politics*, ed. Stephen White, Alex Pravda, and Zvi Gitelman (Hampshire: Palgrave 2001), p. 247.

54. Susan Rose-Ackerman, *Corruption and Government* (Cambridge, UK: Cambridge University Press, 1999), p. 35.

55. Federico Varese, "The Transition to the Market and Corruption in Post-socialist Russia," *Political Studies* 45 (1997), p. 581.

56. Shelley, "Crime and Corruption," p. 244.

57. Eric Hanley, "Cadre Capitalism in Hungary and Poland: Property Accumulation among Communist-Era Elites," *East European Politics and Societies* 14, no. 1 (Winter 2000), pp. 143–80. The study is based on an unusual large-scale survey of the original "nomenklatura lists" naming the individuals who occupied top positions in the party, state, and economy in 1988.

58. Ibid., p. 175.

59. Ibid., pp. 151–52.

60. Goldman, *The Piratization of Russia*, p. 97.

61. Ibid., pp. 101–4, 195–209.

62. William L. Miller, Ase B. Grodeland, and Tatyana Y. Koshechkina, *A Culture of Corruption? Coping with Government in Post-Communist Europe* (Budapest: Central European University Press, 2001), pp. 108–11, report that an average of 85 percent of respondents in their survey said persons needing something from an official would approach the official through a contact, and 52 percent had done so themselves during the last few years.

63. M. Lonkila, "Informal Exchange Relations in Post-Soviet Russia: A Comparative Perspective," *Sociological Research Online* 2, no. 2 (June 1997), p. 19. Retrieved from www.socresonline.org.uk/socresonline/2/2/9.html.

64. Donatella Della Porta, "The Vicious Circles of Corruption in Italy," in *Democracy and Corruption in Europe*, ed. Donatella Della Porta and Yves Meny (London: Pinter, 1997), p. 36.

65. Alena V. Ledeneva, "Non-Transparency of the Post-Communist Economies: The Relationship between the Formal and the Informal," draft paper prepared for Honesty and Trust project of Collegium Budapest, Oct. 2002; the specific statistics are based on a study cited in *Vedemosti*, May 22, 2002.

66. To quote legal scholar Andrej Judin, "our people will not call a lawyer when they have a problem, but will seek out an acquaintance who has had similar difficulties." Presentation at Conference on Law and Society, Riga, May 4, 2002.

67. Ibid.

68. Attila Agh, "From Nomenclatura to Clientura: The Emergence of New Political Elites in East-Central Europe," in *Stabilising Fragile Democracies: Comparing New Party Systems in Southern and Eastern Europe*, ed. Geoffrey Pridham and Paul G. Lewis (London: Routledge, 1996), p. 58.

69. Agh (ibid., p. 59) argues that this counter-elite consists of some 10,000 people.

70. Johnston, "The Political Consequences of Corruption," p. 469.

71. Juan J. Linz and Alfred Stepan, *Problems of Democratic Transition and Consolidation: Southern Europe, South America, and Post-Communist Europe* (Baltimore: Johns Hopkins University Press, 1996), pp. 66, 70.

72. Peter J. Stavrakis, *State-Building in Post-Soviet Russia: The Chicago Boys and the Decline of Administrative Capacity*, Kennan Institute Occasional Paper #254 (Oct. 1993), p. 4.

73. Michael McFaul, "State Power, Institutional Change, and the Politics of Privatization in Russia," *World Politics* 47 (Jan. 1995), pp. 210–43; Varese, "The Transition to the Market and Corruption in Post-socialist Russia," pp. 579–96.

74. Joel S. Hellman, "Winners Take All: The Politics of Partial Reform in Postcommunist Transitions," *World Politics* 50 (Jan. 1998), pp. 203–34.

75. Alena V. Ledeneva, *Unwritten Rules: How Russia Really Works* (London: Centre for European Reform, 2001), p. 12.

76. Marc Morje Howard, *Free Not to Participate: The Weakness of Civil Society in Post-Communist Europe* (Glasgow: Centre for the Study of Public Policy, 2000), p. 36.

Notes to Chapter 6

1. John T. Noonan, *Bribes* (Berkeley: University of California Press, 1984), p. 704.

2. Raymond Guess, *Public Goods, Private Goods* (Princeton, NJ: Princeton University Press, 2001), p. 37.

3. An overview of regime types can be found in Juan J. Linz and Alfred Stepan, *Problems of Democratic Transition and Consolidation: Southern Europe, South America, and Post-Communist Europe* (Baltimore: Johns Hopkins University Press, 1996).

4. I thank Professor Maija Kūle of the University of Latvia for most clearly arguing this point in a personal discussion.

5. Hans Nilsson, "Substantive Criminal Law: Corruption and Money Laundering," in *Corruption and Democracy: Political Institutions, Processes and Corruption in Transition States in East-Central Europe and in the Former Soviet Union*, ed. Duc V. Trang (Budapest: Institute for Constitutional and Legislative Policy, 1994), p. 90.

6. Marie Mendras, "Rule by Bureaucracy in Russia," in *Democracy and Corruption in Europe*, ed. Donatella Della Porta and Yves Meny (London: Pinter, 1997), p. 128; also Ken G. Jowitt, "Soviet Neotraditionalism: The Political Corruption of a Leninist Regime," *Soviet Studies* 35, no. 3 (July 1983), pp. 275–97; and discussion in Chapter 5.

7. Carl J. Friedrich, *The Pathology of Politics: Violence, Betrayal, Corruption, Secrecy and Propaganda* (New York: Harper & Row, 1972), p. 16.

8. Bertolt Brecht, *Mother Courage and Her Children: A Chronicle of the Thirty Years' War* (New York: Grove Press, 1996), p. 61.

9. Lawrence Rosen, *The Culture of Islam: Changing Aspects of Contemporary Muslim Life* (Chicago: University of Chicago Press, 2002), pp. 14–15.

10. William L. Miller, Ase B. Grodeland, and Tatyana Y. Koshechkina, *A Culture of Corruption? Coping with Government in Post-Communist Europe* (Budapest: Central European University Press, 2001), p. 135.

11. Cheng Chen and Rudra Sil, "Bringing Legitimacy Back In: The State of the State in 'Democratic' Russia and 'Authoritarian' China," paper presented at the annual meeting of the American Political Science Association, Boston, Aug. 28–Sept. 1, 2002, p. 6.

12. Philip Pettit, *Republicanism: A Theory of Freedom and Government* (Oxford: Clarendon Press, 1997), p. 129.

13. J. Peter Euben, "Corruption," in *Political Innovation and Conceptual Change*, ed. Terence Ball, James Farr, and Russell L. Hanson (Cambridge, UK: Cambridge University Press, 1989), p. 227.

14. Paul Barry Clarke, *Citizenship* (Boulder, CO: Pluto Press, 1993), pp. 4–11.

15. Euben, "Corruption," p. 228.

16. Ibid., pp. 228–29.

17. Derek Heater, *The Civic Idea in World History, Politics, and Education* (London: Longman, 1990), p. 161.

18. S.M. Shumer, "Machiavelli: Republican Politics and Its Corruption," *Political Theory* 7, no. 1 (Feb. 1979), p. 9.

19. Ibid., pp. 10–11.

20. Joint Project Against Corruption in the Republic of Hungary, *Preliminary Assessment and Feedback on the Corruption Pilot Study*, Global Programme Against Corruption Working Paper (Mar. 2000), p. 43.

21. Michael J. Sandel, *Democracy's Discontent: America in Search of a Public Philosophy* (Cambridge, MA: Belknap Press of Harvard University Press, 1996), p. 130.

22. Bill Brugger, *Republican Theory and Political Thought: Virtuous or Virtual?* (New York: St. Martin's Press, 1999), p. 1.

23. Sandel, *Democracy's Discontent*, p. 5.

24. Ibid.; also Daniel T. Rodgers, "Republicanism: The Career of a Concept," *Journal of American History* 79, no. 1 (June 1992), p. 33.

25. Synthesis of points made by Sandel, *Democracy's Discontent*, pp. 2–24.

26. Albert Hirschman, *Crossing Boundaries: Selected Writings* (New York: Zone Books, 1998), p. 14.

27. Robert D. Putnam, *Making Democracy Work: Civic Traditions in Modern Italy* (Princeton, NJ: Princeton University Press, 1993).

28. Michael Walzer, *What It Means to Be an American* (New York: Marsilio, 1993), p. 100.

29. Pettit, *Republicanism*, p. 134.

30. Rodgers, "Republicanism," pp. 11–38.

31. The exact quote is, "if men were angels, no government would be necessary." Alexander Hamilton, James Madison, and John Jay, *The Federalist Papers* (New York: Bantam, 1982), p. 262. The American founding fathers entertained no idealistic notions of human nature. *The Federalist 37*, written by James Madison, insists that the "infirmities and depravities of the human character" determine most motivations in political life and therefore the core constitutional question was how power can be distributed in such a way as to permit effective government, but preclude despotism or corruption. Compare Arnold A. Rogow and Harold D. Lasswell, *Power, Corruption, and Rectitude* (Englewood Cliffs, NJ: Prentice Hall, 1963), pp. 7, 11.

32. Rogow and Lasswell, *Power, Corruption, and Rectitude*, p. 7.

33. Brugger sees Montesquieu as heralding a rule-based republicanism. *Republican Theory and Political Thought*, p. 117.

34. Andreas Schedler, Larry Diamond, and Marc F. Plattner, eds. *The Self-Restraining State: Power and Accountability in New Democracies* (Boulder, CO: Lynne Rienner, 1999).

35. Sandel, *Democracy's Discontent*, p. 24.

36. Pettit, *Republicanism*, pp. 210–11.

37. Ibid., p. 218, also pp. 211, 216–17.

38. Ibid., p. 250.

39. Ibid.

40. See also Brugger, *Republican Theory and Political Thought*, pp. 172–73.

41. Samuel Huntington, *Political Order in Changing Societies* (New Haven, CT: Yale University Press, 1968), p. 60.

42. Robert Wiebe, *The Search for Order, 1877–1920* (New York: Hill & Wang, 1967); I thank my colleague Professor Andrew McFarland, University of Illinois at Chicago for a concise explanation of the role of the progressive movement in American politics.

43. Wolfgang Seibel, "Institutional Weakness, Ethical Misjudgment: German Christian Democrats and the Kohl Scandal," in *Motivating Ministers to Morality*, ed. Jenny Fleming and Ian Holland (Aldershot: Dartmouth, 2001), pp. 77–90.

44. Ibid., p. 87.

45. Personal notes taken during Walzer's statement at a seminar on corruption issues, Institute for Advanced Study, Princeton, NJ, May 7, 2003.

46. Compare Guillermo O'Donnell, "Horizontal Accountability in New Democracies," *Journal of Democracy* 9, no. 3 (July 1998), pp. 112–28.

47. Seibel, "Institutional Weakness, Ethical Misjudgment," p. 77.

48. Robert D. Behn, *Rethinking Democratic Accountability* (Washington, D.C.: Brookings Institution, 2001), pp. 44–49.

49. Antoni Z. Kaminski, "Coercion, Corruption, and Reform: State and Society in the Soviet-type Socialist Regime," *Journal of Theoretical Politics* 1, no. 1 (1989), p. 83.

50. Paul Q. Hirst, "Introduction," in *The Pluralist Theory of the State*, ed. Paul Q. Hirst (London: Routledge, 1989), p. 2.

51. "Pluralism," in *International Encyclopedia of the Social Sciences*, vol. 12 (1968), p. 165.

52. Gale Stokes, *Three Eras of Political Change in Eastern Europe* (New York: Oxford University Press, 1997), p. 149. Stokes refers to James Madison in *The Federalist Papers*.

53. Putnam, *Making Democracy Work*.

54. Juan Linz, "Transitions to Democracy," *Washington Quarterly* (Summer 1990), p. 152.

55. Daniel H. Levine, "Paradigm Lost: Dependence to Democracy," *World Politics* 40, no. 3 (Apr. 1988), p. 388.

56. Paul Heywood, "Political Corruption: Problems and Perspectives," *Political Studies* 45 (special issue, 1997), pp. 420–21.

57. Ibid., p. 421.

58. James C. Scott, *Comparative Political Corruption* (Englewood Cliffs, NJ: Prentice-Hall, 1972), p. 26.

Notes to Chapter 7

1. Samuel Huntington, *Political Order in Changing Societies* (New Haven, CT: Yale University Press, 1968), p. 59.

2. See for example, Paul Heywood, "Political Corruption: Problems and Perspectives," *Political Studies* 45 (special issue, 1997), p. 423.

3. Susan Rose-Ackerman, "Trust, Honesty, and Corruption: Theories and Survey Evidence from Post-Socialist Societies," toward a research agenda for a project of the Collegium Budapest, draft (Apr. 24, 2001), p. 51.

4. See for example, Jeremy Pope, *Confronting Corruption: The Elements of a National Integrity System* (London: Transparency International, 2000). The Transparency International branch in Latvia has used this approach to evaluate the situation in Latvia: Transparency International–Latvia, *Evaluation of the National Integrity System of Latvia* [in Latvian] (Riga, 2003).

5. Susan Rose-Ackerman, *Corruption: A Study in Political Economy* (New York: Academic Press, 1978), p. 90.

6. Robert Klitgaard, *Controlling Corruption* (Berkeley: University of California Press, 1988), p. 75.

7. Open Society Institute, *Monitoring the EU Accession Process: Corruption and Anti-corruption Policy* (Budapest, 2002), pp. 439–40.

8. Mark Levin and Georgy Satarov, "Corruption and Institutions in Russia," *European Journal of Political Economy* 16 (2000), p. 129.

9. Susan Rose-Ackerman, "Redesigning the State to Fight Corruption," *Public Policy for the Private Sector*, World Bank Note #75 (Apr. 1996), p. 2.

10. Phyllis Dininio, "Political Science and Anti-Corruption Assistance," paper presented at the annual meeting of the American Political Science Association, Boston, Aug. 28–Sept. 1, 2002, pp. 4–6.

11. Agnese Barstad, "Culture of Corruption? Interpreting Corruption in Soviet and Post-Soviet Contexts," M.A. thesis, University of Bergen, Norway (2003), p. 165.

12. Pope, *Confronting Corruption*, p. xxviii.

13. Roberta Ann Johnson, *Whistleblowing: When It Works—and Why* (Boulder, CO: Lynne Rienner, 2003).

14. Open Society Institute, *Monitoring the EU Accession Process*, p. 417.

15. "The use of special investigative technical means in the detection of corrupt behavior" is one of the recommendations made by a team of international experts assessing anti-corruption efforts in Latvia. Council of Europe, Group of States Against Corruption, *Evaluation Report on Latvia* (Strasbourg, Dec. 2001), pp. 26–27.

16. Phyllis Dininio, with Sahr John Kpundeh and Robert Leiken, *A Handbook on Fighting Corruption* (Washington, D.C.: Center for Democracy and Governance, USAID, 1999), p. 13.

17. Rick Stapenhurst, *The Media's Role in Curbing Corruption* (Washington, D.C.: World Bank Institute, 2000), p. 2.

18. Robert D. Behn, *Rethinking Democratic Accountability* (Washington, D.C.: Brookings Institution, 2001), pp. 44–49.

19. Open Society Institute, *Monitoring the EU Accession Process*, p. 207.

20. Behn, *Rethinking Democratic Accountability*, p. 4.

21. Heywood, "Political Corruption," p. 423.

22. Helen Darbishire, "Freedom of Information Laws Promote Honest Government," *Local Governance Brief* (Budapest, Spring 2004), pp. 29–32.

23. Guillermo O'Donnell, "Horizontal Accountability in New Democracies," *Journal of Democracy* 9, no. 3 (July 1998), p. 119; also Andreas Schedler, "Conceptualizing Accountability," in *The Self-Restraining State: Power and Accountability in New Democracies*, ed. Andreas Schedler, Larry Diamond, and Marc F. Plattner (Boulder, CO: Lynne Rienner, 1999), pp. 13–23.

24. Daniel Kaufmann, "Revisiting Anti-Corruption Strategies: Tilt towards Incentive-driven Approaches?" in United Nations Development Programme, *Corruption and Integrity Improvement Initiatives in Developing Countries* (1998), ch. 4, no pagination.

25. World Bank, *Anticorruption in Transition: A Contribution to the Policy Debate* (Washington, D.C., Sept. 2000), p. 15.

26. John Gardiner, "Defining Corruption," in *Coping with Corruption in a Borderless World*, ed. Maurice Punch et al. (Deventer: Kluwer Law and Taxation Publishers, 1993), p. 34.

27. For details, see Chapter 8.

28. Pope, *Confronting Corruption*, pp. 276–77.

29. Several patients and their families in Latvia have sued public health-care doctors in 2003 for declining to operate without unofficial payments.

30. Pope, *Confronting Corruption*, p. 281.

31. Dininio, *A Handbook on Fighting Corruption*, p. 13.

32. *Time Magazine*, Aug. 10, 1998, as cited in Pope, *Confronting Corruption*, p. 279.

33. Robert Klitgaard, "Strategies for Reform," in *New Perspectives on Combating Corruption*, ed. Transparency International and the International Bank for Reconstruction and Development (no place of publication: 1998), p. 232.

34. Janos Kornai and Karen Eggleston, *Welfare, Choice, and Solidarity in Transition: Reforming the Health Sector in Eastern Europe* (Cambridge, UK: Cambridge University Press, 2002), entire, also p. 141.

35. Lena Kolarska-Bobinska, "The Impact of Corruption on Legitimacy and Authority in New Democracies," in *Political Corruption in Transition*, ed. Stephen Kotkin and Andras Sajo (Budapest: Central European University Press, 2002), p. 324.

36. This has been especially true during the early stages of the transition from communism. Compare Steven L. Solnick, *Stealing the State: Control and Collapse of Soviet Institutions*, 2d ed. (Cambridge, MA: Harvard University Press, 1999).

37. For example, William Mishler and Richard Rose, "What Are the Origins of Political Trust? Testing Institutional and Cultural Theories in Post-Communist Societies," *Comparative Political Studies* 34, no. 4 (Feb. 2001), pp. 30–62.

38. Open Society Institute, *Monitoring the EU Accession Process*, p. 205.

39. World Bank Warsaw Office, *Corruption in Poland: Review of Priority Areas and Proposals for Action*, 1999, p. 24.

40. Ibid., p. 23.

41. Janos Kornai, "Hidden in an Envelope: Gratitude Payments to Medical Doctors in Hungary," in *The Paradoxes of Unintended Consequences*, ed. Lord Dahrendorf et al. (Budapest: Central European University Press, 2000), pp. 195–214; also Andras Sajo, "From Corruption to Extortion: Conceptualization of Post-Communist Corruption," *Crime, Law and Social Change* 40 (2003), pp. 171–94, p. 186.

42. Center for Governmental Integrity, *Civil Society Successes in Fighting Corruption in Russia's Regions*, project report (Washington, D.C.: Management Systems International, 2003).

43. A. Cockcroft et al., *Curbing System Leakages: The Health Sector and Licensing in Latvia*, CIET International, draft (Nov. 17, 2002).

44. Michael Johnston and Sahr J. Kpundeh, "Building a Clean Machine: Anti-Corruption Coalitions and Sustainable Reform," World Bank Institute Working Paper #37208 (Washington, D.C., 2002).

45. Arista-Maria Cirtautas, "Anticorruption Campaigns: How to Get Rid of Paradoxes and Inconsistencies," *Transition Newsletter* (Oct./Nov. 2001), pp. 7–9.

46. Bryane Michael, "The Rapid Rise of the Anticorruption Industry," *Local Government Brief* (Spring 2004), p. 20.

47. Mark R. Beissinger, "Introduction," *Soviet Sociology* (May/June 1989), pp. 3–8. Articles from Soviet sources translated in this special volume of the journal make the same point.

48. Levin and Satarov, "Corruption and Institutions in Russia," pp. 113–32.

49. Frank Anechiarico and James B. Jacobs, *The Pursuit of Absolute Integrity:*

How Corruption Control Makes Government Ineffective (Chicago: University of Chicago Press, 1996), p. 179.

50. John M. Kramer, "The Politics of Corruption," *Current History* 97, no. 621 (Oct. 1998), p. 334.

51. David Nelken and Michael Levi, "The Corruption of Politics and the Politics of Corruption," *Journal of Law and Society* 23, no. 1 (Mar. 1996), pp. 1–17, p. 9.

52. Anechiarico and Jacobs, *The Pursuit of Absolute Integrity*, p. xv.

53. Open Society Institute, *Monitoring the EU Accession Process*, p. 177.

54. Rose-Ackerman, "Redesigning the State to Fight Corruption," p. 2.

55. Huntington, *Political Order in Changing Societies*, p. 64.

56. Open Society Institute, *Monitoring the EU Accession Process*, p. 175–76.

57. Ibid., p. 178.

58. Douglass C. North, *Institutions, Institutional Change and Economic Performance* (Cambridge, UK: Cambridge University Press, 1990), p. 4.

59. Open Society Institute, *Monitoring the EU Accession Process*, p. 572.

60. Tony Verheijen and Antoaneta Dimitrova, "Private Interests and Public Administration: The Central and East European Experience," *International Review of Administrative Sciences* 62 (1996), p. 216.

61. Alena V. Ledeneva, *Russia's Economy of Favors: Blat, Networking and Informal Exchange* (Cambridge, UK: Cambridge University Press, 1998). Richard Rose argues that the remaining informal networks in Russia are premodern or antimodern. Richard Rose, "Uses of Social Capital in Russia: Modern, Pre-modern, and Antimodern," *Post-Soviet Affairs* 16, no. 1 (Jan./Mar. 2000), pp. 33–57.

62. Franklin Steves and Alan Russo, *Anti-Corruption Programmes in Post-Communist Transition Countries and Changes in the Business Environment, 1999–2002*, European Bank for Reconstruction and Development, Working Paper # 85 (Oct. 2003), p. 4.

63. Ibid., p. 15.

64. Ibid., p. 16.

65. See Chapter 2, and especially Michael J. Sandel, *Democracy's Discontent: America in Search of a Public Philosophy* (Cambridge, MA: Belknap Press of Harvard University Press, 1996).

Notes to Chapter 8

1. Andreas Schedler, "Conceptualizing Accountability," in *The Self-Restraining State: Power and Accountability in New Democracies*, ed. Andreas Schedler, Larry Diamond, and Marc F. Plattner (Boulder, CO: Lynne Rienner, 1999), p. 17.

2. Douglass C. North, *Institutions, Institutional Change and Economic Performance* (Cambridge, UK: Cambridge University Press, 1990), p. 4.

3. Robert D. Behn, *Rethinking Democratic Accountability* (Washington, D.C.: Brookings Institution, 2001), p. 4.

4. Schedler, "Conceptualizing Accountability," p. 15.

5. Ibid.

6. Larry Diamond, Marc F. Plattner, and Andreas Schedler, "Introduction," in Schedler, Diamond, and Plattner, eds., *The Self-Restraining State*, p. 1.

7. Open Society Institute, *Monitoring the EU Accession Process: Corruption and Anti-corruption Policy* (Budapest: 2002). This report assesses the situation as of the middle of 2002. See also country reports prepared by the Council of Europe's Group of States Against Corruption, 2001 to date, www.greco.coe.

8. Open Society Institute, *Monitoring the EU Accession Process*, p. 16.

9. Ibid., pp. 115–16, 238, 497.

10. Ibid., p. 379.

11. Ibid., pp. 142, 432. Parties can lose a part of their state subsidy equal to three times the amount of the funds illegally raised or spent for four years. They also must pay to the state budget the amount of funds raised illegally.

12. Ivan Krastev, "Corruption, Anti-Corruption Sentiments, and the Rule of Law," in *Reshaping Globalization: Multilateral Dialogues and New Policy Initiatives*, ed. Andrea Krizsan and Violetta Zentai (Budapest: Central European Press, 2003), p. 150.

13. Ibid., p. 68.

14. Ibid., p. 136.

15. Ibid., p. 147; Lubomir Lizal and Evzen Kocenda, "Corruption and Anticorruption in the Czech Republic," William Davidson Institute Working Paper #345 (Ann Arbor, MI, Oct. 2000), p. 22.

16. Open Society Institute, *Monitoring the EU Accession Process*, p. 82; on Poland see p. 68.

17. Ivan Krastev and Georgy Ganev, "Do Uncorrupt Governments in Corrupt Countries Have Incentives to Launch Anticorruption Campaigns?" *East European Constitutional Review* 12, no. 2/3 (Spring/Summer 2003), p. 88.

18. Numerous reports in Latvia's press.

19. See Chapter 2; also Ingrīda Puce, "Reports about Corruption in Latvia by International Organizations (EU, EC, OECD, WB) and Their Influence on the Political Agenda of Political and Economic Elites, 1992–2001" [in Latvian], M.A. thesis, University of Latvia, Department of Communication, Riga (2002), p. 54.

20. Transparency International–Latvia, *Evaluation of the National Integrity System of Latvia* [in Latvian] (Riga, 2003), p. 9, www.delna.lv (accessed Feb. 16, 2004).

21. Open Society Institute, *Monitoring the EU Accession Process*, pp. 83, 109.

22. Ibid., pp. 324, 362, 364, 520–21, 537, 573; Council of Europe, Group of States Against Corruption, *Evaluation Report on Estonia*, Strasbourg, 14 Sept. 2001, pp. 14–15.

23. Open Society Institute, *Monitoring the EU Accession Process*, p. 259.

24. Ibid., pp. 130, 255, 391, 566.

25. Ibid., p. 163.

26. Valts Kalniņš, *Latvia's Anticorruption Policy: Problems and Prospects* (Riga: Institute for International Politics, 2002), ch. 4.

27. Open Society Institute, *Monitoring the EU Accession Process*, pp. 349, 367–68.

28. Numerous press reports and material on the website of the office: www.pretkorupcija.lv.

29. Susan Rose-Ackerman, "Democracy and 'Grand' Corruption," *International Social Science Journal* 48, no. 3 (Sept. 1996), pp. 372–73.

30. Council of Europe, Group of States Against Corruption, *Evaluation Report on Latvia*, Strasbourg, Dec. 2001, p. 21.

31. Valts Kalniņš, *The Justice System and Corruption* [in Latvian] (Riga: Institute for International Politics, 2001), pp. 28–36.

32. Open Society Institute, *Monitoring the EU Accession Process*, p. 531. In the Czech case, seventy-five people were prosecuted and around 11.7 million euros were recovered. Ibid., pp. 149–50.

33. Greco, *Evaluation Report on Estonia*, pp. 36–37.

34. Transparency International, *Global Corruption Report 2004* (London: Pluto Press, 2004), p. 242.

35. *Diena*, May 22, 2004.

36. *Neatkarīgā Rīta Avīze*, Nov. 4, 2003.

37. Petter Langseth et al., "Empowering the Victims of Corruption through Social Control Mechanisms," paper presented at IACC meeting, Prague, Oct. 9, 2001, pp. 3–4.

38. Open Society Institute, *Monitoring the EU Accession Process*, pp. 379, 386.

39. Ibid., p. 524.

40. Mark Levin and Georgy Satarov, "Corruption and Institutions in Russia," *European Journal of Political Economy* 16 (2000), p. 126.

41. Open Society Institute, *Monitoring the EU Accession Process*, pp. 198, 209.

42. Ibid., p. 460.

43. By late 2002 none of the cases mentioned had resulted in a conviction. Open Society Institute, *Monitoring the EU Accession Process*, pp. 103–13, 521.

44. Valentinas Mite, "Lithuania: Paksas Becomes First European President To Be Removed from Office," *RFE/RL Feature Article* (Apr. 6, 2004).

45. The same conclusion is reached in Transparency International–Latvia, *Evaluation of the National Integrity System of Latvia*, p. 8.

46. Open Society Institute, *Monitoring the EU Accession Process*, p. 114.

47. Notes from personal attendance at conference, Riga, May 2–3, 2002.

48. Open Society Institute, *Monitoring the EU Accession Process*, p. 455; on Slovenia, see p. 597.

49. Ibid., pp. 370–71.

50. Ibid., p. 83.

51. Ibid., pp. 103–6.

52. Transparency International–Latvia, *Evaluation of the National Integrity System of Latvia*, p. 67.

53. Corruption Prevention Council, *Strategy for Preventing and Fighting Corruption 2004–2008* [in Latvian], p. 10, www.pretkorupcija.lv (accessed Mar. 2, 2004).

54. Open Society Institute, *Monitoring the EU Accession Process*, pp. 83, 108–9.

55. Ibid., p. 249.

56. Ibid., p. 411; on Lithuania, see pp. 365–66.

57. Transparency International–Latvia, *Evaluation of the National Integrity System of Latvia*, p. 58.

58. Open Society Institute, *Monitoring the EU Accession Process*, pp. 226, 194; references to other countries on pp. 84, 120, 178, 386.

59. Ibid., p. 84.

60. Ibid., pp. 555, 609–10; on Bulgaria, see p. 119.

61. Ibid., pp. 384–86.

62. Council of Europe, Group of States Against Corruption, *Evaluation Report on Latvia*, p. 21.

63. Kalniņš, *Latvia's Anticorruption Policy*. p. 59–76.

64. Transparency International–Latvia, *Evaluation of the National Integrity System of Latvia*, pp. 23, 50, 53, 55.

65. Open Society Institute, *Monitoring the EU Accession Process*, p. 239.

66. Ibid., p. 565; on good results in Bulgaria, see p. 128.

67. Alexandru Grigorescu, "European Institutions and Unsuccessful Norm Transmission: The Case of Transparency," *International Politics* 39 (Dec. 2002), p. 470.

68. Open Society Institute, *Monitoring the EU Accession Process*, p. 130.

69. Press reports.

70. See previous chapters as well as Open Society Institute, *Monitoring the EU Accession Process*, pp. 138, 399, 566, 597.

71. Stefan Batory Foundation, *Annual Report 2002*, www.batory.org (viewed Apr. 30, 2004).

72. Boyko Todorov, "Coalition 2000: A Public-Private Partnership Tackling Corruption in Bulgaria," *Public Management Forum* 5, no. 2 (1999), pp. 1–3; Borislav Tsekov, "Intermediary Groups: A Mechanism for Curbing Corruption Pressure in Municipalities," in *Local Anti-Corruption Initiatives Report 2002*, ed. Center for the Study of Democracy (Sofia: Coalition 2000, 1999), pp. 64–67. See also the coalition's website, www.online.bg/coalition2000.

73. Tālis Tisenkopfs and Valts Kalniņš, "Public Accountability in Passenger Transportation in Latvia," unpublished report (Riga: Baltic Studies Centre, June 2003), p. 7.

74. General program activities of Transparency International–Latvia are outlined on its website, www.delna.lv.

75. Transparency International–Latvia, *Uz Delnas* [in Latvian] 2, no. 7 (May 2002), pp. 1–2; also "NGO Monitoring Efforts: Latvia, Ecuador and India," Transparency International, *Global Corruption Report 2004*, pp. 50–53.

76. This is quite consistent across the region, over time, and in a variety of different surveys. For an analysis, see William Mishler and Richard Rose, "What Are the Origins of Political Trust? Testing Institutional and Cultural Theories in Post-Communist Societies," *Comparative Political Studies*, vol. 34, no. 1 (Feb. 2001), pp. 41–44.

77. Lolita Čigane, "Civil Society Monitoring of Political Party Finance," in *Party Financing: Latvia's Experience in a Global Context* [in Latvian], ed. Jānis Ikstens (Riga: Baltic Institute of Social Sciences, 2003), pp. 93–103.

78. Soros Foundation–Latvia, "Association against Black Cash Boxes," memos, Riga, 2002; also information from various media sources and project leaders in Latvia, July and August 2002.

79. This project was also supported by TI–Latvia and fifty other nongovernmental organizations.

80. Soros Foundation–Latvia, "Association against Black Cash Boxes"; also information from various media sources and project leaders in Latvia, July and August 2002.

81. Transparency International, *Global Corruption Report 2004*, pp. 50–53, Čigane, "Civil Society Monitoring of Political Party Finance"; *Diena*, July 7, 2004.

82. Jānis Ikstens, "Laughter Between Tears and Blood" [in Latvian], www.politika.lv (accessed Feb. 18, 2004).

83. Zuzana Wienk, "Civic Watchdogs Try to Put the Bite on Crooked Politics," *Local Government Brief* (Spring 2004), pp. 35–37.

84. Open Society Institute, *Monitoring the EU Accession Process*, p. 428.

85. Ibid., p. 408.

86. Eugen Tomiuc, "Romania: EU Warns Bucharest over Corruption," *RFE/RL Report* (Apr. 30, 2003), pp. 1–3.

87. See especially the diagnostic surveys and other research sponsored by the World Bank Institute and cited throughout this book. The OECD has created outreach programs to promote its 1999 Convention of Combating Bribery of Foreign Public Officials in International Business. This has focused on creating a network for exchang-

ing information about institutional mechanisms to contain corruption. "Outreach Anti-Corruption Activities in Central and Eastern Europe and the NIS," at www.oecd.org/document/14/ (viewed on Mar. 8, 2004).

88. Open Society Institute, *Monitoring the EU Accession Process*, pp. 18–23.

89. Ibid., pp. 71, 95, 149, 440.

90. Commission of the European Communities, *Communication from the Commission to the Council, the European Parliament and the European Economic and Social Committee on a Comprehensive Policy against Corruption* (Brussels, May 28 2003), p. 10.

91. "Eesti Paevaleht" as reported by the *Latvian News Agency LETA*, Apr. 21, 2004.

92. *New York Times*, June 4, 2004.

93. Puce, "Reports about Corruption in Latvia."

94. See Transparency International, *Global Corruption Report 2004*.

95. Bryane Michael, "The Rapid Rise of the Anticorruption Industry," *Local Government Brief* (Spring 2004), pp. 17–25.

96. See, for example, Transparency International–Latvia, *Evaluation of the National Integrity System of Latvia*.

Notes to Chapter 9

1. Robert Klitgaard, "Strategies for Reform," in *New Perspectives on Combating Corruption*, ed. Transparency International and the International Bank for Reconstruction and Development (no place of publication: 1998), p. 240.

2. See the preceding chapters as well as Stephen Kotkin and Andras Sajo, eds., *Political Corruption in Transition: A Skeptic's Handbook* (Budapest: Central European University, 2002).

3. Peter Eigen, "Combating Corruption around the World," *Journal of Democracy* 7, no. 1 (Jan. 1996), p. 162.

4. Ellen N. Immergut, "The Theoretical Core of the New Institutionalism," *Politics and Society* 26, no. 1 (Mar. 1998), p. 20.

5. Dankwart A. Rustow, "Transitions to Democracy: Toward a Dynamic Model," *Comparative Politics* 2, no. 2 (Apr. 1970), pp. 337–63.

6. Robert Klitgaard, *Controlling Corruption* (Berkeley: University of California Press, 1988), pp. 22–43; also Susan Rose-Ackerman, *Corruption: A Study in Political Economy* (New York: Academic Press, 1978).

7. William A. Clark and Philip H. Jos, "Comparative Anti-Corruption Policy: The American, Soviet and Russian Cases," *International Journal of Public Administration* 23 (2000), pp. 101–48.

8. See Chapter 4; also William Mishler and Richard Rose, "What Are the Origins of Political Trust? Testing Institutional and Cultural Theories in Post-Communist Societies," *Comparative Political Studies* 34, no. 4 (Feb. 2001), pp. 30–62.

9. John Gardiner, "Defining Corruption," in *Coping with Corruption in a Borderless World*, ed. Maurice Punch et al. (Deventer: Kluwer Law and Taxation Publishers, 1993), 25.

10. Klitgaard, *Controlling Corruption*, p. 42.

11. Claus Offe, "Controlling Political Corruption: Conceptual and Practical Issues," draft paper for workshop on Honesty and Trust, Dec. 13–14, 2002, Collegium Budapest, Hungary, pp. 12–13.

12. See Chapters 3 and 4; also William L. Miller, Ase B. Grodeland, Tatyana Y. Koshechkina, "Are the People Victims or Accomplices? The Use of Presents and Bribes to Influence Officials in Eastern Europe," Discussion Paper #6 (Budapest: Open Society Institute, 1998).

13. Susan Rose-Ackerman, "Trust and Honesty in Post-Socialist Systems," *Kyklos* 54, no. 2/3 (2001), p. 424.

14. Eigen, "Combating Corruption around the World," p. 161.

15. Federico Varese, *The Russian Mafia: Private Protection in a New Market Economy* (Oxford: Oxford University Press, 2001), p. 34.

16. In part based on Scott Gehlbach, "Social Networks and Corruption," paper presented at the annual meeting of the American Political Science Association, San Francisco, Aug. 29–Sept. 2, 2001.

17. Transparency International–Latvia, *The Face of Corruption in Latvia*, report [in Latvian] (Riga: Apr. 2000), p. 86.

18. Louise I. Shelley, "Crime and Corruption," in *Developments in Russian Politics*, ed. Stephen White, Alex Pravda, and Zvi Gitelman (Hampshire: Palgrave, 2001), p. 245.

19. See earlier chapters; for astounding revelations about the scope of this practice, see Keith A. Darden, "Blackmail as a Tool of State Domination: Ukraine under Kuchma," *East European Constitutional Review* 10, no. 2/3 (Spring/Summer 2001), pp. 67–71.

20. Vitaly A. Nomokonov, "On Strategies for Combating Corruption in Russia," *Demokratizatsiya* 8, no. 1 (Winter 2000), p. 125.

21. Susan Rose-Ackerman, *Corruption and Government* (New York: Cambridge University Press, 1999), p. 171.

22. World Bank, *Anticorruption in Transition: A Contribution to the Policy Debate* (Washington, D.C., Sept. 2000), p. 22; compare also Chapter 8 and summary argument in Open Society Institute, *Monitoring the EU Accession Process: Corruption and Anti-corruption Policy* (Budapest: 2002), p. 70.

23. Kate Gillespie and Gwenn Okruhlik, "The Political Dimensions of Corruption Cleanups: A Framework for Analysis," *Comparative Politics* 24, no. 1 (Oct. 1991), p. 80; Susan Rose-Ackerman, "Trust, Honesty and Corruption: Reflection on the State-building Process," *Archives Europeans Sociologiques* 17 (2001), p. 556.

24. Frederick Stapenhurst and Sahr J. Kpundeh, "Public Participation in the Fight against Corruption," *Canadian Journal of Development Studies* 19 (1998), p. 502.

25. Elinor Ostrom, "A Behavioral Approach to the Rational Choice Theory of Collective Action," *American Political Science Review* 92, no. 1 (Mar. 1998), pp. 1–22.

26. Richard P. Nielsen, "Corruption Networks and Implications for Ethical Corruption Reform," *Journal of Business Ethics* 42 (2003), pp. 125–49.

27. Ostrom, "A Behavioral Approach," p. 1.

28. Rasma Karklins and Roger Petersen, "Decision Calculus of Protesters and Regimes: Eastern Europe, 1989," *Journal of Politics* 55, no. 3 (Apr. 1993), pp. 588–614.

29. Phyllis Dininio, "Political Science and Anti-Corruption Assistance," paper presented at the annual meeting of the American Political Science Association, Boston, Aug. 28–Sept. 1, 2002, p. 6.

30. Phyllis Dininio, with Sahr John Kpundeh and Robert Leiken, *A Handbook on Fighting Corruption* (Washington, D.C.: Center for Democracy and Governance, USAID, 1999), p. 1.

31. Michael Johnston and Sahr J. Kpundeh, "Building a Clean Machine: Anti-Corruption Coalitions and Sustainable Reform," World Bank Institute Working Paper #37208 (Washington, D.C., 2002), p. 5.

32. See Chapters 3 and 4; also William L. Miller, Ase B. Grodeland, and Tatyana Y. Koshechkina, *A Culture of Corruption? Coping with Government in Post-Communist Europe* (Budapest: Central European University Press, 2001), pp. 64, 69.

33. Gillespie and Okruhlik, "The Political Dimensions of Corruption Cleanups," p. 81.

34. Numerous press reports on investigations; see also Chapter 4.

35. Rose-Ackerman, *Corruption and Government*, p. 227.

36. Eigen, "Combating Corruption around the World," p. 162.

37. Stephen Holmes, "Crime and Corruption after Communism," *East European Constitutional Review* 6, no. 4 (Fall 1997), pp. 1–3, p. 1.

38. *New York Times*, Aug. 24, 2004.

39. Miller et al., *A Culture of Corruption?* entire.

40. Mishler and Rose, "What Are the Origins of Political Trust?"

41. Transparency International–Latvia, *Uz Delnas* [in Latvian], (May 2002), p. 1.

42. Robert Klitgaard, "Strategies for Reform," p. 241.

43. Petter Langseth et al., "Empowering the Victims of Corruption through Social Control Mechanisms," paper presented at IACC meeting, Prague, Oct. 9, 2001, p. 3.

44. Ibid., p. 12.

45. John McMillan and Christopher Woodruff, "Private Order under Dysfunctional Public Order," *Michigan Law Review* 98 (2000), pp. 2431 and 2439, cited in Rose-Ackerman, "Trust and Honesty in Post-Socialist Systems," p. 541.

46. Daniel Kaufmann, "Revisiting Anti-Corruption Strategies: Tilt towards Incentive-Driven Approaches?" in United Nations Development Programme, *Corruption and Integrity Improvement Initiatives in Developing Countries* (1998), ch. 4, no pagination.

47. Eigen, "Combating Corruption around the World," p. 162.

48. Dininio, "Political Science and Anti-Corruption Assistance," pp. 4–6.

49. See also Eigen, "Combating Corruption around the World."

Notes to Chapter 10

1. For an excellent summary, see Alena V. Ledeneva, *Unwritten Rules: How Russia Really Works* (London: Centre for European Reform, 2001).

2. Elmer Hankiss, "Games of Corruption: East Central Europe, 1945–1999," in *Political Corruption in Transition: A Skeptic's Handbook*, ed. Stephen Kotkin and Andras Sajo (Budapest: Central European University Press, 2002), p. 251.

——— Selected Bibliography ———

Primary Sources: Country and Survey Reports, Documents, Anti-Corruption Handbooks

Anderson, James H. *Corruption in Latvia: Survey Evidence.* Washington, D.C.: World Bank, Dec. 16, 1998. Retrieved from www1.worldbank.org/publicsector/Latviasurveyreport.pdf.

———. *Corruption in Slovakia: Results of Diagnostic Surveys.* Washington, D.C.: World Bank, 2000. Retrieved from www.government.gov.sk/bojprotikorupcii/korupcia_na_slovensku-en.doc.

———. *Diagnostic Surveys of Corruption in Romania.* Washington, D.C.: World Bank, 2001. Retrieved from www.worldbank.org/publicsector/anticorrupt/Romenglich.pdf.

Case, Rebecca. *UNDP and Other Anti-Corruption Efforts in Bulgaria,* a case study prepared for the Donor Standards in Anti-Corruption Project, Cambridge, MA, Sept. 2002.

Center for Governmental Integrity, Management Systems International. *Civil Society Successes in Fighting Corruption in Russia's Regions.* Project report, Washington, D.C., Jan. 2003.

Cockcroft, A., et al. *Curbing System Leakages: The Health Sector and Licensing in Latvia.* Draft report, CIET International, Nov. 17, 2002.

Commission of the European Communities. *Communication from the Commission to the Council, the European Parliament and the European Economic and Social Committee on a Comprehensive Policy against Corruption.* Brussels, May 29, 2003.

Corruption Prevention Council. *Strategy for Preventing and Fighting Corruption 2004–2008* [in Latvian]. Retrieved from www.pretkorupcija.lv (accessed Mar. 2, 2004).

Council of Europe, Group of States Against Corruption. *Evaluation Report on Estonia.* Strasbourg, Sept. 14, 2001.

———. *Evaluation Report on Georgia.* Strasbourg, June 15, 2001.

———. *Evaluation Report on Latvia.* Strasbourg, Dec. 2001.

Dininio, Phyllis, with Sahr John Kpundeh and Robert Leiken. *A Handbook on Fighting Corruption.* Washington, D.C.: Center for Democracy and Governance, USAID, 1999.

Gole, Juliet S. *The Role of Civil Society in Containing Corruption at the Municipal Level: Proceedings from the Regional Conference of Transparency International Representatives.* Budapest: Open Society Institute and Transparency International, 1999.

Gray, Cheryl, Joel Hellman, and Randi Ryterman. *Anti-Corruption in Transition 2: Corruption in Enterprise-State Interactions in Europe and Central Asia, 1999–2002.* Washington, D.C.: World Bank, 2004. Retrieved from www.worldbank.org.

Kaufmann, Daniel. "Revisiting Anti-Corruption Strategies: Tilt towards Incentive-driven Approaches?" in United Nations Development Programme, *Corruption and Integrity Improvement Initiatives in Developing Countries,* 1998, ch. 4.

Lizal, Lubomir, and Evzen Kocenda. "Corruption and Anticorruption in the Czech Republic," William Davidson Institute Working Paper #345, Ann Arbor, MI, Oct. 2000.

Miklos, Ivan. *Corruption Risks in the Privatisation Process.* Bratislava, May 1995. Retrieved from www.internet.sk/mesa10/PRIVAT/CORRUPT.htm.

Open Society Institute. *Monitoring the EU Accession Process: Corruption and Anti-corruption Policy.* Budapest, 2002. Retrieved from www.eumap.org/reports/2002/content/50.

Pope, Jeremy. *Confronting Corruption: The Elements of a National Integrity System, TI Source Book 2000.* London: Transparency International, 2000.

RFL/RL Research Report I. Aug. 14, 2000. Retrieved from www.rferl.org.

Sedlenieks, Klāvs. "Corruption Close-Up" [in Latvian]. Unpublished report. Riga: Soros Fund, 2000–2001.

Stavrakis, Peter J. *State-Building in Post-Soviet Russia: The Chicago Boys and the Decline of Administrative Capacity.* Occasional Paper #254, Washington, D.C.: Kennan Institute, Oct. 1993.

Tisenkopfs, Tālis, and Valts Kalniņš. "Public Accountability in Passenger Transportation in Latvia." Unpublished report. Riga: Baltic Studies Centre, June 2003.

Transparency International. *Global Corruption Report 2003.* Retrieved from www.globalcorruptionreport.org.

———. *Global Corruption Report 2004.* London: Pluto Press, 2004.

Transparency International–Latvia. *Evaluation of the National Integrity System of Latvia* [in Latvian]. Riga, 2003.

———. *The Face of Corruption in Latvia.* Report [in Latvian], Riga, Apr. 2000.

World Bank. *Anticorruption in Transition: A Contribution to the Policy Debate.* Washington, D.C., Sept. 2000. Retrieved from www-wds.worldbank.org/servlet/WDSContentServer/WDSP/IB/2000/10/07/ 000094946_00092205320346/Rendered/PDF multi_page.pdf (last verified 10/12/03).

———. *Corruption in Georgia: Survey Evidence.* Report. Washington, D.C., June 2000.

World Bank Institute, ed. *Controlling Corruption: Towards an Integrated Strategy.* Washington, D.C., 2002.

World Bank Warsaw Office. *Corruption in Poland: Review of Priority Areas and Proposals for Action.* Oct. 11, 1999, p. 16, 24. Retrieved from ww.worldbank.org.pl/ECA/Poland.nsf/10f8270b68014d5685256ce100527dc2/85256b560077051e85256aa4007034a2?OpenDocument (last verified Oct. 12, 2003).

Books

Anechiarico, Frank, and James B. Jacobs. *The Pursuit of Absolute Integrity: How Corruption Control Makes Government Ineffective.* Chicago: University of Chicago Press, 1996.

Behn, Robert D. *Rethinking Democratic Accountability*. Washington, D.C.: Brookings Institution, 2001.

Brecht, Bertolt. *Mother Courage and Her Children: A Chronicle of the Thirty Years' War*. Trans. by Eric Bentley. New York: Grove Press, 1966.

Brugger, Bill. *Republican Theory and Political Thought: Virtuous or Virtual?* New York: St. Martin's Press, 1999.

Bunce, Valerie. *Subversive Institutions: The Design and Destruction of Socialism and the State*. Cambridge, UK: Cambridge University Press, 1999.

Chirot, Daniel. *Modern Tyrants: The Power and Prevalence of Evil in Our Age*. New York: Free Press, 1994.

Clarke, Paul Barry. *Citizenship*. Boulder, CO: Pluto Press, 1993.

Djilas, Milovan. *The New Class: An Analysis of the Communist System*. New York: Praeger, 1957.

Evans, Peter B., Dietrich Rueschmeyer, and Theda Skopcol, eds. *Bringing the State Back In*. Cambridge, UK: Cambridge University Press, 1985.

Feige, Edgar L., ed. *The Underground Economies: Tax Evasion and Information Distortion*. Cambridge, UK: Cambridge University Press, 1989.

Friedrich, Carl J. *The Pathology of Politics: Violence, Betrayal, Corruption, Secrecy and Propaganda*. New York: Harper & Row, 1972.

Frydman, Roman, Kenneth Murphy, and Andrzej Rapaczynski. *Capitalism with a Comrade's Face: Studies in Postcommunist Transition*. Budapest: Central European University Press, 1998.

Girling, John. *Corruption, Capitalism and Democracy*. London: Routledge, 1997.

Goldman, Marshall I. *The Piratization of Russia: Russian Reform Goes Awry*. London: Routledge, 2003.

Hamilton, Alexander, James Madison, and John Jay. *The Federalist Papers*. New York: Bantam, 1982.

Heater, Derek. *The Civic Idea in World History, Politics, and Education*. London: Longman, 1990.

Heidenheimer, Arnold J., ed. *Political Corruption: Readings in Comparative Analysis*. New York: Holt, Rinehart and Winston, 1970.

Heidenheimer, Arnold J., and Michael Johnston, eds. *Political Corruption: Concepts and Contexts*. New Brunswick, NJ: Transaction Publishers, 2002.

Heidenheimer, Arnold J., Michael Johnston, and Victor T. Levine, eds. *Political Corruption: A Handbook*. New Brunswick, NJ: Transaction Books, 1989.

Hirschman, Albert. *Crossing Boundaries: Selected Writings*. New York: Zone Books, 1998.

Hirst, Paul Q. ed., *The Pluralist Theory of the State*. London: Routledge, 1989.

Holmes, Leslie. *The End of Communist Power: Anti-Corruption Campaigns and Legitimation Crisis*. New York: Oxford University Press, 1993.

Howard, Marc Morje. *Free Not to Participate: The Weakness of Civil Society in Post-Communist Europe*. Glasgow: Centre for the Study of Public Policy, 2000.

Huntington, Samuel. *Political Order in Changing Societies*. New Haven, CT: Yale University Press, 1968.

Johnson, Roberta Ann. *Whistleblowing: When It Works—and Why*. Boulder, CO: Lynne Rienner, 2003.

Kalniņš, Valts. *The Justice System and Corruption* [in Latvian]. Riga: Institute for International Politics, 2001.

———. *Latvia's Anticorruption Policy: Problems and Prospects*. Riga: Institute for International Politics, 2002.

Kaminiski, Bartlomiej, ed. *Economic Transition in Russia and the New States of Eurasia.* Armonk, NY: M.E. Sharpe, 1996.

Klitgaard, Robert. *Controlling Corruption.* Berkeley: University of California Press, 1988.

Kornai, Janos. *The Socialist System: The Political Economy of Communism.* Princeton, NJ: Princeton University Press, 1992.

Kornai, Janos, and Karen Eggleston. *Welfare, Choice, and Solidarity in Transition: Reforming the Health Sector in Eastern Europe.* Cambridge, UK: Cambridge University Press, 2002.

Kotkin, Stephen, and Andras Sajo, eds. *Political Corruption in Transition: A Skeptic's Handbook.* Budapest: Central European University Press, 2002.

Lazear, Edward P. *Economic Transition in Eastern Europe and Russia: Realities of Reform.* Stanford, CA: Hoover Institution Press, 1995.

Ledeneva, Alena V. *Russia's Economy of Favors: Blat, Networking and Informal Exchange.* Cambridge, UK: Cambridge University Press, 1998.

———. *Unwritten Rules: How Russia Really Works.* London: Centre for European Reform, 2001.

Ledeneva, Alena V., and Marina Kurkchiyan, eds. *Economic Crime in Russia.* The Hague: Kluwer Law International, 2000.

Levi, Margaret. *Consent, Dissent, and Patriotism.* Cambridge, UK: Cambridge University Press, 1997.

Linz, Juan J., and Alfred Stepan. *Problems of Democratic Transition and Consolidation: Southern Europe, South America, and Post-Communist Europe.* Baltimore: Johns Hopkins University Press, 1996.

Los, Maria, and Andrzej Zybertowicz. *Privatizing the Police-State: The Case of Poland.* New York: St. Martin's Press, 2000.

Lu, Xiaobo. *Cadres and Corruption: The Organizational Involution of the Chinese Communist Party.* Stanford, CA: Stanford University Press, 2000.

Miller, William L., Ase B. Grodeland, and Tatyana Y. Koshechkina. *A Culture of Corruption? Coping with Government in Post-Communist Europe.* Budapest: Central European University Press, 2001.

Noonan, John T. *Bribes.* Berkeley: University of California Press, 1984.

North, Douglass C. *Institutions, Institutional Change and Economic Performance.* Cambridge, UK: Cambridge University Press, 1990.

Pettit, Philip. *Republicanism: A Theory of Freedom and Government.* Oxford: Clarendon Press, 1997.

Portes, Alejandro, Manuel Castells, and Lauren A. Benton, eds. *The Informal Economy: Studies in Advanced and Less Developed Countries.* Baltimore: John Hopkins University Press, 1989.

Putnam, Robert D. *Making Democracy Work: Civic Traditions in Modern Italy.* Princeton, NJ: Princeton University Press, 1993.

Rogow, Arnold A., and Harold D. Lasswell. *Power, Corruption, and Rectitude.* Englewood Cliffs, NJ: Prentice-Hall, 1963.

Rose, Richard, William Mishler, and Christian Haerpfer. *Democracy and Its Alternatives.* Cambridge, UK: Cambridge University Press, 1998.

Rose-Ackerman, Susan. *Corruption: A Study in Political Economy.* New York: Academic Press, 1978.

———. *Corruption and Government.* Cambridge, UK: Cambridge University Press, 1999.

Rosen, Lawrence. *The Culture of Islam: Changing Aspects of Contemporary Muslim Life*. Chicago: University of Chicago Press, 2002.

Sandel, Michael J. *Democracy's Discontent: America in Search of a Public Philosophy*. Cambridge, MA: Belknap Press of Harvard University Press, 1996.

Schedler, Andreas, Larry Diamond, and Marc F. Plattner, eds. *The Self-Restraining State: Power and Accountability in New Democracies*. Boulder, CO: Lynne Rienner, 1999.

Scott, James C. *Comparative Political Corruption*. Englewood Cliffs, NJ: Prentice-Hall, 1972.

Simis, Konstantin M. *USSR, The Corrupt Society: The Secret World of Soviet Capitalism*. New York: Simon and Schuster, 1982.

Solnick, Steven L. *Stealing the State: Control and Collapse of Soviet Institutions*, 2d ed. Cambridge, MA: Harvard University Press, 1999.

Steinmo, Sven, Kathleen Thelen, and Frank Longstreth, eds. *Structuring Politics: Historical Institutionalism in Comparative Analysis*. Cambridge, UK: Cambridge University Press, 1992.

Stokes, Gale. *Three Eras of Political Change in Eastern Europe*. New York: Oxford University Press, 1997.

Trang, Duc V., ed. *Corruption & Democracy: Political Institutions, Processes and Corruption in Transition States in East-Central Europe and in the Former Soviet Union*. Budapest: Institute for Constitutional and Legislative Policy, 1994.

Varese, Federico. *The Russian Mafia: Private Protection in a New Market Economy*. Oxford: Oxford University Press, 2001.

Verba, Sidney, Kay Lehman Schlozman, and Henry E. Brady. *Voice and Equality: Civic Voluntarism in American Politics*. Cambridge, MA: Harvard University Press, 1995.

Voslensky, Michael. *Nomenklatura: Anatomy of the Soviet Ruling Class*. London: Bodley Hall, 1984.

Walzer, Michael. *What It Means to Be an American*. New York: Marsilio, 1993.

Wiebe, Robert. *The Search for Order, 1877–1920*. New York: Hill & Wang, 1967.

Willerton, John P. *Patronage and Politics in the USSR*. Cambridge, UK: Cambridge University Press, 1992.

Zielonka, Jan, ed. *Democratic Consolidation in Eastern Europe: Volume 1, Institutional Engineering*. Oxford: Oxford University Press, 2001.

Articles, Chapters in Books, Working Papers

Agh, Attila. "From Nomenclatura to Clientura: The Emergence of New Political Elites in East-Central Europe," in *Stabilising Fragile Democracies: Comparing New Party Systems in Southern and Eastern Europe*, Geoffrey Pridham and Paul G. Lewis, eds. London: Routledge, 1996, pp. 44–68.

Barstad, Agnese. "Culture of Corruption? Interpreting Corruption in Soviet and Post-Soviet Contexts," M.A. thesis, University of Bergen, Norway, 2003.

Beissinger, Mark R. "Introduction," *Soviet Sociology* (May–June 1989), pp. 3–8.

Ben-Dor, Gabriel. "Corruption, Institutionalization, and Political Development: The Revisionist Theses Revisited," *Comparative Political Studies* 7, no. 1 (1974), pp. 63–83.

Bruszt, Laszlo. "Market Making as State Making: Constitutions and Economic Development in Post-Communist Eastern Europe," *Constitutional Political Economy* 13 (2002), pp. 53–72.

Bunce, Valerie. "The Postsocialist Experience and Comparative Politics," *PS: Political Science & Politics* 34, no. 4 (Dec. 2001), pp. 793–95.

———. "Rethinking Recent Democratization: Lessons from the Postcommunist Experience," *World Politics* 55 (Jan. 2003), pp. 167–92.

Carasciuc, Lilia. "Fighting Corruption to Improve Governance: Case of Moldova," Transparency International Working Paper, Chisinau, 2002. Retrieved Jan. 29, 2002 from www.transparency.org/documents/work-papers/carasciuc/index.html.

Chen, Cheng, and Rudra Sil. "Bringing Legitimacy Back In: The State of the State in 'Democratic' Russia and 'Authoritarian' China," paper presented at the annual meeting of the American Political Science Association, Boston, Aug. 28–Sept. 1, 2002.

Cirtautas, Arista-Maria. "Anticorruption Campaigns: How to Get Rid of Paradoxes and Inconsistencies," *Transition Newsletter*, World Bank and William Davidson Institute (Oct.–Nov. 2001), pp. 7–10.

———. "Corruption and the New Ethical Infrastructure of Capitalism," *East European Constitutional Review* 10, no. 2/3 (Spring/Summer 2001), pp. 79–84.

Clark, William A. "Crime and Punishment in Soviet Officialdom, 1965–90," *Europe-Asia Studies* 45, no. 2 (1993), pp. 259–79.

———. "Soviet Official Corruption under Perestroika: A Balance Sheet," *Current Politics and Economics of Russia* 2, no. 3 (1992), pp. 205–16.

Clark, William A., and Philip H. Jos. "Comparative Anti-Corruption Policy: The American, Soviet and Russian Cases," *International Journal of Public Administration* 23 (2000), pp. 101–48.

Darbishire, Helen. "Freedom of Information Laws Promote Honest Government," *Local Governance Brief* (Budapest, Spring 2004), pp. 29–32.

Darden, Keith A. "Blackmail as a Tool of State Domination: Ukraine under Kuchma," *East European Constitutional Review* 10, no. 2/3 (Spring/Summer 2001), pp. 67–71.

Della Porta, Donatella. "The Vicious Circles of Corruption in Italy," in *Democracy and Corruption in Europe*, Donatella Della Porta and Yves Meny, eds. (London: Pinter, 1997), pp. 35–49.

Diamond, Larry, Marc F. Plattner, and Andreas Schedler. "Introduction," in *The Self-Restraining State: Power and Accountability in New Democracies*, Andreas Schedler, Larry Diamond, and Marc F. Plattner, eds. Boulder, CO: Lynne Rienner, 1999, pp. 1–14.

DiFranceisco, Wayne, and Zvi Gitelman. "Soviet Political Culture and 'Covert Participation' in Policy Implementation," *American Political Science Review* 78, no. 2 (June 1984), pp. 603–21.

Dininio, Phyllis. "Political Science and Anti-Corruption Assistance," paper presented at the annual meeting of the American Political Science Association, Boston, Aug. 28–Sept. 1, 2002.

Doig, Alan, and Stephanie McIvor. "Corruption and Its Control in the Developmental Context: An Analysis and Selective Review of the Literature," *Third World Quarterly* 20, no. 3 (1999), pp. 657–76.

Eigen, Peter. "Combating Corruption around the World," *Journal of Democracy* 7, no. 1 (Jan. 1996), pp. 158–68.

Eisenstadt, S.N., and Luis Roninger. "Clientelism in Communist Systems: A Comparative Perspective," *Studies in Comparative Communism* 14, no. 2 /3 (Summer/Autumn 1981), pp. 233–45.

Euben, J. Peter. "Corruption," in *Political Innovation and Conceptual Change*, Terence Ball, James Farr, and Russell L. Hanson, eds. Cambridge, UK: Cambridge University Press, 1989, pp. 220–46.

Frye, Timothy. "Corruption: The Polish and Russian Experiences," USIA Electronic Journal *Economic Perspectives* 3, no. 5 (Nov. 1998), pp. 1–2.

Galtung, Fredrik, and Jeremy Pope. "The Global Coalition against Corruption: Evaluating Transparency International," in *The Self-Restraining State: Power and Accountability in New Democracies*, Andreas Schedler, Larry Diamond, and Marc F. Plattner, eds. Boulder, CO: Lynne Rienner, 1999, pp. 257–83.

Ganev, Venelin I. "Notes on Networking in Postcommunist Societies," *East European Constitutional Review* 9, no. 1/2 (Winter/Spring 2000), pp. 101–7.

Gardiner, John. "Defining Corruption," in *Coping with Corruption in a Borderless World*, Maurice Punch et al., eds. Deventer: Kluwer Law and Taxation Publishers, 1993, pp. 21–38.

Gehlbach, Scott. "Social Networks and Corruption," paper presented at the annual meeting of the American Political Science Association, San Francisco, Aug. 30–Sept. 2, 2001.

Gillespie, Kate, and Gwenn Okruhlik. "The Political Dimensions of Corruption Cleanups: A Framework for Analysis," *Comparative Politics* 24, no. 1 (Oct. 1991), pp. 77–96.

Glinkina, Svetlana P. "The Ominous Landscape of Russian Corruption," *Transitions* (Mar. 1998).

Gong, Ting. "Dangerous Collusion: Corruption As a Collective Venture in Contemporary China," *Communist and Post-Communist Studies* 35, no. 1 (Mar. 2002), pp. 85–103.

Granville, Johanna. "'Demokratizatsiya' and 'Prikhvatizatsiya': The Russian Kleptocracy and Rise of Organized Crime," *Demokratizatsiya* 11, no. 3 (Summer 2003), pp. 449–57.

Grigorescu, Alexandru. "European Institutions and Unsuccessful Norm Transmission: The Case of Transparency," *International Politics* 39 (Dec. 2002), pp. 467–89.

Gupta, Sanjeev, Hamid Davoodi, and Erwin Tiongson. "Corruption and the Provision of Health and Education Services," in *The Political Economy of Corruption*, Arvind K. Jain, ed. London: Routledge, 2001, pp. 111–41.

Hanley, Eric. "Cadre Capitalism in Hungary and Poland: Property Accumulation among Communist-Era Elites," *East European Politics and Societies* 14, no. 1 (Winter 2000), pp. 143–80.

Hellman, Joel S. "Winners Take All: The Politics of Partial Reform in Postcommunist Transitions," *World Politics* 50 (Jan. 1998), pp. 203–34.

Heywood, Paul. "Political Corruption: Problems and Perspectives," *Political Studies* 45 (special issue, 1997), pp. 417–35.

Immergut, Ellen N. "The Theoretical Core of the New Institutionalism," *Politics & Society* 26, no. 1 (Mar. 1998), pp. 5–34.

Jacobs, James B. "Dilemmas of Corruption Control," in *Political Corruption in Transition*, Stephen Kotkin and Andras Sajo, eds. Budapest: Central European University, 2002, pp. 81–90.

Johnston, Michael. "Corruption as a Process," in *Coping with Corruption in a Borderless World*, Maurice Punch et al., eds. Deventer: Kluwer Law and Taxation Publishers, 1993, pp. 39–58.

———. "Historical Conflict and the Rise of Standards," in *New Perspectives on Com-*

bating Corruption, Transparency International and the International Bank for Reconstruction and Development, 1988, ch. 18, pp. 193–205.

———. "Patrons and Clients, Jobs and Machines: A Case Study of the Uses of Patronage," *American Political Science Review* 73, no. 2 (June 1979), pp. 385–98.

———. "The Political Consequences of Corruption: A Reassessment," *Comparative Politics* 18, no. 4 (July 1986), pp. 459–77.

Johnston, Michael, and Sahr J. Kpundeh. "Building a Clean Machine: Anti-Corruption Coalitions and Sustainable Reforms," World Bank Institute Working Paper #37208, Washington, D.C., 2002.

Jowitt, Ken G. "Soviet Neotraditionalism: The Political Corruption of a Leninist Regime," *Soviet Studies* 35, no. 3 (July 1983), pp. 275–97.

Józsa, Gyula. "Politische Seilschaften in der Sowjetunion," *Berichte des Bundesinstituts für ostwissenschaftliche und internationale Studien*, no. 31 (1981).

Kaliyev, Roustam. "Russia's Organized Crime: A Typology, Part I," *Eurasia Insight* (Feb. 6, 2002), p. 1.

Kaminski, Antoni Z. "Coercion, Corruption, and Reform: State and Society in the Soviet-type Socialist Regime," *Journal of Theoretical Politics* 1, no. 1 (1989), pp. 77–102.

Karklins, Rasma. "Explaining Regime Change in the USSR," *Europe-Asia Studies* 46, no. 1 (Jan. 1994), pp. 29–45.

———. "Typology of Post-Communist Corruption," *Problems of Post-Communism* 49, no. 4 (July–Aug. 2002), pp. 22–32.

Karklins, Rasma, and Roger Petersen. "Decision Calculus of Protesters and Regimes: Eastern Europe, 1989," *Journal of Politics* 55, no. 3 (Aug. 1993), pp. 588–614.

Kassof, Allen. "The Administered Society: Totalitarianism without Terror," *World Politics* 16, no. 4 (July 1964), pp. 558–75.

Kaufmann, Daniel, and Paul Siegelbaum. "Privatization and Corruption in Transition Economies," *Journal of International Affairs* 50, no. 2 (Winter 1996), pp. 419–58.

Klitgaard, Robert. "Strategies for Reform," in *New Perspectives on Combating Corruption*, Transparency International and the International Bank for Reconstruction and Development. No place of publication: 1998, ch. 21, pp. 230–44.

Kolarska-Bobinska, Lena. "The Impact of Corruption on Legitimacy and Authority in New Democracies," in *Political Corruption in Transition*, Stephen Kotkin and Andras Sajo, eds. Budapest: Central European University Press, 2002.

Kornai, Janos. "Hidden in an Envelope: Gratitude Payments to Medical Doctors in Hungary," in *The Paradoxes of Unintended Consequences*, Lord Dahrendorf et al., eds. Budapest: Central European University Press, 2000, pp. 195–214.

Kramer, John M. "Political Corruption in the U.S.S.R.," *Western Political Quarterly* 30, no. 2 (June 1977), pp. 213–24.

———. "The Politics of Corruption," *Current History* 97, no. 621 (Oct. 1998), pp. 329–34.

Krastev, Ivan, and Georgy Ganev. "Do Uncorrupt Governments in Corrupt Countries Have Incentives to Launch Anticorruption Campaigns?" *East European Constitutional Review* 12, no. 2/3 (Spring/Summer 2003), pp. 87–93.

Kryshtanovskaya, Olga, and Stephen White. "From Soviet *Nomenklatura* to Russian Elite," *Europe-Asia Studies* 48, no. 5 (July 1996), pp. 711–33.

Langseth, Petter, et al. "Empowering the Victims of Corruption through Social Control Mechanisms," paper presented at IACC meeting, Prague, Oct. 9, 2001.

Ledeneva, Alena V. "Non-transparency of the Post-Communist Economies: The Relationship between the Formal and the Informal," draft Oct. 2002.

Levin, Mark, and Georgy Satarov. "Corruption and Institutions in Russia," *European Journal of Political Economy* 16 (2000), pp. 113–32.

Levine, Daniel H. "Paradigm Lost: Dependence to Democracy," *World Politics* 40, no. 3 (Apr. 1988), pp. 377–94.

Linz, Juan. "Transitions to Democracy," *Washington Quarterly* 13, no. 3 (Summer 1990), pp. 143–64.

Lipset, Seymour Martin, and Gabriel Salman Lenz. "Corruption, Culture, and Markets," in *Culture Matters: How Values Shape Human Progress*, L.E. Harrison and S.P. Huntington, eds. New York: Basic Books, 2000, pp. 112–24.

Lonkila, M. "Informal Exchange Relations in Post-Soviet Russia: A Comparative Perspective," *Sociological Research Online* 2, no. 2 (June 1997). Retrieved from www.socresonline.org.uk/socresonline/2/2/9.html.

Magdashian, Pyotr. "Battling Corruption in Armenia," *Local Government Brief* (Summer 2003), p. 13.

Maidanik, Kiva. "Corruption, Criminalization, Kleptocracy: 'Transition Phase'? Dead-End Branch? Foundational Structures?" *Russian Politics and Law* 36, no. 1 (Jan./Feb. 1998), pp. 5–35.

March, James G., and Johan P. Olsen. "The New Institutionalism: Organizational Factors in Political Life," *American Political Science Review* 78, no. 3 (1984), pp. 734–49.

Mauro, Paolo. "Corruption and Growth," *Quarterly Journal of Economics* 110 (Aug. 1955), pp. 681–712.

McFaul, Michael. "State Power, Institutional Change, and the Politics of Privatization in Russia," *World Politics* 47 (Jan. 1995), pp. 210–43.

Mendras, Marie. "Rule by Bureaucracy in Russia," in *Democracy and Corruption in Europe*, Donatella Della Porta and Yves Meny, eds. London: Pinter, 1997, pp. 118–31.

Millar, James R. "The Little Deal: Breshnev's Contribution to Acquisitive Socialism," *Slavic Review* 44, no. 4 (1985), pp. 694–706.

———. "What's Wrong with the Mafia Anyway? An Analysis of the Economics of Organized Crime in Russia," in *Economic Transition in Russia and the New States of Eurasia*, Bartlomiej Kaminiski, ed. Armonk, NY: M.E. Sharpe, 1996, pp. 206–19.

Miller, William L., Ase B. Grodeland, and Tatyana Y. Koshechkina. "Are the People Victims or Accomplices? The Use of Presents and Bribes to Influence Officials in Eastern Europe," Discussion Paper #6, Budapest: Open Society Institute, 1998.

Miller, William L., Tatyana Koshechkina, and Ase Grodeland. "How Citizens Cope with Postcommunist Officials: Evidence from Focus Group Discussions in Ukraine and the Czech Republic," *Political Studies* 45 (1997), pp. 597–625.

Mishler, William, and Richard Rose. "What Are the Origins of Political Trust? Testing Institutional and Cultural Theories in Post-Communist Societies," *Comparative Political Studies* 34, no. 4 (Feb. 2001), pp. 30–62.

Moreno, Alejandro. "Corruption and Democracy: A Cultural Assessment," *Comparative Sociology* 1, no. 3/4 (2002), pp. 495–507.

Mungiu-Pippidi, Alina. "Culture of Corruption or Accountability Deficit?" *East European Constitutional Review* 11, no. 4 and 12, no. 1 (Fall 2002/Winter 2003), pp. 80–85.

Nielsen, Richard P. "Corruption Networks and Implications for Ethical Corruption Reform," *Journal of Business Ethics*, 42 (2003), pp. 125–49.

Nilsson, Hans. "Substantive Criminal Law: Corruption and Money Laundering," in *Corruption and Democracy: Political Institutions, Processes and Corruption in Transition States in East-Central Europe and in the Former Soviet Union*, Duc V. Trang, ed. Budapest: Institute for Constitutional and Legislative Policy, 1994, pp. 89–104.

Nomokonov, Vitaly A. "On Strategies for Combating Corruption in Russia," *Demokratizatsiya* 8, no. 1 (Winter 2000), pp. 123–28.

O'Donnell, Guillermo. "Horizontal Accountability in New Democracies," *Journal of Democracy* 9, no. 3 (July 1998), pp. 112–28.

Offe, Claus. "Controlling Political Corruption: Conceptual and Practical Issues," draft paper for workshop on Honesty and Trust, Dec. 13–14, 2002, Collegium Budapest, Hungary.

Ostrom, Elinor. "A Behavioral Approach to the Rational Choice Theory of Collective Action," *American Political Science Review* 92, no. 1 (Mar. 1998), pp. 1–22.

Pateman, Carole. "Political Culture, Political Structure and Political Change," *British Journal of Political Science* 1 (July 1971), pp. 291–305.

Pidluska, Inna. Ukrainian Center for Independent Research, conference presentation as reported in Robert Lyle, "Ukraine under Corruption Spotlight," *RFE/RL Newsline*, Part II (Feb. 26, 1999).

Pleines, Heiko. "Large-scale Corruption and Rent-seeking in the Russian Banking Sector," in *Economic Crime in Russia*, Alena V. Ledeneva and Marina Kurkchiyan, eds. The Hague: Kluwer Law International, 2000, pp. 191–208.

Polishchuk, Leonid. "Decentralization in Russia: Impact for Quality of Governance," paper presented at the IRIS Center Conference on Collective Action and Corruption in Emerging Economies, Washington, D.C., May 1999.

Puce, Ingrīda. "The Corruption Theme in Agenda Setting and the Journalist's Role in It" [in Latvian], thesis for attainment of the bachelor's degree, University of Latvia, Department of Communication, Riga, 1999.

———. "Reports about Corruption in Latvia by International Organizations (EU, EC, OECD, WB) and Their Influence on the Political Agenda of Political and Economic Elites, 1992–2001" [in Latvian], M.A. thesis, University of Latvia, Department of Communication, Riga, 2002.

Radaev, Vadim. "Corruption and Violence in Russian Business in the Late 1990s," in *Economic Crime in Russia*, Alena V. Ledeneva and Marina Kurkchiyan, eds. The Hague: Kluwer Law International, 2000, pp. 63–82.

Remmer, Karen L. "Theoretical Decay and Theoretical Development: The Resurgence of Institutional Analysis," *World Politics* 50 (Oct. 1997), pp. 34–61.

Rodgers, Daniel T. "Republicanism: The Career of a Concept," *Journal of American History* 79, no. 1 (June 1992), pp. 11–38.

Rose, Richard. "Uses of Social Capital in Russia: Modern, Pre-modern, and Anti-modern," *Post-Soviet Affairs* 16, no. 1 (Jan./Mar. 2000), pp. 33–57.

———. "What are the Origins of Political Trust? Testing Institutional and Cultural Theories in Post-Communist Societies," *Comparative Political Studies* 34, no. 1 (Feb. 2001), pp. 30–62.

Rose-Ackerman, Susan. "Democracy and 'Grand' Corruption," *International Social Science Journal* 48, no. 3 (Sept. 1996), pp. 365–80.

———. "Redesigning the State to Fight Corruption," *Public Policy for the Private Sector*, World Bank Note #75, Apr. 1996, pp. 21–28.

———. "Reducing Bribery in the Public Sector," in *Corruption and Democracy:*

Political Institutions, Processes and Corruption in Transition States in East-Central Europe and in the Former Soviet Union, Duc V. Trang, ed. Budapest: Institute for Constitutional and Legislative Policy, 1994, no pagination.

———. "Trust and Honesty in Post-Socialist Systems," *Kyklos* 54, no. 2/3 (2001), pp. 415–44.

———. "Trust, Honesty and Corruption: Reflection on the State-building Process," *Archives Europeans Sociologiques* 17 (2001), pp. 626–70.

———. "Trust, Honesty, and Corruption: Theories and Survey Evidence from Post-Socialist Societies, Toward a Research Agenda for a Project of the Collegium Budapest," draft, Apr. 24, 2001.

Rustow, Dankwart A. "Transitions to Democracy: Toward a Dynamic Model," *Comparative Politics* 2, no. 2 (Apr. 1970), pp. 337–63.

Sajo, Andras. "Corruption, Clientelism, and the Future of the Constitutional State in Eastern Europe," *East European Constitutional Review* 7, no. 2 (Spring 1998), pp. 37–46.

Schedler, Andreas. "Conceptualizing Accountability," in *The Self-Restraining State: Power and Accountability in New Democracies*, Andreas Schedler, Larry Diamond, and Marc F. Plattner, eds. Boulder, CO: Lynne Rienner, 1999, pp. 13–23.

Schwartz, Charles A. "Corruption and Political Development in the USSR," *Comparative Politics* (July 1979), pp. 425–43.

Schwartz, Herman. "Surprising Success: The New Eastern European Constitutional Courts," in *The Self-Restraining State: Power and Accountability in New Democracies*, Andreas Schedler, Larry Diamond, and Marc F. Plattner, eds. Boulder, CO: Lynne Rienner, 1999, pp. 195–214.

Seibel, Wolfgang. "Institutional Weakness, Ethical Misjudgement: German Christian Democrats and the Kohl Scandal," in *Motivating Ministers to Morality*, Jenny Fleming and Ian Holland, eds. Aldershot: Dartmouth, 2001, pp. 77–90.

Shelley, Louise I. "Corruption in the Post-Yeltsin Era," *East European Constitutional Review* 9, no. 1/2 (Winter/Spring 2000), pp. 70–74.

———. "Crime and Corruption," in *Developments in Russian Politics*, Stephen White, Alex Pravda, and Zvi Gitelman, eds. Hampshire: Palgrave, 2001, pp. 239–53.

———. "Crime, Organized Crime and Corruption in the Transitional Period: The Russian Case," paper presented at the Law and Society conference, Budapest, July 4–7, 2001, p. 1.

Shlapentokh, V. "Russia's Acquiescence to Corruption Makes the State Machine Inept," *Communist and Post-Communist Studies* 36, no. 2 (June 2003), pp. 151–61.

Shumer, S.M. "Machiavelli: Republican Politics and Its Corruption," *Political Theory* 7, no. 1 (Feb. 1979), pp. 5–34.

Sik, Endre. "Network Capital in Capitalist, Communist and Post-Communist Societies," *International Contributions to Labour Studies* 4 (1994), pp. 73–93.

Solnick, Steven L. "The Breakdown of Hierarchies in the Soviet Union and China: A Neoinstitutional Perspective," *World Politics* 48 (Jan. 1996), pp. 209–38.

Solomon, Peter H., Jr., and Todd S. Foglesong. "The Two Faces of Crime in Post-Soviet Ukraine," *East European Constitutional Review* (Summer 2000), pp. 70–75.

Srubar, Ilja. "War der reale Sozialismus modern? Versuch einer strukturellen Bestimmung," *Kölner Zeitschrift für Soziologie und Sozialpsychologie* 43, no. 3 (1991), pp. 415–32.

Staats, Steven J. "Corruption in the Soviet System," *Problems of Communism* 21 (Jan./Feb. 1972), pp. 40–47.

Stapenhurst, Frederick, and Sahr J. Kpundeh. "Public Participation in the Fight against Corruption," *Canadian Journal of Development Studies* 19 (1998), pp. 491–508.

Steen, Anton. "How Elites View Corruption and Trust in Post-Soviet States," in Transparency International, *Global Corruption Report 2004*. London: Pluto Press, 2004, pp. 323–25.

Symposium on David Stark and Laszlo Bruszt, *Postsocialist Pathways: Transforming Politics and Property in East Central Europe* (New York: Cambridge University Press, 1998), in *East European Constitutional Review* 9, no. 1/2 (Winter/Spring 2000), pp. 101–20.

Szymanderski, Jacek. "Moral Order and Corruption in Transition to the Market: Popular Beliefs and Their Underpinnings," *Communist Economies and Economic Transformation* 7, no. 2 (1995), pp. 249–57.

Taagepera, Rein. "Baltic Values and Corruption in Comparative Context," *Journal of Baltic Studies* 33, no. 3 (2002), pp. 243–58.

Tarkowski, Jacek. "Patronage in Centralized Socialist Systems," *International Political Science Review* 4 (1983), pp. 495–518.

Thelen, Kathleen. "Historical Institutionalism in Comparative Politics," *Annual Review of Political Science* 2 (1999), pp. 369–404.

Todorov, Boyko. "Coalition 2000: A Public-Private Partnership Tackling Corruption in Bulgaria," *Public Management Forum* 5, no. 2 (1999), pp. 1–3.

Tomiuc, Eugen. "Romania: EU Warns Bucharest over Corruption," *RFE/RL Report* (Apr. 30, 2003).

Tucker, Aviezer. "Higher Education on Trial," *East European Constitutional Review* 9, no. 3 (Summer 2000), pp. 88–89.

———. "Networking," *East European Constitutional Review* 9, no. 1/2 (Winter/Spring 2000), p. 110–11.

Varese, Federico. "The Transition to the Market and Corruption in Post-socialist Russia," *Political Studies* 45 (1997), pp. 579–96.

Verheijen, Tony, and Antoaneta Dimitrova. "Private Interests and Public Administration: The Central and East European Experience," *International Review of Administrative Sciences* 62 (1996), pp. 197–218.

Volkov, Vadim. "Violent Entrepreneurship in Post-Communist Russia," *Europe-Asia Studies* 51, no. 5 (July 1999), pp. 741–54.

Weingast, Barry R. "The Political Foundations of Democracy and the Rule of Law," *American Political Science Review* 91, no. 2 (June 1997), pp. 245–64.

Yavlinsky, Grigory. "Russia's Phony Capitalism," *Foreign Affairs* 77, no. 3 (May–June 1998), pp. 67–79.

Index

Rasma Karklins is professor of political science at the University of Illinois at Chicago. A noted scholar of East European and comparative politics, Karklins is the recipient of many awards. Her work on post-communist corruption has been recognized by a fellowship at the Institute for Advanced Study in Princeton in 2002–3 and an Ed A. Hewett Policy Fellowship from the National Council for Eurasian and East European Research in 2003–4. She has published widely on comparative ethnopolitics and transitions to democracy. Her first book, *Ethnic Relations in the USSR*, won the Ralph E. Bunche Award of the American Political Science Association.